MATERIALS ON
THE MEMORIAL TO THE MURDERED JEWS OF EUROPE

Robert Vermes, from Topolcany
in Slovakia, was born in 1924.
Arrested on 27 March, 1942, he was
deported to the Majdanek concentration
camp and murdered there.

MATERIALS ON THE MEMORIAL TO THE MURDERED JEWS OF EUROPE

PUBLISHED BY THE FOUNDATION
FOR THE MEMORIAL TO THE
MURDERED JEWS OF EUROPE

nicolai

PUBLISHER'S INFORMATION

Information Centre exhibition (E)
Material Anthology (M)

Managing Director of the Foundation for the Memorial to
the Murdered Jews of Europe (www.stiftung-denkmal.de):
Hans-Erhard Haverkampf

1. Foundation employees

Eva Brücker: Room of Dimensions, picture series foyers 1+2, portal to the sites
of remembrance (all E), picture series "Documentation of Suffering" (M)
Ulrich Baumann: Room of Families (E), Overview texts foyers 1+2 (E/M)
Jürgen Lillteicher: Room of Names, portal to the sites of remembrance (both E)
Uwe Neumärker: Room of Sites (E)
Sibylle Quack: Managing Director until February 2004 (E)
Stefanie Fischer: educational concept, rights (E/M)
Uwe Seemann: information technology (E/M)

2. Advisory Bodies

Commission of experts, "Information Centre" and "Design" working groups:
Aleida Assmann, Wolfgang Benz, Ulrich Herbert, Eberhard Jäckel,
Salomon Korn, Andreas Nachama, Sibylle Quack, Monika Richarz,
Richard Rosson, Reinhard Rürup, Günter Schlusche, Peter Steinbach,
Christoph Stölzl, Dagmar von Wilcken

Advisory Board:
Max Bächer, Wolfgang Benz, Wacław Długoborski, Günter Dworek,
Bernd Faulenbach, Detlef Garbe, Norbert Kampe, Adam König,
Sonja Lahnstein-Kandel, Margret Hamm, Manfred Messerschmidt,
Horst Möller, Jörg Skriebeleit, Hans-Jochen Vogel

3. External contributors and contractors

Exhibition design: F217, Dagmar von Wilcken with Claudia Franke (E)
Multimedia hardware: luxoom, PIK (E)
Multimedia production: MMCD (E)
Lighting scheme: Kardorff Ingenieure, Lichtvision (E)
Acoustics: ADA (E)
Exhibition construction: museumstechnik (E)
Display case construction: Ausstellungsmanufaktur Hertzer (E)
Photo printing: PPS Farbfotocenter (E)
Screen printing: Heerlein (E)
Book design: buschfeld.com – graphic and interface design (M)
Image management: Yara-Colette Lemke Muniz de Faria (E/M)
Editing: Jeannine Fiedler (M)
Copy-editing: Claudia Allen (E/M) Bettina Hüllen (E),
Almut Otto (E), Susanne Wind (E/M)
Translation: Toby Axelrod (E/M), Noah Mkayton (M),
Günter Schlusche (M), James Taylor (E), Bill Templer (E)
English version: Richard Bessel (E/M), James Taylor (M)
Printing and binding: Passavia Druckerei, Passau (M)

4. Student assistants and interns

Axel Bangert, Henry Becker, Martin Both, Katharina Christoffers,
Rebecca Denz, Markus Falk, Diana Fisch, Katharina Friedla, Lukas Imhof,
Florian Kemmelmeier, Viktor Kucharski, Jana Mechelhoff-Herezi, Ulrike Möller,
Joanna Nalewajka, Doron Oberhand, Marino Otté, Katarzyna Pawlak,
Daniel Ratner, Grzegorz Rossolinski, Alexander Sewohl, Kim Wünschmann

Material presented in this volume relates
to the level of information as of 31 January, 2005.
Trade Edition ISBN 3-89479-223-X

© 2005 Nicolaische Verlagsbuchhandlung GmbH, Berlin

Foundation for the
Memorial to the Murdered
Jews of Europe

PREFACE

On 25 June, 1999, the Bundestag – the German parliament – approved the construction of a central "Memorial to the Murdered Jews of Europe" in the centre of Berlin. It is dedicated to the six million victims of the Holocaust and will keep alive the memory of the most horrific crimes in German history. The memorial honours the victims and warns future generations to protect human rights, to defend the constitutional state, and to safeguard the equality of all people under the law. Through its honesty, the memorial provides a space for personal reflection, remembrance and mourning.

In the "Information Centre", victims of the Holocaust have names and faces. Here, the fate of individual victims and their families is the focal point. Here, their lives, their suffering and their deaths are documented. The personalization and individualization of the horrors connected with the Holocaust is intentional. It is the central thread running through the entire exhibition. It will lift the victims out of the anonymity of a scale of death so enormous as to be incomprehensible to us, connecting personal memories with real life stories. In text and images, the exhibition traces the monstrous scale of the mass murder perpetrated against European Jewry. It shows the enormous number of killing sites, it documents the escalation of the National Socialist extermination policy and it names the perpetrators.

Peter Eisenman's design for the memorial has a history, which dates back 15 years. The initial impetus came from a grass-roots initiative. This sparked years of controversial debate that reflected the way Germany saw itself at the end of the 20th century, and in which the pros and cons of individual design entries were discussed. This debate was essential. It showed that the passage of time had not made it easier, but had, in fact, made it more difficult to reach a consensus about appropriate forms of remembrance and respect.

Eisenman's spacious sculpture is accessible. Whoever passes through this seemingly endless sea of stone blocks, leaves the noise of the street behind, is on their own, is hardly able to avoid a feeling of distress, a palpable sense of anxiety. One senses a great emotional and physical energy in the memorial and the meaning of loneliness, helplessness and despair.

The integration of the memorial site into the new parliamentary and government district is an acknowledgment of our political responsibility. We are making it clear that we are not connecting the fortunate outcome for us of the post-war period with an unspoken wish to be finally able to close the worst chapter of our history. On the contrary, the memorial contributes to our society's self-awareness. It is, in the best sense of the word, provocative: it will continue to stir emotions and to prompt discussion.

This catalogue traces the origins of the "Memorial to the Murdered Jews of Europe" and explains its creative concept. At the same time, it serves as a guide through the rooms of the "Information Centre".

WOLFGANG THIERSE
PRESIDENT OF THE BUNDESTAG

Claire Brodzki from Lyons, France,
survived the deportation to Auschwitz,
but died a few months after the liberation
of the camp, on 20 June, 1945.

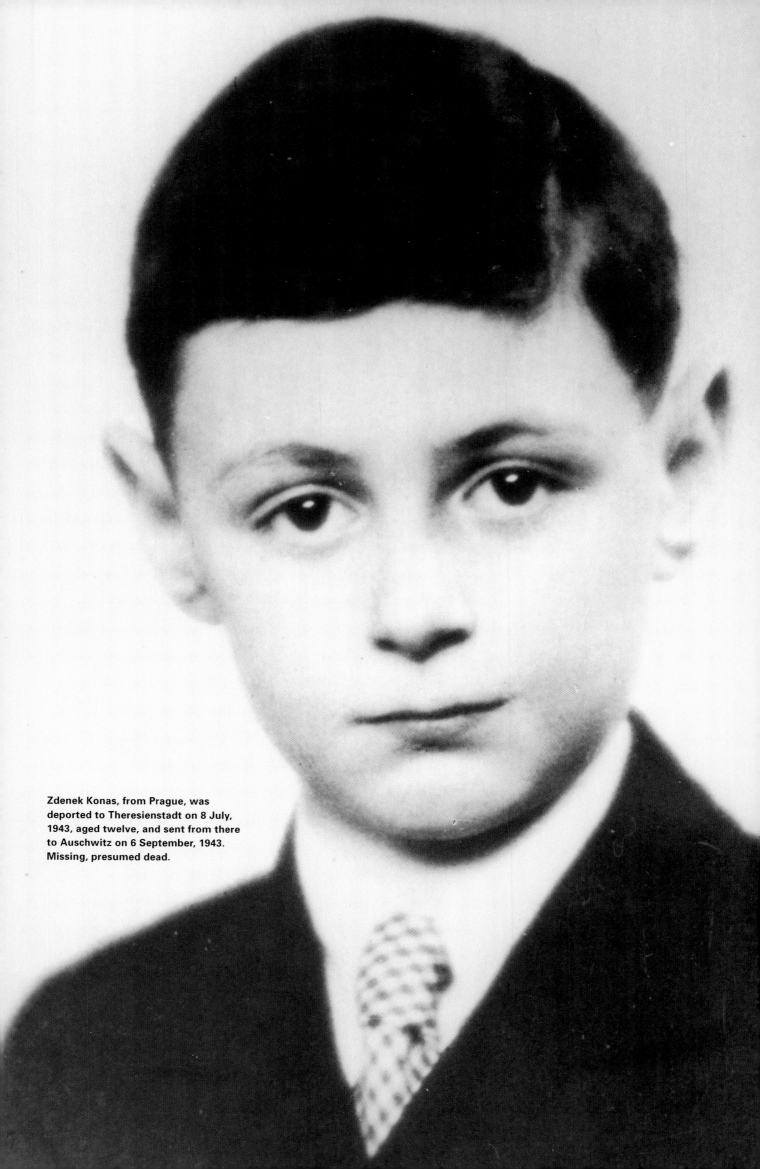

Zdenek Konas, from Prague, was deported to Theresienstadt on 8 July, 1943, aged twelve, and sent from there to Auschwitz on 6 September, 1943. Missing, presumed dead.

FROM THREE TO FOUR YEARS, INTO SEVENTEEN

When we started thinking about the memorial, first Eberhard Jäckel, then myself, and finally the citizens' initiative "Perspective Berlin e.V.", we figured: it will take three or four years, but then we will have the memorial. Or maybe not. But 17 years? Why did it take so long from conception in 1987 to dedication in 2005?

We – a citizens' initiative, residents of West Berlin – had neither money nor political power. We simply had an idea and had to convince others of it: our goal was to create a memorial to the murdered Jews of Europe. We wanted to remember the crime, the million-fold murder, and to honour the memory of the dead, to give them back their names. We wanted to prevent Germany from simply getting down to the business of reunification, rebuilding, affluence – as if nothing had happened. But that would not be easy. Because at no other time in history had a nation, a people, admitted to and visibly documented such a tremendous crime committed in its name.

We looked for allies, supporters. Our first signatory was Willy Brandt. It was he who pronounced the words that would become our motto: "our honour demands an immense expression of remembrance of the murder of European Jewry". We campaigned for our project with advertisements; we stood in wind and rain on the street, gathering signatures for petitions and collecting money in biscuit tins. We had soon collected 100,000 Deutschmark and about 10,000 signatures. And we received contributions from people with large and small pocketbooks. For some, it was enough to donate 10 Euro per month. But they have been contributing this sum, loyally, for many years. The discussion grew more heated and we found ourselves having to clarify our position time and again: why a memorial for the murdered Jews alone? Why not also for other victim groups? Or even for all of them? We argued: because the central goal of National Socialist genocide policy was the destruction of Jewry. This was Hitler's most important aim, more important to him than winning the war. The consummation of 2,000 years of anti-Semitism on this continent and the figure of six million Jewish victims demanded a memorial dedicated to the Jews.

The debate lasted years. There were two competitions with hundreds of entries. The decisive breakthrough came with the parliamentary resolution of 25 June, 1999. Back in 1988, we had called on the Parliament to deal with this issue. Finally it had done so. With a majority of 314 to 209 votes, the Lower House of the German Parliament approved the memorial to the murdered Jews of Europe, for which we had campaigned. We had done it: "the State" had adopted our grass-roots initiative and taken responsibility for honouring the memory of those murdered in the name of its predecessor.

Jakob Schulze-Rohr, co-founder of the citizens' initiative and the Society for the Promotion of the "Memorial to the Murdered Jews of Europe", could finally say after all those years: "Now it is easier to live in this land."

LEA ROSH, PRESIDENT,
SOCIETY FOR THE PROMOTION OF THE MEMORIAL TO THE MURDERED JEWS OF EUROPE

MEMORIAL TO THE MURDERED JEWS OF EUROPE

Site model.

Architecture is about monuments and graves, said the Viennese architect Adolf Loos at the turn of the 20th century. By this he meant that an individual human life could be commemorated by a stone, a slab, a cross, or a star. The simplicity of this idea ended with the Holocaust and Hiroshima and the mechanisms of mass death. Today, an individual can no longer be certain to die an individual death, and architecture can no longer remember life as it once did. The markers that were formerly symbols of individual life and death must be changed, and this has a profound effect on the idea of memory and the monument. The enormity and horror of the Holocaust are such that any attempt to represent it by traditional means is inevitably inadequate. The memory of the Holocaust can never be one of nostalgia.

The context of the Memorial to the Murdered Jews of Europe is the enormity of the banal. The project manifests the instability inherent in what seems to be a system, here a rational grid, and its potential for dissolution in time. It suggests that when a supposedly rational and ordered system grows too large and out of proportion to its intended purpose, it in fact loses touch with human reason. It then begins to reveal the innate disturbances and potential for chaos in all systems of seeming order, the idea that all closed systems of a closed order are bound to fail. In searching for the instability inherent in an apparently stable system, the design begins from a rigid grid structure, composed of some 2,700 concrete pillars, or stelae, each 95 centimetres wide and 2.375 metres long, with heights varying from zero to four metres. The pillars are spaced 95 centimetres apart to allow for only individual passage through the grid. In addition, while the difference between the ground plane and the top plane of the pillars may appear to be random and arbitrary, a matter of pure expression, this is not the case. Each plane is determined by the intersections of the voids in the pillar grid and the gridlines of the larger site context of Berlin. In effect, a slippage occurs in the grid structure, causing indeterminate spaces to develop within the seemingly rigid order of the monument. These spaces condense, narrow, and deepen to provide a multilayered experience from any point in the gridded field. The agitation of the field shatters any notions of absolute axiality and instead reveals an omni-directional reality. The illusion of order and security in the internal grid and the frame of the street grid are thus destroyed.

Remaining intact, however, is the idea that the pillars extend between two undulating grids, forming the top plane at eye level. The way these two systems interact describes a zone of instability between them. These instabilities, or irregularities, are superimposed on both the topography of the site and on the top plane of the field of concrete pillars. A perceptual and conceptual divergence between the topography of the ground and the top plane of the stelae is thus created. This divergence denotes a difference in time, between what the philosopher Henri Bergson called chronological, narrative time and time as duration. The monument's registration of this difference makes for a place of loss and contemplation, elements of memory.

The "Ort der Information" is subdued in manner, effectively designed to minimize any disturbance to the Memorial's field of pillars. Its mass, weight, and density seem to perceptibly bear down and close in on individuals. The organization of the space of the Ort extends the stelae of the field into the structure, provoking a continued state of reflection and contemplation once inside. The stelae are manifested in the form of a coffered ceiling with rib spacing that matches the spacing of the field above. The presence of these elements is subverted by the Ort's walls, which are set on a classical nine-square grid. This grid is rotated against the logic of the field, thereby thwarting any paradigmatic understanding of its formal arrangement. The uncertain frame of reference that results further isolates individuals in what is intended to be an unsettling, personal experience. Juxtaposed against the hard, concrete materiality of the Ort will be a series of exhibitions that will

Early conceptual diagrams of site topography.

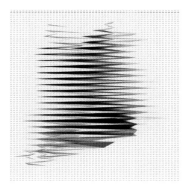
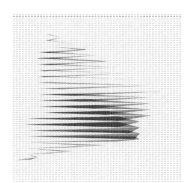
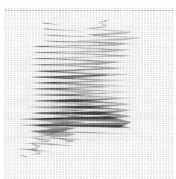
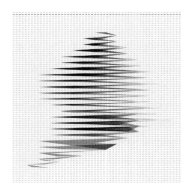

use state-of-the-art technologies to create an ephemeral and visceral dimension appropriate for reflection. The glow of the illuminated images and text is intended to dematerialize the walls of the Ort, allowing the stelae to reveal themselves as a topographical extension of the field.

Early conceptual model of ground topography.

In a prescient moment in "In Search of Lost Time", Marcel Proust identifies two different kinds of memory: a nostalgia located in the past, touched with a sentimentality that remembers things not as they were, but as we want to remember them, and a living memory, which is active in the present and devoid of nostalgia for a remembered past. The Holocaust cannot be remembered in the first, nostalgic mode, as its horror forever ruptured the link between nostalgia and memory. Remembering the Holocaust can, therefore, only be a living condition in which the past remains active in the present.

In this context, the monument attempts to present a new idea of memory as distinct from nostalgia. We propose that the time of the monument, its duration, is different from the time of human experience and understanding. The traditional monument is understood by its symbolic imagery, by what it represents. It is not understood in time, but in an instant in space; it is seen and understood simultaneously. Even in traditional architectures such as labyrinths and mazes, there is a space-time continuum between experience and knowing; one has a goal to work one's way in or out.

In this monument there is no goal, no end, no working one's way in or out. The duration of an individual's experience of it grants no further understanding, since understanding is impossible. The time of the monument, its duration from top surface to ground, is disjoined from the time of experience. In this context, there is no nostalgia, no memory of the past, only the living memory of the individual experience. Here, we can only know the past through its manifestation in the present.

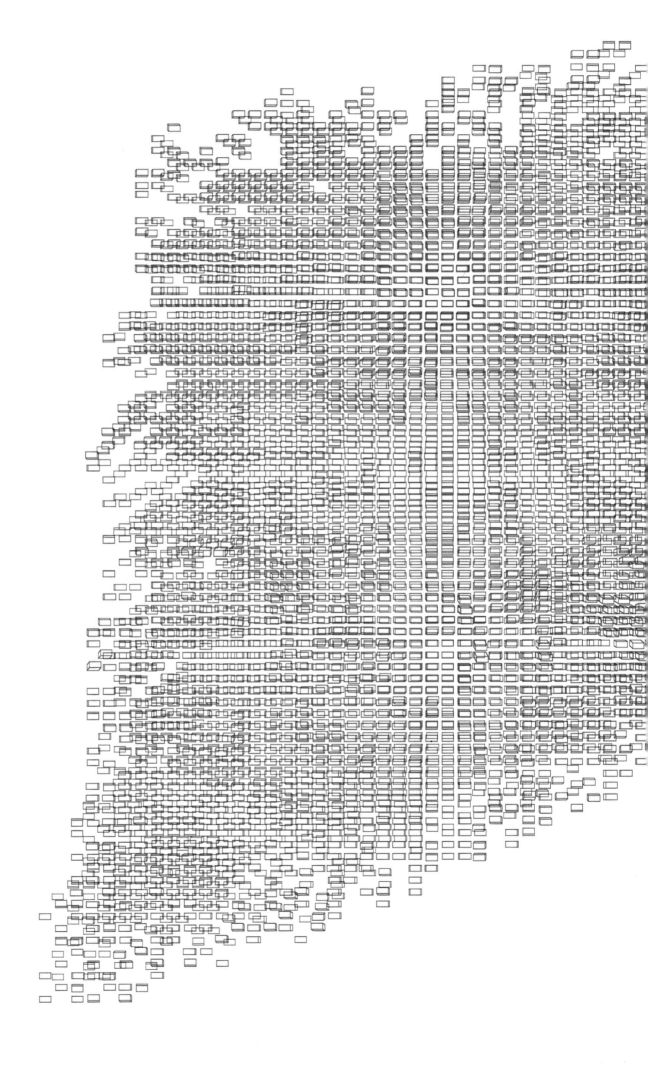

A MEMORIAL IS BUILT
HISTORY, PLANNING AND ARCHITECTURAL CONTEXT

Aerial photograph of the construction site from the south with Ebertstrasse (on the far left), the Brandenburg Gate, Pariser Platz and the Reichstag (at the top), October 2004.

When journalist Lea Rosh proposed a "higly visible symbol" to remember the murder of European Jewry, at a public forum held on 24 August, 1988 to decide the future of the Prince-Albrecht site, she sparked mixed reactions, ranging from enthusiastic approval to sharp rejection. While the plan met with growing sympathy among the public, and soon also among political circles, it received a generally negative reception from experts and some sections of the Berlin public. The argument for an artistically conceived memorial did not sit well with developments in the culture of memory at the time, which had been influenced by a genuine scepticism regarding modern art in general and the concept of memorials in particular. Memorials were characterized as affirmative and statuary and the preference was for prompting reflection, for more active forms of remembrance.

Moreover, with their proposal, Rosh and the other members of the citizens' initiative "Perspective Berlin" – the forerunner of today's "Society for the Memorial to the Murdered Jews of Europe" –, put themselves in opposition to the concept behind the "Topography of Terror" exhibition, which since 1987 has been located in the area between Wilhelmstrasse and Stresemannstrasse. Intended as a temporary display on Berlin's

750th anniversary, and set up following an unsuccessful artistic competition, this exhibition was the culmination of almost ten years of work by a circle of people from the "Active Museum Association", whose goal it was to pave the way for new encounters with the suppressed history of National Socialism. They saw this site, in the shadow of the Berlin Wall, as the place where desk-bound perpetrators had worked. The "Active Museum Association" would turn it into a "place for learning and thinking" by protecting the traces of the past they found underground. It would be a place where one could confront the existence and workings of the most important National Socialist instrument of terror, located there from 1933 to 1945, alongside what is today the Martin-Gropius-Bau. The unexpectedly positive response to this project helped build support, from 1987 onward, for this new way of tackling Nazi history. But the controversy about the character and design of the site, named after the former Prince-Albrecht Palace, came to a head in the following years, as support for Lea Rosh's initiative grew dramatically.

Not until the fall of the Berlin Wall and reunification of East and West Germany did things change. In the spring of 1990, the "Society for the Memorial to the Murdered Jews of Europe" suggested a new location for their project: the land "between the Brandenburg Gate and the former Reich Chancellery... on the ruins of the centre of Nazi power" (1). The tearing down of the Berlin Wall brought new life to an area that had been cut off and inaccessible for decades. The German federal government, as proprietor of the former border zone, had, in 1992, already signalled its readiness to make part of this land available for a memorial project, on the condition that the contours of the project would be in keeping with the new design for Berlin, which was once again to be the capital city.

The fact that this land is now the location of the completed memorial should not lead one to assume that the site for the memorial was chosen irrevocably in 1992. Just as there were questions about the nature of the memorial and its typological and iconographic character, there were also many fundamental doubts about its location, with serious alternatives being recommended in the years that followed. These matters would not be resolved until a Bundestag resolution in 1999. Firstly, however, the urban planning structure of the entire site had to be clarified, as well as the memorial's relationship to the nearby Bundestag and other government sites. A major step in this regard was presented in an urban planning study "Ministergärten" ("Ministry Gardens"), which was compiled for the Berlin Senate in 1993 and 1994 (2). In this document, the authors developed a relatively robust urban planning structure for the site. Priority was given to the restoration and modular development of the city's ground plan. This meant that the memorial's location would be in the centre, offering the highly important services which only a capital city can provide, from foreign embassies and representatives of the German states to urban housing. It also clearly rejected the idea of bringing the memorial into direct contact with the future legislative and executive centres on the Spree River. Choosing to locate the memorial next to the Tiergarten park on the western side, only 170 metres from the Brandenburg Gate and the premium development on the southern side of Pariser Platz, it was clear that the planners sought to forge very strong links to the network of public spaces and to the multi-use urban environment with all its benefits.

The study's title highlighted the connection with the former "Ministry Gardens", an area on the western edge of Friedrichstadt, created in 1688 as the third baroque extension of medieval Berlin. The main axis of this area was Wilhelmstrasse, which the "Soldier King" Friedrich Wilhelm I laid out from 1732, in keeping with plans drawn up by Johann Philipp Gerlach. The development of the northernmost section between Leipziger Strasse and the Linden resulted, as the King demanded, in so-called "Immediatbauten" (literally "immediate buildings"). Thus, seven palatial apartment buildings were constructed on the west side on long, self-contained plots. They were situated in the right-hand corner of the northern section, in a row along the street and had ornamental gardens that extended up to the customs wall between the Brandenburg Gate and Potsdam Gate. The distinguished character of this quarter changed in the course of the 19th century, particularly with the growth sparked in 1871, when Berlin was declared the capital of the German Reich.

The history of the construction and use of the two plots at Wilhelmstrasse 72 and 73, which today form the location of the memorial, make this development easy to understand (3). The site at Wilhelmstrasse 72

City map of Berlin by Schmettau, 1748 (turned upside down); detail of Pariser Platz - Potsdamer Platz.

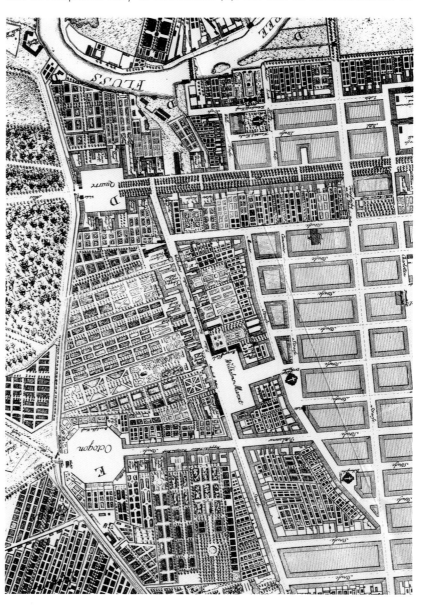

was purchased and developed in 1737 by the chief judge, Hans Christoph von Görne. In 1816, it came into the possession of the Prussian royal family, who hired architect Karl Friedrich Schinkel to alter and improve the palace before it was used until 1918 as the residence of the princes of Hohenzollern. After its purchase by the German Reich in 1919, the building became the headquarters of the newly founded Reich Food Ministry, and later housed the Prussian Ministry for Food and Agriculture. As of 1937, an extension was built in the western part of the garden. This was used as the office villa of the Reich Propaganda Minister, Joseph Goebbels. Two years later, an underground bunker was added to the east side of the villa, which today is the only remaining structural trace of the pre-1945 site.

Wilhelmstrasse 73 was turned into the palace of the Count of Schwerin in 1737 and – after temporary ownership by the family of the book dealer Reimer – it was used from 1858 as the ministry of the Prussian royal

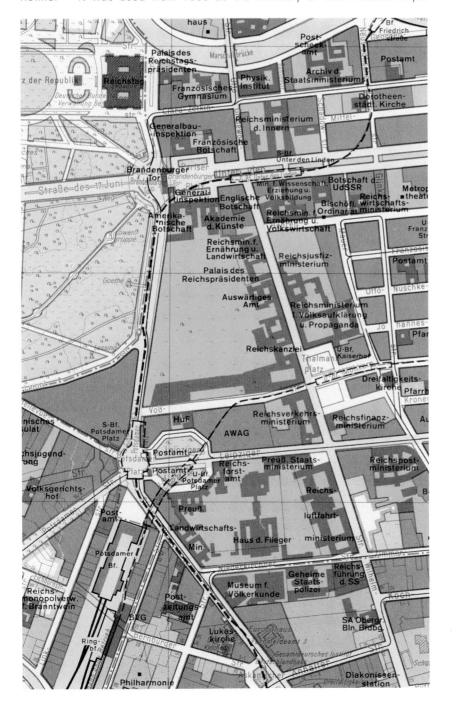

Berlin around 1940 (detail of Pariser Platz - Askanischer Platz) on a 1986 Berlin map, including historical structures and names of buildings. Violet: common spaces (public buildings, etc.), brown: business zones (shops), green: parkland.

Reich President von Hindenburg taking a walk with his grandchildren in the park of the Reich President's Palace (site of today's memorial), 1932.

household. By 1918, it had become the office and home of the newly created department of the Reich President and from 1939 to 1945, after a costly renovation, it was the office of the Reich Foreign Minister, Joachim von Ribbentrop. The adjacent, formerly baroque Palace Gardens, became the "Ministry Gardens", with access restricted to an exclusive circle. The public was never allowed to go into the "Ministry Gardens".

Both buildings were severely damaged during air raids in 1944-45, but were preserved after the war for the time being – unlike the other buildings on the west side of Wilhelmstrasse. One reason for this was that in the German Democratic Republic, those in charge of the preservation of historic monuments rated the buildings as valuable and, furthermore, possibly useful. In 1961, however, during the construction of the Berlin Wall, they were completely torn down. The gardens had already been left abandoned by the 1950s. With the gradual development of the "border security system", the site became part of the so-called "death strip", the mined, strictly controlled no-man's-land between East and West Berlin. Practically all relics of the distinct architecture and landscaping were erased.

Current layout of the memorial site, including the historical bunker configurations:

1 – Bunker of the Adlon Hotel
2 – Bunker of the "Reich Ministry for Arms and Munitions"
3 – Goebbels' Service Villa with bunker extension
4 – Bunker of the "Ministry for Nutrition and Agriculture"
5 – Underground power station
6 – Bunker layout for the Foreign Ministry
7 – "The Führer Bunker" and Main Bunker
8 – Drivers' Bunker and underground garages
9 – Terraced Bunker (waterworks)
10 – Large Bunker for the New Reich Chancellery
11 – Adjudants' Bunker for the New Reich Chancellery
12 – Bunker- and Air Defence Construction of the "Reich Ministry of Transportation"
13 – "Kaiserhof-Bunker"
14 – Bunker of the "Reich Aviation Ministry".

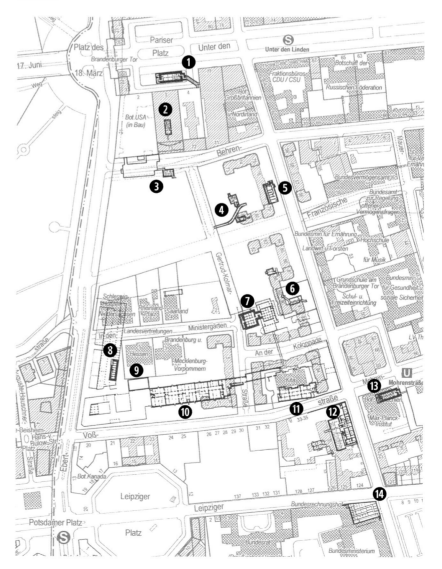

The site was condemned to nearly total historical oblivion by the GDR government's decision to build apartment buildings of seven or eight storeys on the western side of Wilhelmstrasse. Some of these were completed only after the fall of the Berlin Wall. Their U-shaped structures and their construction from large concrete blocks contribute to their being regarded as trivial and not in keeping with the quality of the area today. This is an error of judgment where urban planning is concerned, because housing in this inner city area makes sense and contributes to the revival of the city centre.

Public interest, however, focused in the mid-1990s on the open – and anonymous – artistic competition, held from April 1994 by the Berlin Senate's Office for City Redevelopment, on behalf of the federal government, the Berlin Senate and the "Society for the Memorial to the Murdered Jews of Europe". The drawn-out preparations for this competition were indicative of conceptual difficulties and tensions between the three groups planning the award. Only after tough negotiations did they succeed in reaching an agreement on an open competition, which would keep within legal regulations, and twelve well-known international artists were invited to pitch for the project. These included Rebecca Horn, Dani Karavan, Fritz Koenig, Gerhard Merz and Richard Serra. Further attempts by the "Society for the Memorial" to influence who could compete and the composition of the jury

Aerial photograph taken from the southeast, showing the destroyed Reich Chancellery bordered to the north by the Ministry Gardens (today the location of the memorial), and Wilhelmstraße (below right), Ebertstrasse (above left) and Pariser Platz (above right), 1945.

TIERGARTEN
GEWÄCHSHAUS
AUSSENMINISTERIUM
VERBRENNUNGSSTELLE
BUNKER NOTAUSGANG
FÜHRERWOHNUNG
ALTE REICHSKANZLEI
NEUE REICHSKANZLEI
WILHELMSTRASSE
EHRENHOF

View toward the south from the Reichstag toward the Brandenburg Gate and the Berlin Wall (the front wall is in the lower part of the image, and the back wall in the upper part) with what would become the site of today's memorial, 1986.

were prevented. A description of the project, together with a sketch for a design, by Swiss exhibition designer Harald Szeemann, who had already been consulted by the "Society for the Memorial" in 1991, was given in a supplement to the competition brochure – a rather unusual step in the process. Parallel to the competition, there were efforts to defuse the equally controversial question concerning the fact that the memorial would be specifically dedicated to murdered Jews. The attempt to resolve the issue through simultaneous political commitments to the construction of a memorial for the murdered Sinti and Roma in the northern area of the Tiergarten park was, however, inconclusive for the time being, because it proved impossible to come to a decision on the matter within a Berlin Senate dominated by the Christian Democrats and the Social Democrats.

The judging panel, headed by the former president of the Academy of Art, Walter Jens, needed a lot more time than was originally planned for the viewing of the 528 entries which were submitted. In March 1995, they finally recommended awarding two first prizes of equal value to Simon Ungers of Cologne and the team of Christine Jackob-Marks, Hella Rolfes, Hans Scheib and Reinhard Stangl of Berlin. Ungers proposed an 85 x 85 metre horizontal steel sculpture, surrounding a plaza accessible by stairs. The names of all the extermination camps would be perforated into the six-metre high steel girders. The entry from the Jackob-Marks group consisted of a large concrete platform that would cover the entire site, slanting upwards towards the east and on which, gradually, the known names of all the murdered Jews would be engraved. On the platform, 17 boulders from Massada, Israel, would be placed at irregular intervals.

Aerial photograph of the property between Pariser Platz and Potsdamer Platz (today's memorial site is outlined in colour) with the ruins of Wilhelmstraße 72 and 73 above right, 1959.

The final choices met with heavy public criticism. This increased when – after the presentation of a feasibility study – the panel decided three months later that the Jackob-Marks design should be implemented. When Chancellor Helmut Kohl registered his veto two days later, confusion reigned. Clearly, the decision process had not been prepared carefully enough. The participants evidently had misjudged the likely public reaction and, on top of everything else, they were arguing amongst themselves. The project slipped into an existential crisis that would last for more than a year. The new start, to which the panel agreed in 1996 after a pause for reflection, was heralded by an open public colloquium, where both critics and supporters dealt with all the issues debated over the previous years, subject by subject. There were three meetings: the first, on 10 January, 1997, dealt with the conception and scope of the memorial's dedication; the second, on 14 February, 1997, looked at the question of location; and the final meeting on 11 April concentrated on proposed iconography and on how the project should move forward. The meetings made it clear that there was less public support for this project than had been supposed. Despite controversies about matters of procedure, which occasionally pushed debate about content into the background, the colloquium made the advantages and disadvantages of the various positions transparent and justified a new beginning. After renewed expert evaluation of all alternative locations named in the course of the debate, the judging panel chose to hold a second competition, albeit one which would

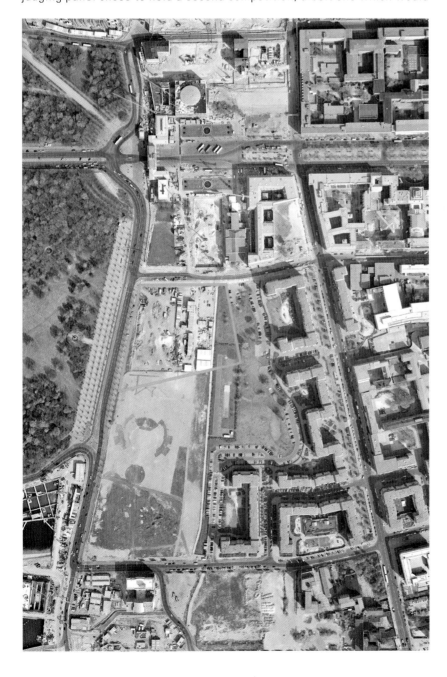

Aerial photograph of the property between Pariser Platz and Potsdamer Platz (today's memorial site is outlined in colour), 1997. On the right-hand side are the prefabricated concrete apartment buildings constructed on Wilhelmstraße between 1989 and 1991.

contain fundamental changes in comparison with its predecessor. The terms of reference of the competition were reformulated, but the dedication of the memorial and its location in the north-west of the former "Ministry Gardens", remained unchanged. The award panel opted for a narrower competition, with invited participants only. It was to be directed by a commission of experts consisting of Prof. Dr. Werner Hofmann, Prof. Josef Paul Kleihues, Prof. Dr. Dieter Ronte, Prof. Dr. Christoph Stölzl and Prof. Dr. James E. Young.

Of the 25 participants invited to compete – 16 of them artists and architects recommended by the finding commission and nine of them winners from the first competition – 19 submitted entries. In November 1997, surprisingly, not one work but rather a so-called realization shortlist of four works was presented. The finding commission recommended the design by New Yorkers Peter Eisenman and Richard Serra, as well as that of the young Berlin architect Gesine Weinmiller, while the representatives of the federal and state governments put forward the work of Daniel Libeskind and the members of the "Society for the Memorial to the Murdered Jews of Europe" championed the work of Jochen Gerz. The advantages to this step-by-step procedure were highlighted even more by the suggestion that these designs should be shown in an exhibition before any final

decision was made, and that the designers of the four selected projects should be invited to Berlin to present their entries in order to shape public opinion. This was clearly a consequence of the failed decision-making process of 1995. The closely followed public discussions generated the first cautious public approval of the process, together with an obvious confidence in the artistic strength of the favoured works. Above all, the proposal of architect Eisenman and sculptor Serra for a field of some 4,000 stelae, some up to five metres high ("Eisenman I"), received positive feedback and was considered by experts to be both appropriate and workable.

A photograph of the model for the memorial designed by Eisenman Architects and Richard Serra ("Eisenman I"), as seen from the south, November 1997.

In this sensitive phase, however, the political factor came into play with irritating consequences that only delayed matters. In early 1998, Chancellor Kohl interjected in the process. He suggested, after viewing his favoured proposal – that of Eisenman and Serra – that it be reworked so as to improve its integration into the urban landscape. Serra, who as a sculptor was not accustomed to making compromises in the execution of his work, took this request by the client as a reason to withdraw from the project. The proposal, reworked by Eisenman alone ("Eisenman II"), was presented in Berlin in the summer of 1998. Although the field of stelae was reduced to 2,700 in number, the pattern and size of the design remained unchanged. Its outer edges would fit precisely into its surroundings by means of occasional open spaces and trees. Meanwhile,

A photograph of the model for the memorial, designed by Eisenman Architects ("Eisenman II"), as seen from the southwest, July 1998.

a general election was approaching at an alarming speed, and Kohl saw that he was unable to push through another resolution on what was a controversial project within his own party. At the instigation of the Mayor of Berlin, Eberhard Diepgen (CDU), who never missed an opportunity to articulate his rejection of the project, the decision was postponed.

The Bundestag elections of September 1998 brought an end to the 16-year-long Kohl government, replacing it with the Red-Green administration of Chancellor Gerhard Schröder, who, in his election campaign, had announced a reappraisal of Germany's cultural policies. In keeping with this, the Red-Green coalition government decided in its programme to give the Bundestag the final say on the memorial project. This was a demand that experts had made for years: only the Bundestag was equipped to deliver a decision, in view both of the fundamental importance of this project and of the significant, constant, and ever-increasing divisions of opinion running across party lines regarding the sovereignty of the final decision. But ventures in this direction by individual members of the Bundestag in previous years had been fruitless. They included a debate in the Bundestag in May 1996, which was primarily the initiative of SPD-Parliament member Peter Conradi. It led to no real progress, however, other than to garner ground-level support in the Bundestag for the project.

The Federal government's new cultural representative, the publisher Michael Naumann, who, in the election campaign, had spoken out vehemently against the Eisenman proposal and would have preferred to drop the project entirely, wavered soon after the new coalition administration took office. Accordingly, he passed his own resolution with the newly created Bundestag Committee for Culture and Media, but not without adding his own twist to the existing options. Together with architect Eisenman, in January 1999 Naumann presented the latest proposal ("Eisenman III"), in which the field of stelae would be further reduced by several hundred stelae in favour of a huge "House of Remembrance" to be placed on the northern side of the site, facing Behrenstrasse. Naumann, a man of letters, bore a certain mistrust towards the educational potential of fine arts and architecture, and wanted to combine the aesthetic value of Eisenman's field of stelae with the classical medium of information,

A photograph of the model for the memorial, designed by Eisenman Architects ("Eisenman III"), as seen from the northwest, January 1999.

literature and other educational elements. To fill the rather voluminous "House of Remembrance", which would have 13,000 square metres of floor space over seven storeys, he recommended a museum, a library, a research department and such illustrious partners as the Leo Baeck Institute, the Shoah Foundation or the Genocide Watch Institute.

It was up to the Bundestag Committee for Cultural Affairs, under its head, SPD representative Elke Leonhard, to thin out the thicket of procedural and design options, which were threatening to get ever more unfathomable, and to sift from those the best options. The models from the initial selection and the three Eisenman designs were presented in the foyer of the Plenary Chamber in Bonn. Several expert opinions were gathered and noted and specialists were invited to hearings. At these hearings, the preference for the Eisenman entry was confirmed, while Naumann's variant encountered scepticism. In particular, representatives of existing memorial sites saw in his proposal a threat of competition with the educational work they were doing at authentic locations of National Socialist crimes. They feared a centralization of the memorial site landscape that had grown over the previous ten years and were concerned that the new project would siphon away from them hard-won financial support – a not unwarranted suspicion given conservative construction cost estimates of 80 million for the "House of Remembrance" alone.

The looming decision was additionally burdened by the controversy over a speech by the author Martin Walser, who declared himself fundamentally against the memorial in October 1998, referring to the "Never-ending Presentation of Our Shame". By doing so, he drove many undecided people onto the side of the memorial's supporters – surely unintentionally. In the closing phase, there was yet another recommendation, from theologian Richard Schröder, who suggested instead of a memorial a very simple "warning memorial" bearing the Hebrew inscription, "Thou shalt not kill".

On 25 June, 1999, in one of the last meetings of the Bundestag to take place in Bonn, a surprisingly clear majority of 314 to 209 voted in favour of creating the "Eisenman II" memorial at the "Ministry Gardens", which would include the dedication. By making this decision, they were rejecting the Naumann design with the "House of Remembrance" ("Eisenman III"). The latter would have meant the further reduction of the field of stelae and had clearly caused the debate over the memorial to drag on. Through the course of the debate, much support had grown for the idea of adding an element, which would give information about the Holocaust, thereby explaining the reason for the memorial and its dedication. So it was not only a tactical compromise, but also a decision on values, when the Bundestag committed itself to adding an information centre to the field of stelae. This would enable visitors to learn about the victims whose memories were to be honoured, as well as to inform them about authentic memorial locations. It should, however, be achieved "within the framework of the concept". In other words, it should in no way encroach upon the expressly recognized artistic quality of the Eisenman design, and certainly not by reducing the number of stelae.

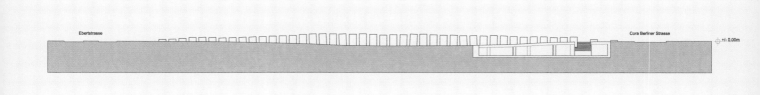

The Bundestag assumed responsibility for clearing up these issues, as well as the future funding and development. It set up, for the project, a special designated foundation, whose structure and composition would be determined in an additional law, passed nine months later. It became fundamentally clear that the Federal government would cover the full budget of the project, the precise cost of which had to be determined again with the inclusion of the "Information Centre".

This was one of the most urgent tasks of the newly constituted Board of Trustees along with reaching a decision about the location and size of the "Information Centre". In mid-2000, on behalf of the foundation, architect Peter Eisenman inspected several locations and development possibilities both inside and outside the field of stelae, which encompassed some 19,000 square metres. He very quickly dismissed all options for the site due to conceptual inconsistencies and the risk of unforeseeable costs and construction delays. If, however, the field of stelae was to remain intact and not be further reduced, the pressing question arose as to whether the "Information Centre" could be located underground, beneath the field of stelae. On this basis, the architect looked into two possible underground sites, at the south-eastern and north-western corners of the field of stelae. He chose the south-eastern option, not least because the north-western corner was situated on the busy Ebertstrasse and the field of stelae would thus become an appendix, particularly if the entrances to the "Information Centre" were accessible from the public footpath.

Parallel to this process, the Board of Trustees dealt with important decisions regarding the planned character and content of the "Information Centre". A small working group was set up, consisting for the most part of historians. The group delivered its first outline proposal in July 2000. According to this proposal, the "Information Centre" would be a self-contained project taking a non-museal stance towards information, in which the abstract memorialization of victims in the field of stelae would be made concrete and personalized. With that in mind, the working group recommended that there be four "theme rooms", each laid-out differently and covering in total 500 square metres, as well as a multi-functional entrance foyer of 300 square metres. The proposal clarified the foundation's plan for the use of rooms in terms of the need for lobby areas, as well as rooms for technical and office space, resulting in a gross floor space of about 1,800 square metres. In the summer of 2000, the Board of

A west-east slice through the field of stelae and the Information Centre, by Eisenman Architects, 2004.

Trustees tied together all these threads, so that the architect could formally begin planning the field of stelae and the "Information Centre". The corresponding cost estimate that the architect presented in the autumn of 2000 came to 25.3 million for the construction of the field of stelae and the "Information Centre", plus 2.3 million for the interior design of the "Information Centre". With the consent of the Board of Trustees, the economic committee of the Bundestag approved the sum of 27.6 million in November 2000 and thus opened the way, as far as finance was concerned, for the realization of the project.

With these conditions established, a decision could be taken in November 2000, as to what shape the exhibition in the "Information Centre" would take. Following a competition, the foundation chose Berlin exhibition planner Dagmar von Wilcken, whose basic idea convinced the foundation's representatives, primarily because she managed to effect a continuation of the architecture of the field of stelae into that of the "Information Centre" in a way that was both intelligent and minimal in form, and also rejected melodramatic gimmicks. The decision recognised the basic principle that the interior architecture, the delivery of the historical concept, and the exhibition design were to be developed at the same time – almost a concurrent process – an ambition that would be fully achieved in the four-year, extremely positive cooperation between architect and exhibition designer.

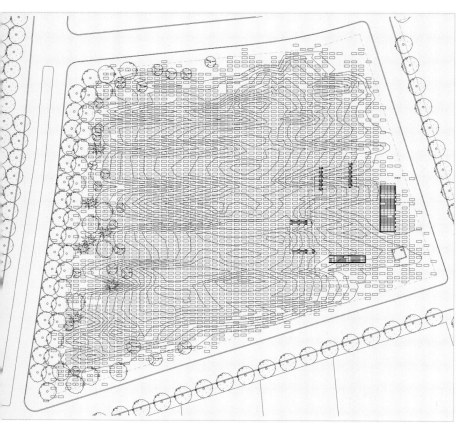

Layout of the memorial by Eisenman Architects, including the foundation contours for the field of stelae and the outline of the Information Centre, 2004.

The project management process entailed only small changes to the entire concept. According to the premise, "First the field of stelae, then the Information Centre", the architect moved the "Information Centre", positioned in the south-east corner, about ten to 20 metres into the field of stelae, so that the two stairways originally meant to be alongside the public footpath were now surrounded by, or partially occupied by, stelae. Additionally, a lift was added, whose access above-ground would, however, be to a great extent integrated into the field of stelae. To improve access to the field of stelae for people with disabilities, particularly for those in wheelchairs, the narrow gap between the stelae, and the width of the stelae, was increased from 0.92 centimetres to 0.95 centimetres. Apart from that, the general size and number of the stelae remained unchanged. The varying depth of the paved field, on which one crossed the field of stelae, was reduced from a maximum of – 3.2 metres to a maximum of – 2.4 metres, in order to reduce the danger that some of the stelae would stand on very steep inclines. But the heights of the approximately 2,700 stelae remained unchanged; the maximum height of the stelae from the ground was to be about 4.7 metres.

The intention to plant 41 trees on the field of stelae was also reworked, with concentration now on the west side. It would thus provide a transition from the urban setting, through the arrangement of trees by landscape architect Peter Josef Lenné, reconstructed in 1993 on the west side of Ebertstrasse, to the broad, open landscape of the Tiergarten. And another element, one already in the original design proposal for the field of stelae, was detailed in this planning phase: the continuation of the grid of stelae in the form of ground-level concrete slabs, each in the size of a stele, which would converge with the public footpaths surrounding all four sides of the field of stelae.

The paths belong to the four streets adjacent to the field of stelae. Only one of the streets, namely Ebertstrasse, has been a constant element in the city's outline for almost 300 years. The section of Behrenstrasse between Wilhelmstrasse and Ebertstrasse, with its heavy traffic, was, in contrast, built in 1993-94. Its course was shifted in 2004 by about 20 metres toward the south, in order to meet the growing security challenges in the construction of the US Embassy, which would extend from the northern border of the memorial up to Pariser Platz. The Founda-

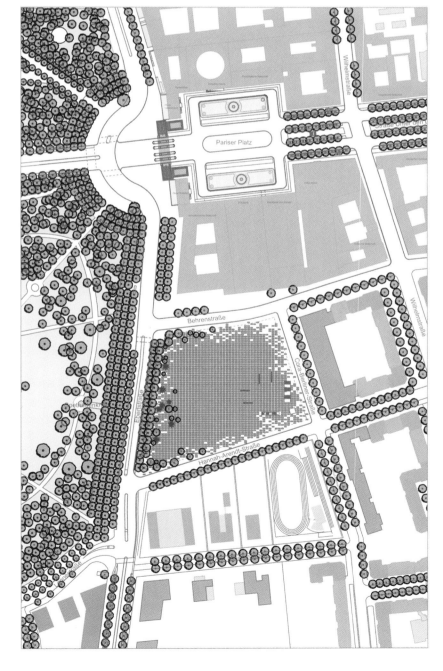

Urban planning map for the memorial property, showing nearby construction projects, 2004.

tion had approved this adjustment back in 2000, and changed the memorial plans accordingly. And on Cora-Berliner-Strasse, a residential street bordering the eastern side of the memorial site and built in 2004-05, a new apartment building will be constructed which will close off the U-shaped courtyard on Wilhelmstrasse. Likewise, on the southern side of the memorial, the Hannah-Arendt-Strasse was built in 2004-05. Because of its function as an entrance road, it is of great importance, primarily for bus traffic heading towards the "Information Centre". The fact that these two streets, as well as the Gertrud-Kolmar-Strasse to the south, are named after Jewish women persecuted by the National Socialists follows, by the way, decisions reached by the Berlin-Mitte District Administration in 1998 and 1999 — noteworthy decisions that sit well with the memorial and whose naming anchors these streets in the collective memory (4).

The planned start of construction in the late summer of 2002, following the approval of planning documents and extensive revision of the related development plan I-202-a, was postponed by eight months. The process of awarding the contract for the manufacture of the stelae had to be stopped and new tenders had to be issued. In March 2003, all essential building contracts, encompassing 80 percent of net building costs, had been awarded, so that construction could begin as of 1 April, 2003. The completion of the building project was achieved within the projected time and budget. The public confrontation in autumn 2003 concerning the use of Degussa products to safeguard the concrete stelae and their surfaces and to protect against graffiti, changed little in principle, but made it clear that this was never going to be a normal construction process. After intensive examination of all alternatives, the Board of Trustees of the Foundation decided, in November 2003, to continue construction, that is, to go on using the Degussa products. The main motivation for this decision was the fact that, in the country responsible for the Holocaust, there could be no clinically pure memorial that would be completely free, down to the last detail, of associations and burdens related to the past.

The memorial, consisting of the field of stelae and underground "Information Centre", is, in terms of building typology, a mixtum compositum, containing elements of various building and art forms. It is a national memorial in so far as it is aimed at German society and built in its name. But it memorializes not the great acts of a people, a ruler or dynasty, but rather a singular crime against humanity, committed in the name of Germany. In form, too, it breaks from the tradition of national memorials of the 19th and early 20th centuries, because its language bears absolutely no relation to traditional, hierarchical monumental forms (5). The difference from classical sculptural, memorial art, which depicts Germany as a nation of culture and civilization, is clear when one considers Fritz Schaper's Goethe Memorial, erected in 1880 on the west side of Ebertstrasse, in the Tiergarten – a memorial that also resulted from a civic initiative. Eisenman's memorial design is a large, abstract sculpture that, with its intensive links to the network of roads and its complete accessibility to pedestrians, sits within a tradition of art in public spaces. In its anti-monumentality, this horizontal force field stands in clear formal opposition to the densely populated, vertically-stacked buildings and apartment houses around it.

The memorial is a place of remembrance dedicated to an unimaginably large number of dead human beings. In that respect, it represents the tradition of the gravestone or tomb. The memorial incorporates several elements of sepulchral culture (6). It makes use of the stele form, in other words an upright, stone-like shape that points upward toward the heavens, constructed in remembrance of the dead. It also takes as a reference the sarcophagus, as a block-shaped, reclining form, as well as the ground-level grave slab, whose proportions approach that of a human body. With its sequential, patterned rows, the field of stelae is, in addition, reminiscent of a cemetery. But it is no cemetery, in the true sense of the word, as there are no human remains to be protected here. It can be interpreted as a symbolic cemetery, which employs elements of tombstone culture in serial and abstract form. The manner in which these various forms of building and tombstone art are joined in a varied and novel way, constitutes the artistic quality of the design (7).

The descending floor that leads, so to speak, through the field of stelae into the past, forcing the visitor's usual sensory relationships with the immediate environment into the background as he or she walks through, expresses the contemplative character of this space in an unusual manner. The formal rigidity of the field of stelae corresponds to its wordlessness. In view of the immense number of victims, every attempt to relate the individual concrete shapes to a particular person in the usual way is fundamentally rejected. The field of stelae, without any words, strengthens at the same time the memorial's dialogue with its visitor, because it demands a certain "shaping of memory that pulls the visitor inside" (8). One awaits with great interest the different ways in which the visitor will use the memorial after its completion.

The formal features and references of the memorial can unfold in a special manner in the memorial's chosen location. Through this site, with its complex integration into the network of spaces, buildings and levels of meaning in the centre of Berlin, the memorial will become a public space for remembrance with numerous connotations. The memorial location breaks up the historic inaccessibility of the former "Ministry Gardens", in that it overcomes and makes porous the nearly 300-year-old city borders, recently delineated by the Berlin Wall. The memorial will turn this space into a link between the Tiergarten – the city's central park – and the historic city centre.

The formal metaphors and arguments for the memorial developed up to now will be only the beginning. With its formal quality, its diverse typology and its openness, the memorial allows plenty of room for new interpretations. It is to be hoped that a good portion of the interpretations and meanings assigned to the memorial and which it will require in the future, will develop in concert with the changing urban environment. Only then will the memorial have an impact on coming generations and show the enduring strength of its message.

(1) Lea Rosh, *Ein Denkmal für die ermordeten Juden Europas* (Berlin, 1990), p. 6.

(2) Hildebrand Machleidt, Wolfgang Schäche, Christos Papathanasiou, Cornelia Müller, Städtebauliche Studie *"Ministergärten"* in: Ute Heimrod/ Günter Schlusche/Horst Seferens (eds.), *Der Denkmalstreit – das Denkmal?* (Berlin, 1999), p. 785 ff.

(3) On the building history of the area s. Laurenz Demps, *Berlin-Wilhelmstrasse Eine Topographie preussisch-deutscher Macht* (Berlin, 1996); Wolfgang Schäche, *Zur Geschichte and stadträumlichen Bedeutung der "Ministergärten"* (Berlin, 1992), in: Heimrod/Schlusche/Seferens, loc. cit., p. 780 ff. and Peter R. Fuchs (Landesdenkmalamt Berlin), *Die Bunkeranlage auf dem Grundstück Wilhelmstrasse 72 – Ministergärten – in Berlin-Mitte* (Berlin, 1998).

(4) Sibylle Quack, *Drei Strassen in Berlin*, in: Marion Kaplan/Beate Meyer (ed.), *Jüdische Welten – Juden in Deutschland vom 18. Jahrhundert bis in die Gegenwart* (Göttingen, 2005).

(5) Nikolaus Pevsner, *A History of Building Types*, London 1979; Thomas Nipperdey, *Nationalidee und Nationaldenkmal in Deutschland im 19. Jahrhundert*, in: Jutta Schuchard/Horst Claussen (eds.), *Vergänglichkeit und Denkmal* (Bonn, 1985).

(6) Rainer Sörries, *Großes Lexikon der Bestattungskultur*, vol. 1 (Kassel, 2002).

(7) Werner Hofmann, *Stellungnahme zum "Denkmal für die ermordeten Juden Europas"*, in: Heimrod/Schlusche/Seferens, loc.cit., p. 935.

(8) James E. Young, *Die Zeitgeschichte der Gedenkstätten und Denkmäler des Holocaust*, in: James E. Young (ed.), *Mahnmale des Holocaust* (München, New York, 1993).

A MEMORIAL FOR WHOM?

THE DEBATE ABOUT THE MEMORIAL TO THE MURDERED JEWS OF EUROPE, ABOUT VICTIMS
OF PERSECUTION UNDER NATIONAL SOCIALISM, AND ABOUT MEMORIAL SITES

Memorial at Sachsenhausen, 23 April 1995:
Russian and Israeli survivors of the camp during
a ceremony marking the 50th anniversary of
the liberation, on the grounds of the memorial.
In the foreground is Ignatz Bubis.

The debate about a central site of remembrance for the victims of National Socialist ideology and rule has been going on for more than ten years. This debate originally began on the initiative of just a few people, but it has now taken on national dimensions. It was a constant crystallization point in the discourse on National Socialism, one of central importance to the Federal Republic of Germany. With its resolution of 25, June 1999, the German Bundestag made the debate its own concern. By doing so, it was also reaching a decision on the intellectual and moral doubts as to whether a memorial dedicated to the genocide of the Jews – with the other victims of the National Socialist regime somehow included, but not expressly mentioned – could or should be built in Germany.

But the Bundestag resolution did not put an end to the discussion. The ongoing debate over the pros and cons of this memorial proved to be an appropriate form of remembrance – perhaps even the best form of remembrance – the cause and nature of which are imprinted deeply on the general consciousness. And this was not least because the heated arguments during construction in 2003 – about the use of materials from a firm whose sister company had produced, of all things, Zyklon B, the poison gas used to murder people in Auschwitz – led once more right into the heart of the matter: whether and for whom should the memorial be built and, if the answer were yes, then which resources might be used and who might take part in the construction. The impact of this confrontation on the public revealed once again a principle function of the post-war discourse on remembrance: the memory of the National Socialist crimes is divided. On the one hand, the survivors of persecution and their descendants, and on the other, members of the dominant society at the time and their descendants, live with different sensibilities that flowed into the debate, and continue to do so (1).

Determining the Location
The Dedication

The lengthy debate would also clarify whether the memorial should be dedicated to the victims of National Socialist persecution (and if so, which victims should be included) or whether it should be built as a warning against the crimes of the National Socialist state. Salomon Korn, with his skills both as an architect and a Jewish intellectual, highlighted the dual problem of making this decision in his article, "The wrong label". Does the "Memorial to the Murdered Jews" preclude a central memorial against crime and perpetrators?", in which he pointed out that the state's support for a "Memorial to the Murdered Jews of Europe" made it less likely that a "central memorial in Germany to the crime and the perpetrators" would ever be realized: "It is certainly more pleasant for descendants of the perpetrators to have a memorial to the victims than to construct a warning against the crimes committed by their own people. The memorial to the victims could then – seen in psychoanalytic terms – easily become a "cover" for the unbuilt central memorial and thereby disguise the necessity for such a memorial. The parcelling out of memorials to individual groups of victims appears to make the central German memorial superfluous". (2) Aside from the fragmentation of remembrance, he emphasizes here another pattern of public and private confrontation with the National Socialist past, which emerged clearly in the discussion about the memorial: identification with the victims prevented confrontation with the perpetrators.

The political decision favoured a memorial dedicated to the Jewish victims, but, in the public mind, the connotation of this decision was soon seen in relative terms. One speaks generally of the "Holocaust Monument" or "Holocaust Memorial". All National Socialist crimes are often subsumed under the term "Holocaust", and remembrance is, at the same time, understood as remembrance of the guilt of the perpetrators. Intellectually and morally, this certainly left something to be desired, but as a form of acceptance, it was valueable in paving the way towards building societal consensus. Of course, part of that consensus is widespread public rejection of forms of remembrance that focus on crimes committed in their name.

The philosopher Jürgen Habermas posed the crucial questions regarding the sense of the monument, thereby highlighting the essence of the public debate: "Are we turning the self-critical remembrance of 'Auschwitz' – the ongoing reflection on the events connected with this name – into an explicit element of our political self-image? Are we, who were born later, taking on the disturbing political responsibility for the departure from civilization that Germans perpetrated, supported and tolerated, as an element in our fractured national identity?" The answer corresponds exactly to the political reason for setting up the monument: "As descendants who share responsibility, we tell ourselves, 'Never again'. A break with old traditions is the prerequisite for the recovery of self-esteem". (3) Political reasoning, philosophical and public opinion were widely in agreement here.

Habermas defines the citizens as the creators and sponsors of such a memorial. This is meant in the original sense of the word: citizens as the society of politically emancipated individuals, who bear responsibility for their state: "The sponsor is every citizen who finds himself the clear inheritor of a culture in which this was possible – in the context of a tradition that they share with the generation of perpetrators. With their memorial, they establish at once a connection with the perpetrators, the victims and their descendants". On the one hand, it should become clear that the sponsors of the memorial do not include citizens who are survivors or their descendants living in Germany, such as Jews and others who were persecuted for "racist", religious, social or political reasons, nor do they include post-war immigrants, but rather those who represent a traditional connection with the dominant society of that time. At the same time, Habermas says a connection to the victims and to remembrance of victims is necessary: " (...) an exclusive concentration on what crime and perpetrators mean to us would undermine the moral core of compassion for the victims. The unconditional moral impulse towards remembrance must not be qualified through the context of self-assurance. We can only think of the victims seriously, and properly, when we think of them for their own sake". The planned memorial could thus be understood as helping create those connections and overcome the fragmentation of remembrance.

The historian Reinhart Koselleck, a precise and unswerving champion of clear definitions and decisions – not only with regard to the monument – took up the problem of this optimism and referred to three overlapping and contradictory goals with which memorials, memorial sites, and museum projects have been dogged since the 1980s, particularly in Berlin. These include the finished designs of the former Gestapo site at Prinz-Albrecht-Strasse in Berlin-Mitte, the "House of the Wannsee Conference" in Berlin-Zehlendorf, the "Neue Wache" [literally "New Guardhouse"] in Berlin-Mitte, as well as the "Memorial to the Murdered Jews of Europe", the Berlin "Jewish Museum" and the "House of the Topography of Terror", which were still at the conceptual stage only. Without looking for compromises, Koselleck focused on the problem of the dedication and the societal and political points of view that it would express: "The latest attempt to establish a death-cult of memorials – to present remembrance and remorse, warning and reminder, in a lasting manner – point toward three different realms of the dead that reach into our lives in various manners. Either all dead are victims, as inscribed on the national memorials" – the "Neue Wache" in Berlin, centrally situated on Unter den Linden, is dedicated without qualification to all "victims of war and tyranny" – "or victims are only those killed as innocent civilians or as defenceless prisoners, particularly by the Nazis" – a definition on which numerous historic memorial sites are based – "or these groups of victims must once again be differentiated from one another" – which addresses the demands of individual groups that their dead be commemorated specifically (4).

The Bundestag's decision on 25 June, 1999 to build the memorial was an attempt to reconcile these positions: the memorial would be dedicated to the main group of victims – European Jewry. But allied to this there was a brief to include remembrance of all other victims of National Socialist persecution at the site. Not expressly formulated, but established through discussion about the Bundestag resolution, was the intention to involve all parts of the population in the process of realizing the memorial. This ultimately resulted in a confrontation of central importance, cited in the introduction, about the involvement of a chemical firm in the construction. The Bundestag's resolution had left room for a hierarchy of victims, which later would find expression in a collection of forms of remembrance for various victim groups, starting with the Sinti and Roma. The representative of the Sinti and Roma rejected the position offered him on the board of the "Foundation for the Memorial to the Murdered Jews of Europe", in protest against the exclusivity of the inscription and thus the accompanying classification of victims. Representatives of other victim groups chose to express their interests and wishes for their own memorial sites or monuments under the umbrella of the board of the Foundation.

Hierarchies and forgotten victims of National Socialism

In order to emphasize that the memorial inscription should not be understood as shutting out other victim groups, the statutes of the "Foundation for the Memorial to the Murdered Jews of Europe" stated that all those persecuted under National Socialism were to be included. In other words, the aim was to cultivate remembrance of discrimination, persecution, expulsion and extermination of people and to seek ways to anchor this remembrance in the national cultural memory. The victims of National Socialist persecution are numerous. In addition to the Jews, those targeted by National Socialist racist ideology included above all Sinti and Roma and members of Slavic peoples such as Poles, Ukrainians, Belorussian forced labourers or Soviet prisoners of war. Political opponents of the National Socialist regime were also persecuted, as well as ideological and religious groups such as the Jehovah's Witnesses, pacifists, Confessional Protestants. Proponents of democracy and communism were also declared enemies. Other groups are the victims of National Socialist military justice, "euthanasia", and medical experiments in concentration camps; and those who were shut out and persecuted for social and ideological reasons, including homosexuals and so-called anti-social people, whose behaviour offended the norms of the unconstitutional state. These victim groups often have no lawyers to help them secure their place in the public memory. For example, there is little public awareness of the fate of Soviet prisoners of war, of whom some three million did not survive the German camps, either because they were allowed to die or were deliberately murdered. Even when politicians mention the National Socialist crimes in their speeches, they seldom refer to Russian, Ukrainian and Belorussian victims.

National Socialist criminal, special justice and military courts condemned about 46,000 people to death for desertion, conscientious objection to military service, or "Wehrkraftzersetzung" – undermining the military. This was an order of magnitude by far surpassing the punishments meted out by all other states. Only in October 1990 was an "Interest Group for Victims of Military Justice" founded to fight for the acceptance into society of these victims and for their due place in the public memory. Post-war justice and policies have, in keeping with widespread attitudes towards "deserters", continued, as a rule, to look upon those who refused to serve as traitors to the fatherland, deserving of draconian punishment. The fact that most victims of this military justice had refused to serve an unjust state, and were thus committing individual acts of resistance, must still be conveyed to the general public. Not until the autumn of 1996 did the Upper House of the German Bundestag determine that sentences handed down during the National Socialist dictatorship regarding acts of desertion, "undermining the military" and refusal to serve, were not valid in law, because the sentences were the acts of a terror state. The Bund-

estag expressed respect and sympathy for the victims and urged the federal government to compensate them. The commitment of those victims to public memory is still to come. The creation of a travelling exhibition planned by the "Foundation for the Memorial to the Murdered Jews of Europe" could help here. First of all, the requisite information is to be prepared and presented throughout Germany. The intention is that the exhibition should finish up at Torgau on the Elbe. This former central location of National Socialist military justice, with its two military prisons, the seat of the Reich's wartime court – where many death sentences were carried out – could be the appropriate site for remembrance of this group of victims.

Berlin, Nollendorfplatz, 2005: Memorial plaque commemorating homosexuals who were persecuted and murdered during the Nazi period.

Until very recently, the general public, both in the former East Germany and West Germany, also had difficulty honouring the memory of homosexual victims of National Socialist persecution. Discrimination against this group existed both in criminal law and general attitudes in society. It persisted beyond the period of National Socialism, hindering public awareness of the injustice committed against them. There was also discrimination against homosexuals from other victims, who for a long time refused to include homosexual survivors in events marking the anniversary of liberation from concentration camps, or would not accept the creation of monuments, thereby barring homosexuals from the discourse on remembrance. The demand for a memorial for persecuted and murdered homosexuals, which would also be an information centre, will be met in the coming years. The Bundestag accepted the recommendation and the Board of the "Foundation for the Memorial to the Murdered Jews of Europe" agreed to meet the demand as well.

Another category of prisoner in the National Socialist concentration camp system was the Jehovah's Witnesses, then better known as "Ernste Bibelforscher", or "serious Bible scholars". Members of this religious group were more consistently opposed to the ideology of National Socialism than members of other religious communities, refusing to perform

military service, or give the "Hitler salute", and resisting the subjugation expected by the regime. Of an estimated 25,000 active Jehovah's Witnesses before the persecution, some 10,000 fell victim to the National Socialists. The persecution ranged from the loss of home and job to the denial of the right to childcare and imprisonment in jails and concentration camps. In the camps, the "serious Bible scholars" were stigmatized by having to wear a purple triangle. Of some 4,000 prisoners, 1,400 died and 360 were executed. After liberation, this victim group was gradually forgotten, resurfacing only in the early 1990s due both to efforts by the Jehovah's Witnesses themselves and the groundbreaking work of historian Detlef Garbe (5).

Moers, 28 April 1999:
Ceremonial erection of street sign for the road named after Franz Saumer, a Jehovah's Witness. For religious reasons, he had refused to serve in the armed forces and was therefore executed.

Also without a lobby were the victims of medical experiments. This was a particularly difficult group to define. The victims were not objects of systematic persecution clearly defined by National Socialist ideology. Common identifying aspects are also difficult to find. Often, they were members of other victim groups, including Sinti and Roma, Soviet prisoners of war and homosexuals. Victims of medical experiments in the concentration camps fell into the hands of unscrupulous doctors for the most varied of reasons: either by accident or because of unusual physical characteristics. They included twins, people who fell under the "Law for Protection Against Hereditary Defects" (such as blindness or deafness), or those who stood out for other reasons. Historical research has long concentrated on victims of the "euthanasia" programme and only gradually turned its focus to experiments related to illnesses such as tuberculosis, scarlet fever, malaria and so on, and to surgical, toxicological and gynaecological experiments. In such experiments, participating doctors were quite prepared to accept the death of the victim. When it came to sterilization experiments, these doctors caused permanent damage. People were murdered because scientists wanted to use their organs, skeletons or skulls for the purposes of research. Scholars in academia and at memorial sites have only just begun to explore this complex subject. New research has been presented in recent years, primarily under the auspices of the Max Planck Society and, since the autumn of 2004, at the memorial at Sachsenhausen. There are no figures for this victim group, not least because of the difficulty of definition when compared with other groups.

Hadamar, 1999: Dedication of a bell made at the behest of survivors, in memory of victims of the National Socialist crimes of forced sterilization and "euthanasia".

The group of victims to whom the memorial is explicitly dedicated, represented by the Central Council of Jews in Germany, exercised restraint in the discussions. It was always stressed that the Jewish community at no point asked for such a memorial and that the memorial would in no way transmit demands from Jews to perpetrators of the genocide and their descendants. Prominent Jews continued to criticize the memorial in general, or the exclusiveness of its dedication, and will surely go on doing so. When the plans for the memorial began to take shape, Ignatz Bubis, then president of the Central Council, delivered a talk about the artistic competition in 1995 in which he thanked the initiators for their commitment, and particularly for the fact "that it was non-Jews who took the initiative". At the same, he emphasized his hope, linked to the memorial, that the memory of both the genocide and its victims would be preserved, without the imposition of guilt on others. He also expressed the expectation that "the victims, their representatives, the heirs of the victims [should] not remain completely apart [from the project], for they also have their own feelings to contribute". (6) Given his own background, this position was understandable: born in Breslau and raised in Poland; deported to a ghetto by the National Socialists; robbed of his family. Bubis lived in Germany after the war and became involved in the community. He became president of the Central Council in 1992 – around the time of the xenophobic riots in Mölln, Rostock, Solingen and elsewhere, a time that also saw the events marking the 50th anniversary of the end of the war and the liberation of the National Socialist concentration camps. This clearly shows how diverse positions were regarding the memorial within the individual groups involved.

Centralization, and memorials at historic locations

It remained to be clarified where the memorial should be sited, both in concrete and institutional terms. Where should it be built and what should its relationship be to memorials at historical sites, as well as to museums and similar projects providing information and education? Not only was there concern about classification of victim groups through the dedication; the location was also controversial because of fears of centralizing a diverse, federally organized landscape of memory [see Rürup in this volume].

As of 1989, the debate over the memorial ran concurrently with the difficult process of rapprochement and confrontation with German unification. In addition to confronting the aforementioned riots, there was also the need to confront the vastly different ways that East and West Germany had dealt with the National Socialist past. In 1989, the newly founded citizens' initiative, which was established to create a memorial to the murdered Jews, chose the unused land of Prinz-Albrecht-Strasse in Berlin, former location of the National Socialist machinery of persecution, including the administration of the Reich Security Main Office and the Gestapo. The former site of the Gestapo complex, which another group, the association "Active Museum, Fascism and Resistance in Berlin", had claimed since the early 1980s, with the goal of presenting the "Topography of Terror" there, highlighted again the pattern of conflict related to the memorial. The argument in brief: could victims be memorialized in, of all places, a site once occupied by perpetrators? Or should one not focus on the crimes and on the support for them, meaning inevitably a cognitive consideration rather than an emotional connection? With the fall of the Berlin Wall, a prominent area in what had been a no-man's-land became available; for the sponsors of the "Memorial to the Murdered Jews of Europe", the area near the former Reich Chancellery had even more symbolic power than the former Gestapo complex. The symbolism of this location near the Brandenburg Gate and the destroyed Reich Chancellery – the former centre of power of the dictatorship – corresponded with widespread visions for the memorial.

It was not only its location that placed the memorial project at the centre of diverse efforts associated with the culture of memory, which in the early 1990s was in a period of growth in Berlin. In January 1992, the "House of the Wannsee Conference" was opened to the public as a memorial and educational centre; at the same time, the Foundation "Topography of Terror" was set up with the goal of documenting and interpreting for future generations, the "historical experience of National Socialism and its crimes" on the site of the Prinz-Albrecht complex. Two prominent locations were thereby dedicated to remembering the crimes and perpetrators. Many memorials to the victims were set up in Berlin: at the Grunewald train station, in memory of the deportation of Jewish citizens (1991); at the Reichstag, for persecuted members of parliament (1992); at the site of the satellite concentration camp on Sonnenallee (1994); at the location of the Columbiahaus concentration camp (1994); at the site of the book burnings on Bebelplatz (1995); and at the former location of the synagogue on Lindenstrasse, and elsewhere. The rededication of the "Neue Wache" memorial on Unter den Linden as a central national site, dedicated to the memory of all victims of war and tyranny, was accompanied by incessant controversy regarding its aesthetics and the political purpose behind its message. This revealed how difficult it was to reach a consensus, when diverse and contradictory views in German society were breaking out with some vehemence in the course of trying to reach that consensus. At the same time, the intensity and breadth of the debate demonstrated how urgent the need was for communication on the issue.

Another expression of the culture of remembrance based on monumentality and symbolism, the Berlin "Jewish Museum", began to raise a furore at the same time, both from the architectural and artistic standpoints. Daniel Libeskind, who in June 1989 had won first prize in a competition for the project, constructed the "Jewish Museum" as a kind of memorial sculpture to the Holocaust. Admirers of his architectural philosophy were astonished and when the building was opened to the public in 1999, it was acclaimed as a work of art that delivered a message through diverse expressions and metaphors, and was seen as a revelation. This structure was the real Holocaust memorial, said many who eagerly followed the architect's line of thought. Thousands of people visited the building, which presented itself as an expressive gesture – it was not yet a museum, for only the dramatic external form, with its claim to meaning, existed – and there were many who insisted that the structure should remain empty. In September 2001, the "Jewish Museum" assumed its intended role, with the opening of its exhibition and then with numerous additional programmes. It presented Jewish history and Jewish culture and is a dominant institution in the culture of remembrance, embraced by a wide public. The museum clearly met, and continues to meet, a profound need for information and discussion.

Realization

The difficulties in dealing with the National Socialist past were also reflected in the numerous competitions held regarding the planned memorial, in the texts of the invitations to tender, and in the apparent impossibility of evaluating the choices, with their attendant processes. Above all, it was clear how difficult the task that had been set was [see Schlusche in this volume]. The competition entry of concept artist Horst Hoheisel, who had long been involved in confronting National Socialism in various artistic projects (7), revealed how the debate pierced the very core of societal identity. His concept, which naturally had no chance of being realized, was to "tear down the Brandenburg Gate and grind its stone and bronze into dust. The dust will be scattered over the memorial area. The plaza will be covered in the old granite paving stones that are common on Berlin pavements. The names of the European countries with their corresponding numbers of murdered Jews will be engraved there." The artist questioned just how serious people were about the memorial's location: "Would the nation of the perpetrators, considering the genocide of European Jews and Sinti and Roma, be prepared to sacrifice a national symbol as a memorial? Can the Germans bear a second void? The empty space of Pariser Platz, without the Brandenburg Gate, and the empty space of the "Ministry Gardens" without an exonerating memorial out of stone, steel or bronze?" (8)The debate continued. Finally, 19 writers and intellectuals demanded, at the beginning of February 1998, "Renunciation through Insight" and collated numerous objections and doubts concerning the memorial: "Every form and every dedication that does not apply to all victims of the National Socialist racist and master-race madness, has an artificial feel and stands in crass disproportion to existing sites of authentic history, to eye-witness and to remembrance". The intellectuals feared that, as opposed to the historic sites of the crimes, a "gigantic 'national' memorial would more likely remain a place of distraction, of dissociation from reality, of cold abstraction" (9). At the same time, Walter Jens, head of the artistic competition of 1994-95, also turned against the memorial with the observation: "The horror of horrors cannot be grasped through the medium of monumental art." (10) But the time was long since past when "Renunciation through Insight" could be brought into line with the requirements of historical politics, that is, public presentation, perception and a responsible confrontation with history. Besides, as far as those responsible for political culture were concerned, it had given rise to misinterpretations, particularly abroad.

The development of a private initiative into a matter of public interest is as much a part of the memorial concept as is the public discussion today about subliminally, rather than consciously perceived patterns of remembrance; the reassessment, modification or confirmation of established official forms of remembrance in the East and West; and the ongoing disputes which break out time and again. This coincides with a need that has arisen in Europe as a whole after the end of the Cold War to

Bayreuth, November 2001: "Memorial Stone Collection". In connection with a concept drawn up by Horst Hoheisel, pupils, students and soldiers in the German Army together carried a sign of remembrance of 145 Jews from Bayreuth, who died in the Holocaust. Each stone bears the name of a victim, with whose life story the participants became engaged as they compiled, the collection.

clarify how one deals with World War II, the National Socialist occupation of Europe, and the mass crimes committed, a catastrophe that almost everywhere awakened dubious national traditions. Memorials at historical sites, which exist all over Europe – Theresienstadt, Auschwitz, Belzec, Majdanek, Sachsenhausen, Dachau, Bergen-Belsen, to name only a few – have been newly designed and shaped. In many places, new memorials and museums are under construction. Like the Berlin memorial, they will be open in 2005 to coincide with ceremonies marking the 60th anniversary of the end of the war.

In the meantime, the memorial itself is more than an abstract sign of remembrance that appeals to emotions. With the "Information Centre", it becomes a site for cognitive experience that includes all victim groups. The monument acts as a portal for memorials at authentic sites. Located near the Foundation "Topography of Terror" at the former Gestapo site, which serves as a reminder of crimes and perpetrators, the "Memorial to the murdered Jews of Europe" is – with all its emotional and cognitive aspects – dedicated to the victims. This again distinguishes it from the "Jewish Museum", which endeavours to present Jews to the public not as victims, but as a culture. The Foundation will keep memory alive, through the memorial's artistic essence and the scholarly contribution of the "Information Centre"; through programmes, lectures on literary, scholarly and aesthetic subjects, and always in cooperation with representatives of victims groups and with memorials at authentic locations across Europe. The goal of all these activities is to bring the confrontation with National Socialism into everyday life. Only then does the memorial become a living institution.

(1)   Salomon Korn, *Geteilte Erinnerung* (Berlin, 1999), p. 201.

(2)   Salomon Korn, *Mit falschem Etikett*, in: *Frankfurter Rundschau*, 4 September 1997.

(3)   Jürgen Habermas, *Der Zeigefinger. Die Deutschen und ihr Denkmal*, in: *Die Zeit*, 31 March 1999.

(4)   Reinhart Koselleck, *Vier Minuten für die Ewigkeit*, in: *Frankfurter Allgemeine Zeitung (FAZ)*, 9 January 1997.

(5)   Detlef Garbe, *Zwischen Widerstand und Martyrium: die Zeugen Jehovas im "Dritten Reich"* (Oldenburg, 1993).

(6)   Ute Heimrod/Günter Schlusche/Horst Seferens (eds.), *Der Denkmalstreit – das Denkmal?*, (Berlin, 1999), p. 246.

(7)   Compare Horst Hoheisel & Andreas Knitz, *Zermahlene Geschichte. Kunst als Umweg* (Weimar, 1999).

(8)   ibid, p. 379.

(9)   *Offener Brief*, in: *FAZ*, 5 February 1998.

(10) Walter Jens, *In letzter Minute*, in: *FAZ*, 7 February 1998.

CREATING AN EXHIBITION ABOUT THE MURDER OF EUROPEAN JEWRY

CONFLICTS OF SUBJECT, CONCEPT AND DESIGN IN THE "INFORMATION CENTRE"

Making history tangible

How can an exhibition about the history of the murder of European Jewry do justice to the subject in a condensed form, especially when it is in a different location from the historical sites where the Holocaust took place? How can one avoid intimidating or making excessive emotional demands on the visitors, while at the same time neither playing down nor trivializing the crimes? How – at this central place of remembrance in Germany's capital city – can one overcome the dangers of descending into empty symbolism or preaching historical "dogmas"? These and other questions came up during the process of creating the historical concept for the "Information Centre". The decisions that had to be made during the planning phase were not easy ones; and naturally, in view of the extremely difficult subject matter, there were passionate disagreements over both the content and the creative means of expression.

The Bundestag's resolution of 1999 brought to an end the long debate about a memorial dedicated to the murdered Jews of Europe. The addition of an "Information Centre about the victims whose memory was being honoured and about memorials at authentic sites" represented a compromise between those who wanted a Holocaust museum on the one hand and supporters of a pure memorial with no additional information on the other. Yet the task of giving this compromise a meaningful form and of developing it into an effective exhibition, presented great challenges to all those involved. The first question to be answered was where the "Information Centre" should be situated in relation to the memorial. The decision of the Foundation's Board of Trustees to locate it underground, resulted above all from the following considerations: The "Information Centre" would be subordinate to the memorial; it should not disturb Peter Eisenman's huge accessible sculpture and draw visitors away from the memorial; at the same time, however, it had to be integrated into the overall artistic concept.

The Board of Trustees additionally decided that the main function of the "Information Centre", as regards content, would be to "personalize and individualize the horrors of the Holocaust" (1). The exhibition would make it clear that individual fates lay behind the unfathomable number of six million murdered European Jews, whom one wished to commemorate. A working group set up by the Board of Trustees, which included the historians Eberhard Jäckel, Andreas Nachama, Reinhard Rürup and the Foundation's Executive Director, Sibylle Quack, developed the fundamental principles for the exhibition's historical conception and established two essential content-related issues, both of which had to be taken into consideration: how to tell the story of the murder of European Jewry and how to inform about memorials at authentic sites. Needless to say, the basic concept for the "Information Centre" was modified and altered many times, and this process, too, was subject to much criticism and heated debate among experts (2). It was precisely the diverse and some-times competing demands on a relatively small exhibition space, which one knew would probably attract hundreds of thousands of visitors, that required a great deal of patience and precision from those responsible. The result, the exhibition that we see today, shows that the debates, though sometimes difficult, were completely worthwhile.

As already stated, individuals and their families from all over Europe are the focus of the "Information Centre". Their lives, suffering and death are documented here. By presenting personal stories of people who were per-secuted and murdered, the victims receive, in the eyes of the visitor, real faces, names and lives as individuals, which clearly convey their diverse cultural and national heritages. Because by far the greatest proportion of those murdered came from central and Eastern Europe, their life stories and fates are in the foreground. This is particularly important because it will contribute to deepening the visitors' knowledge about the cultural diversity of European Jewry before the Holocaust, knowledge that is par-ticularly lacking in Germany.

While the exhibition is dedicated to the victims of the genocide against the Jews, it also provides a historical orientation for the actions and responsibility of Germans. The display starts with a summary of the events that took place between 1933 and 1945. This summary gives an historical overview and guide for the detailed information, which is to follow in four thematically designed rooms. The "Information Centre" entrance foyer shows the escalation of the politics of murder, provides context and names the perpetrators, constantly emphasizing the effects of this policy on individuals and their families at this early stage in the exhibition.

Statements by eye-witnesses, family stories, names and short biogra-phies of murdered Jews form the essence of the exhibition.

Visitors experience a dramatic peak in the third room of the exhibi-tion, the only one to contain sound. The names of murdered individuals, together with brief biographical sketches, are featured in the centre of the presentation, which highlights just how limited our knowledge is of those who were murdered. In their incomplete and fragmentary nature, the biographies show the extent of the destruction of people and their property, often the destruction of all the traces that make memory pos-sible. Even today, a vast number of names of those murdered remain unknown. That it has been possible to make accessible, via the "Informa-tion Centre" database, the most extensive collection of names and biog-raphies of murdered Jews — compiled by the Israeli memorial Yad Vashem — underscores the importance of this central place of remembrance in the German capital.

The exhibition also tells visitors about the course and spread of National Socialist terror across the European continent and gives detailed informa-tion about the multifaceted and cruel face of the persecution and murder of European Jewry: deportations throughout Europe; incarceration in ghettos; mass shootings; extermination camps; and death marches. The question of what one finds today at the historic sites, of whether and how these terrible events are to be remembered, is presented at the very conclusion of the exhibition, in the exit hall. This final "portal" focuses on the present, providing information about memorial sites throughout Europe. In addition, visitors get the chance to learn more about the history of the debate on the memorial itself.

The process of creating the memorial has been accompanied not only by socially significant discussions, such as that about the Degussa company's involvement in the memorial construction. In November 2001, at a symposium involving an international gathering of historians and other scholars, the content and design concept for the "Information Centre" were also severely criticized. The disagreements revolved primarily around the balance between the memorial and information-led elements of the future exhibition, and honed in on the "Information Centre" being a creation borne of compromise. If it was not a museum, then what was it? Did it represent simply an extension of the memorial and should therefore avoid providing extensive information? To what extent were the elements of the work of art above-ground to be carried through into the "Information Centre"? The specific arrangement of the ensemble prompted associations: some critics suspected that the "Information Centre" was meant as a kind of underground "tomb", a "crypt" or even a "memory cave" under the memorial designed by Peter Eisenman, which for many brought to mind a burial ground. This did not bode well for the claim that information would be presented here, that would provide cognitive, educational access to the subject. Most specialists agreed with the words of the President of the Bundestag and Chairman of the Foundation, who had emphasized that "honest remembering" was for him "inseparable from critical enlightenment" (3). Most experts promoted a sober, factual and sensitive delivery of knowledge, with an emphasis on informative rather than on memorial aspects. They argued against the "duplication" of the memorial character of the field of stelae, and warned against using overpowering artistic and/or architectural elements in the "Information Centre".

The exhibition concept still incorporates the memorial's stelae into the design of the "Information Centre" – and with good reason. It was a special challenge to balance the relationship between content and design so that these impressive creative elements would not be divorced from the content, but rather would support and strengthen it.

Bench

Illuminated glass
floor panels with texts

Hanging rectangles
with illuminated
photographs and texts

Projection surface
Monitor
Touchscreen

Loudspeaker
Audiostation

Illuminated wall display case

In the exhibition, the content – particularly the individual stories illustrating and representing the murder of European Jewry – stands in the foreground. The stories speak to the visitor both emotionally and cognitively, avoiding an empty or depersonalized presentation of events, or one that is too abstract. By citing Eisenman's stele form and "grid", the design of the "Information Centre" makes present and evident its connection to the memorial dedicated to the murdered Jews. And that is as it should be: the close relationship and ensemble with the memorial above is the chief characteristic of this place of remembrance.

Giving the victims an identity
The exhibition's design concept

The task of forming an exhibition in the "Information Centre" presented a special challenge, because it involved bringing the Centre's impressive historical content into harmony with Peter Eisenman's unusual, architectural memorial design. The Bundestag resolution of 25 June, 1999, demanded that the architect created space for an exhibition that would complement his memorial and explain its dedication. In order to carry this out in as integrated and "invisible" a manner as possible, Peter Eisenman planned to locate the "Information Centre" below the field of stelae.

In early 2000, after consulting with historians, the Foundation's Board of Trustees agreed on four main themes for the future exhibition, each of which would be presented in a room of approximately equal size:

Room 1: the European dimension
of the mass murder of the Jews;
Room 2: representative family histories,
before, during and after the Holocaust;
Room 3: the presentation of known names of victims;
Room 4: a cartographic overview of the sites
of persecution and extermination in Europe.

In addition, the exhibition was to mention non-Jewish victims. An important, final task was to make reference to other memorials and museums with the same theme. The foyer area was designated to perform this function.

Working on this basis, Peter Eisenman drew up four square exhibition rooms of equal size, as well as several foyers or lobby areas. In order to make clear the overlapping of the two levels of time – on one level the historical and on the other, the actual memorial – he turned the walls of the exhibition rooms five degrees from the grid of the field of stelae. This grid is repeated in the curved coffered ceiling and, even underground, reflects the movement of the sweeping blanket of stelae above. This important correspondence between what is above and what lies below it – between present and past – became the central, pivotal element of the exhibition design for the "Information Centre".

The challenge of the exhibition's design was to produce a connection between the content requirements and the structurally set framework, creating an unmistakably unified whole. It seemed completely logical to take up the language of the field of stelae and to continue it in different variations. In each exhibition space, visitors are to be reminded constantly, through various manifestations of the stele motif – on the floor, down from the ceiling, from the walls – that they are beneath the memorial. This concept met with the full approval of the architect, and led to a constructive collaboration between Peter Eisenman and Dagmar von Wilcken over the several years it took to plan and to realize the "Information Centre".

The tension between "above" and "below" derives from the fact that the memorial, as an abstract work of art, is experienced by the visitor both physically and emotionally, while the exhibition presents the context of and background to the Holocaust. The resulting tension is expressed in the exhibition's structure.

Every cement stele on the site symbolizes the destruction of human life. Because the edges of the field of stelae appear to blend into the surface of the city, the field seems to the observer to be borderless and thus symbolizes the incomprehensible. The suffering and tragic fates of the persecuted and murdered are also endless and incomprehensible. There is no space large enough to show the full scale of each individual's humiliation, persecution and extermination. And that is exactly what the exhibition also means to highlight, by making the information panels appear to extend indefinitely behind the walls. By repeating the motif of the stele as a bearer of information and transmitting the stele pattern to the exhibition space below, the sealed cement pillars of the memorial open themselves and allow glimpses of the stories and testimonies of people who were obliterated.

In the second theme room, the stelae of the memorial appear to press downwards from above, transforming themselves into informational displays. (Model photo)

Characteristic of the exhibition's concept is the rhythmic exchange between contemplative atmosphere and explanatory information. This is illustrated in the four exhibition rooms. With the generosity and openness of their design, the first and third rooms permit a contemplative approach to their contents; in the second and fourth rooms, on the other

The illuminated glass panels, set into the floor in the first theme room, pick up the pattern of the memorial above. (Model photo)

hand, the denser exhibition structure represents a larger amount of content with a more informative character. This rhythm raises the artistic tension and offers visitors various ways in which to approach or explore the theme more deeply.

The start of the exhibition consists of six large-format portraits, which confront the visitors on their way into the first room. These represent the six million murdered people – men, women and children. The way to the first exhibition space follows a long, extended hall that leads past a 24-metre-long timeline. A rear-lit panel of text and images shows a condensed historical overview of the events of 1933 to 1945. Here the visitors, depending on what they already know, can choose whether to get information from the text or the images. By doing so, they can prepare themselves for the theme rooms ahead.

The task of the first theme room is to show the European dimensions of the genocide, by naming all affected countries along with the number of victims in each. This information is provided on a continuous frieze that runs along the length of the walls. Set into the floor are illuminated glass plates reflecting the pattern of the stelae above-ground. On these plates, one can read personal statements and diary quotations of those persecuted. In this way, the delivery of information comes from the perspective of the victim. With their eyes cast downwards to read these words, visitors also may look reflectively within themselves.

In the second theme room, the stelae of the memorial appear to press downwards from above, transforming themselves into informational displays. Photographs and documents of persecuted families will be illuminated from behind, through openings in the perforated cubes. In this way, the visitors have a glimpse of the extremely varied biographies of families from different European countries. The rectangular spot of light, that each stele casts on the floor, again picks up the pattern of the memorial above.

At first sight, the third room appears to be completely empty. As one approaches, one hears a voice, which fills the room, reading out the names of murdered European Jews and their biographies. One by one, each name is projected onto the four walls while the person's life story is told briefly and succinctly. Individual life stories are thereby lifted out of the anonymity of the enormous numbers of victims. This succession of individual fates makes it clear that, even if only 20 seconds was dedicated to each person, it would take years to read aloud the names and short biographies of every one of those six million murdered individuals. In the adjacent hallway, visitors can use a database connected with Yad Vashem in Jerusalem to research the approximately 3.5 million victims, whose names are known.

The names of victims will be projected, one after another, onto the walls of the third theme room, while their recorded biographies are heard. (Model photo)

In the fourth and last theme room, the stelae come through the walls, converging in the centre of the space and confronting the visitors directly with information. With the help of a series of short films, the broad sides of the stelae show the enormous number of extermination centres and how they are related. The narrow sides of the stelae provide images and texts about the largest of the organized extermination centres.

Away from the stream of people, in the niches between the narrow stelae, visitors have the opportunity to listen, at audio stations, to accounts of the viewpoints of victims facing extermination.

In the fourth theme room, the stelae seem to emerge from the walls, bearing information about the geographic dimension of the genocide. (Model photo)

This personalized perspective is a theme that threads its way through the entire exhibition, lifting the victims out of anonymity. It increases one's readiness to encounter an individual fate, with attention and empathy. Thus the door is opened for cognitive processing of the exhibition's content, particularly important for younger generations.

When visitors leave the final exhibition space, they step into the day-lit exit hall. Here they find information about memorials located in Germany and elsewhere in Europe. The bridge from past to present is highlighted through a change in colour scheme: while the historical part of the exhibition is presented predominantly in black and white and discreet colours, here the more intensive use of colours refers to the present.

The dramatic use of light plays an important role in the exhibition's overall design concept. Light serves less as a way of illuminating a room and more as way of delivering information. Texts and photos are either lit from behind or projected, thus drawing attention to themselves. The use of general room lighting is kept to a minimum. In order to allow the powerful content of the exhibition to speak for itself, cool and austere building materials were chosen, such as glass, steel and smoothly polished surfaces. All in all, the colour, light, material and design of the exhibition spaces refer to the architecture of the memorial, and, through this relationship, the memorial and the "Information Centre" together become an unmistakable place of remembrance.

(1)   See the minutes of the third meeting of the Board of Trustees of the Foundation for the Memorial to the Murdered Jews of Europe, 24 February 2000.

(2)   Individual criticisms can be read in the first volume of the Foundation's series: Sibylle Quack (ed.), *Auf dem Weg zur Realisierung. Das Denkmal für die ermordeten Juden Europas und der Ort der Information. Architektur und historisches Konzept* (Stuttgart/München, 2002).

(3)   Wolfgang Thierse, *Foreword*, in: ibid, p. 11.

Etty Hillesum, born in 1914, lived in Amsterdam. She was deported to Auschwitz and murdered there in 1943.

CHRONOLOGY OF GENOCIDE
ESCALATION OF THE EXTERMINATION POLICY

1933 - 1937

As soon as the National Socialists assumed power in Germany, they began persecuting political opponents and Jews. For the first time, anti-semitism was part of the governmental policy of a modern state. German Jews were turned into foreigners in their own country, and the persecution was intensified step-by-step. Official decrees, acts of violence by supporters of the regime and incitement by the National Socialist press were intertwined. Jews' legal rights were rescinded one after the other. For example, after the "Nuremberg Laws" were proclaimed in 1935, marriage between Jews and non-Jews was prohibited. These laws were also applied to German Sinti and Roma who, as "Gypsies", were deprived of their rights and persecuted. At the same time, those in power forced the removal of Jews from trade and industry. Thus, already in 1933 and increasingly so from 1937, pressure was brought to bear on Jews to emigrate.

1938

The November Pogrom in 1938 marked a new stage in the National Socialist persecution of the Jewish population. On the night of 9-10 November and throughout the following day, synagogues were destroyed and Jewish-owned businesses ransacked across the German Reich, which by then included Austria and the Czech Sudetenland. National Socialists and their supporters attacked Jewish families and laid waste their homes. Between 25,000 and 30,000 Jews were held for several weeks in concentration camps. Pressure was put on them to emigrate. Tens of thousands of German and Austrian Jews decided to flee.

1939

The Second World War began with the Wehrmacht's attack on Poland on 1 September, 1939. Both within Germany and in the occupied territories, the war enabled the German leadership to extend radically and intensify their persecution of the Jews, Sinti and Roma, political opponents, the disabled and others.

From the very first weeks after Poland was invaded, German military and police units shot thousands of people. The Polish upper class and Catholic Church dignitaries were victims; later, the targets came to include ever-wider sections of the non-Jewish population. At the same time, the violent persecution and first mass shootings of Polish Jews began.

1940

Jews within the German Reich also faced persecution on a new scale when the war broke out in 1939. The German leadership gradually abandoned its policy of pressing Jews to emigrate, and began deportations to outlying areas under German control: In the autumn of 1939 and in the course of 1940, Austrian, Czech, and German Jews from various towns and regions were deported to France and to occupied Poland. Sinti and Roma were deported as well.

Not long after the Wehrmacht occupied Poland, the occupation authorities issued decrees aimed at isolating Polish Jews from the rest of the population. Jews were forced to wear an armband or yellow star for identification. Later, the German administration began to force the Jewish population to move to separate residential areas, so-called ghettos. Some of these ghettos, such as those in Lodz and Warsaw, were sealed off from the rest of the city with fences and walls shortly after they had been established; others were cordoned off only shortly before the deportations to the extermination camps began in 1942.

1941

The German attack on the Soviet Union on 22 June 1941 marked the launch of a war of extermination. The conquered territory was to be plundered ruthlessly to supply the German Reich; German leaders planned that millions of people would starve as a result. Soviet prisoners of war received no food. Already by the end of the winter of 1941/42, some two million soldiers had perished in German camps.

Immediately following their attack, the German occupiers carried out the first mass murders of Jews and Soviet Roma. Already in June, the Einsatzgruppen (mobile killing squads) of the Security Police and the Security Service (SD) of the SS, of the Waffen-SS as well as of other police and military units, had begun rounding up and shooting Jewish men and, from late summer 1941, women and children, too. By the end of 1941, nearly 500,000 Soviet Jews had been murdered. These crimes mark the transition to genocide.

As the war continued, the plight of the Jews also deteriorated in those countries where those in power cooperated with or were dependent upon the German leadership. Most of these regimes issued racist regulations and began to imprison Jews in camps. In Romania, which had been allied with the German Reich since 1940, the persecution escalated after the German attack on the Soviet Union. Military and police fomented pogroms. Together with German units, Romanian soldiers carried out mass shootings of Romanian and Ukrainian Jews. Within the first few weeks alone, some 160,000 people were murdered. In the autumn of 1941, the Romanian government deported more than 145,000 Jews to the area captured on the other side of the Dniestr (Transnistria). Well over half died of hunger and disease or were shot. Romanian Roma and Ukrainian civilians also were victims of persecution in Transnistria.

The summer of 1941 saw increased resistance against the German occupiers and their collaborators in various parts of Europe. In reprisal for attacks, the German Military Administration began to arrest uninvolved civilians and to murder them. The victims of these crimes were, in the first instance, Jews. In August 1941, the German Army leadership in France had thousands arrested and ordered shootings time and again. In the Serbian part of shattered Yugoslavia, the German occupiers expanded this policy in the autumn of 1941 into a war against the civilian population. The most frequent targets were minorities. Within a few weeks, nearly all Jewish and thousands of Roma men had been the victims of mass shootings in Serbia.

The German occupation authorities pursued a deliberate policy of impoverishment of the Polish Jews. By the autumn of 1941, the situation in the ghettos had worsened dramatically. Increasing numbers of people were starving or dying from disease. Under conditions of increasing poverty and violence, ghetto inhabitants tried to maintain a strategy of self-assertion: they organized schools for their children, cultural events, and their own press. The occupiers considered the misery that they themselves had caused in the ghettos as a "problem", to be got rid of by means of violence. Thus developed a logic of supposed practical necessity: the Germans met the increasingly catastrophic conditions with increasingly brutal methods and finally, by preparing for mass murder. For the first time, German authorities developed plans to murder Jews with poison gas.

In the summer of 1941, the German occupiers in Poland began to prepare the mass murder of the Jewish population with poison gas. Occupation authorities developed their plans for these crimes locally. Heinrich Himmler, Reichsführer-SS and head of the German police, approved the plans. Murder with poison gas had already been carried out on handicapped people within Germany and in the occupied territories since 1939. Members of an SS Special Task Force, who had previously participated in these crimes, were transferred to western Poland in 1941. There they murdered Jews in gas vans – rebuilt lorries, in whose airtight containers people were poisoned by redirected exhaust fumes. In November 1941, the task force set up a base for murder near Chelmno (Kulmhof); there, from December 1941, they killed Jews from the immediate region and from the Lodz ghetto with motor exhaust fumes. Between 150,000 and 320,000 Jews and 4,300 Sinti and Roma were murdered in Chelmno.

While the mass murder of Jews was under way in various parts of Eastern Europe, the German leadership developed step-by-step their plans for a pan-European policy of extermination. At the end of 1940, Hitler charged Reinhard Heydrich, director of the Reich Security Main Office, head of the Security Police and of the SS Security Services, with the task of developing a "final solution project". This was envisaged as a gigantic programme of deportation that would include all Jews within the territories under German control. In October 1941, on Hitler's orders, the systematic deportation began of German, Austrian and Czech Jews to the occupied areas of Eastern Europe. In the months that followed, Hitler repeatedly confirmed to leading National Socialists his intention to now realize the plan to murder all European Jews.

1942

At the invitation of Reinhard Heydrich, head of the Reich Security Main Office, senior ministerial civil servants and high-level Nazi Party and SS functionaries met in a villa at Berlin's Wannsee Lake on 20 January, 1942. This meeting later would be referred to as the Wannsee Conference. Heydrich explained the plans for a programme to murder all European Jews. The only matter for discussion was how this was to be implemented. The decision to commit genocide had already been made at a higher level. This programme of extermination was intended to encompass more than 11 million people, including Jews in countries beyond the German sphere of influence such as Switzerland, Great Britain and Turkey.

In the first half of 1942, the German administration stepped up its programme of genocide. In the Polish cities of Lvov and Lublin and in nearby towns, German SS and police units herded Jews together and deported them to the extermination camp, Belzec. Immediately upon their arrival at the camp, they were killed in gas chambers with motor exhaust fumes. In the spring of 1942, the German occupation authorities established two further extermination camps in Poland at Sobibor and Treblinka. From July 1942, the programme of murder was broadened to include all of central and southern Poland. Heinrich Himmler, Reichsführer-SS, had ordered that the ghettos in these regions be dissolved and that all the Jews considered "unfit for work" be killed. Sinti and Roma were also among those murdered in the extermination camps. The crimes committed in these three camps were given the code-name "Action Reinhardt". By the time the camps were closed down in 1943, some 1.75 million Jews from Poland, the German Reich and numerous other European countries under German occupation had been murdered in Belzec, Treblinka and Sobibor.

Between July and December 1941, German units in eastern Poland and the Soviet Union murdered several hundred thousand Jews. Starting in December 1941, people in this occupied region, too, were killed with the exhaust fumes of mobile gas vans. After a period when, for a few weeks at the end of winter 1941/42, the German occupation authorities had reduced the scale of their criminal activities, they then began the second wave of the mass murder of Soviet Jews in the spring of 1942. Throughout the occupied area, German units carried out further mass shootings. The number of Soviet Jews murdered by the end of the war is estimated at more than one million.

In April 1940, Heinrich Himmler ordered the construction of a concentration camp near the Polish city of Auschwitz, where over the following years an extensive camp complex and an extermination camp arose. The beginning of 1942 saw the start of systematic mass murder in gas chambers in the Auschwitz-Birkenau camp complex. Auschwitz became the final destination for deportations from almost the whole of Europe. In the spring of 1942, this was where deportations of Jews from France, Slovakia and the German Reich ended. All those prisoners not channelled into forced labour were murdered immediately. In the course of 1942 and 1943, the SS constructed additional gas chambers in the camp area. At the same time, the German leadership extended the programme of deportation and murder to include Jews in Belgium, Luxembourg, and Holland, as well as Italy, Greece, Hungary and other countries. By 1945, approximately one million European Jews, up to 75,000 Polish political prisoners, about 21,000 Sinti and Roma, 15,000 Soviet prisoners of war and at least 10,000 prisoners of other nationalities had been murdered in Auschwitz.

Right from the start of the war, the German rulers had used slave labour as a means to oppress, exploit and murder Jews, particularly in the ghettos and concentration camps. The hope of many of those interned, that as forced labourers they would be seen as useful by the Germans, and therefore protected from the programme of murder, proved deceptive. In the second half of 1942, the German occupation authorities began to replace the Jewish forced labourers with non-Jews and to murder the Jews. In Germany, too, all the Jews still working in armaments factories were picked up and deported to the extermination camps in 1943. In the last phase of the war, however, the German leadership again employed Jewish forced labourers – most of them from Hungary – in factories within Germany, mainly in underground armaments plants. For this purpose, numerous new camps were established and placed under the control of existing concentration camps.

1943

During 1943, the German administration broadened its extermination programme to include a large part of southern Europe. As of the spring of 1943, some 55,000 Jews were deported from northern Greece and Macedonia to the extermination camps in occupied Poland. After German forces occupied Italy in September 1943, deportations began here too, as well as in the Mediterranean areas that had been occupied by Italy. By the end of 1944, some 15,000 people had been deported from these regions to Auschwitz. Determined to destroy Jewish life in Europe completely, the National Socialist leadership committed increasing logistical resources to the programme of murder. Thus, Jewish inhabitants of the islands of Rhodes and Kos were brought by ship to the Greek coast in July 1944 and deported from there by train to Auschwitz, a journey of several days.

Time and again, small groups of people suffering persecution tried to escape the liquidation of ghettos and mass murders by fleeing into the forests. There, the struggle to survive often pitted them against both German occupying forces and antisemitic partisan groups. At the same time, underground cells in some ghettos managed to obtain weapons and to defend themselves. In September 1942, Jewish ghetto inhabitants and forced labourers in eastern Poland united for the first time to form a substantial armed resistance. In April 1943, ghetto residents in Warsaw rose against the German occupiers. In late summer, the same occurred in Bialystok and Vilnius. In August 1943, Jewish forced labourers rebelled in the Treblinka extermination camp, and in October they did so in Sobibor.

1944

In March 1944, the Wehrmacht occupied Germany's ally, Hungary. The approximately 800,000 Hungarian Jews comprised the largest Jewish community still intact within the German sphere of influence. Until the occupation, the government in Budapest had opposed the German plans for deportation and murder. Immediately after the Germans marched in, the first deportations from Hungary to Auschwitz were organized under the direction of Adolf Eichmann, who, as, the "Expert for Jewish Questions" in the Reich Security Main Office in Berlin, was responsible for the Europe-wide deportations to the death camps. The mass deportations from Hungary and the areas occupied by Hungary, which ensued within a few weeks, affected some 500,000 people. Only one in four survived.

1945

Aware of the approaching Red Army, the German occupiers forced massive numbers of prisoners to evacuate the concentration camps in the east and move towards camps in the interior of the German Reich. Many prisoners were murdered in mass shootings during these death marches. The number of Jewish and non-Jewish prisoners, who died during the death marches and evacuation transports, is estimated at 300,000. The survivors were moved mostly to the concentration camps of Sachsenhausen, Buchenwald, Neuengamme, Bergen-Belsen, Dachau and their satellite camps. The large number of prisoners in close quarters, the catastrophic hygienic conditions, and the total exhaustion of the internees led to the spread of disease. Many thousands died in the days before or shortly after their liberation in the spring of 1945. With the capitulation of the Wehrmacht on 7-8 May 1945, the war in Europe came to an end. The total number of Jews murdered in the area under German control is between 5.4 and 6 million.

DOCUMENTATION OF SUFFERING

A CHRONOLOGICAL SEQUENCE OF PHOTOGRAPHS ABOUT THE HOLOCAUST 1933-1945

← ↓ Heppenheim (Hesse), 6 March, 1933:
As a political opponent of the new regime,
George Mainzer, a Social Democrat and son
of Jewish department store owner, Berthold
Mainzer, is publicly humiliated. SA men force
him to wash off symbols of social democratic
organisations from walls and doorposts.

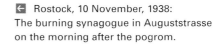 Norden (East Frisia), 24 July, 1935:
SA men lead Christine Neemann and her Jewish boyfriend through the city. They have to wear placards on which are written "I am a German girl and I have let myself be defiled by a Jew" and "I am a race defiler."

← Rostock, 10 November, 1938:
The burning synagogue in Auguststrasse on the morning after the pogrom.

↑ Hamburg, 1 April, 1933:
SA men and sympathisers block the door to the shop of a Jewish businessman. The National Socialists had called for a boycott against Jewish traders, doctors and lawyers across the Reich for the day.

↑ Berlin-Tiergarten, 10 November, 1938:
In Potsdamer Strasse Jewish shop-owners remove traces of the pogrom night.

↑ → ↘ Czestochowa (Poland), 4 September, 1939: Immediately after the invasion of Poland, soldiers of the Wehrmacht herd Polish civilians together, amongst them Jews. Many of them are shot. The last photograph was originally captioned: "The dead on the street."

⬇ Hohenasperg, 22 May, 1940: Sinti and Roma families are herded through the streets and deported to Poland.

⬆ Gurs internment camp (France) 1940/41: Frau Althausen from Mannheim (Germany) cooks on a makeshift oven. Photographed during the visit of an American aid organisation.

⬆ Dubossary (Moldavia, Soviet Union), 14 September, 1941: Mass shooting of Jewish women by a detachment of Einsatzgruppe D (mobile killing squad).

⬆ Probably the Radom Ghetto (Poland), around 1941: Senta and Sonja Birkenfelder were deported in 1940 with a group of German Sinti and Roma from Ludwigshafen to Poland.

↑ Targu-Frumos (Romania), July 1941:
After the pogrom in Jassy, over 4,400 survivors
are crammed into two goods trains in baking
heat and without food or water. More than half
of the deportees had died of thirst or suffocated
by the time the trains reached their respective
destinations several days later.

↑ Banks of the Dniestr, 1941/42: Jews from
Germany's ally, Romania, are deported by local
troops over the river to "Transnistria" (the
Romanian occupied territory in Ukraine).

↑ Jassy (Romania), pogrom on
29/30 June, 1941: In the centre of
the city lie the corpses of Jewish
inhabitants, who were murdered
by German and Romanian
soldiers, police and civilians.

↑ Warsaw Ghetto, June/August 1941.

⬇️ ➡️ Warsaw, 15 October, 1941:
Ajzyk and Jakob Wierzbicki (left picture, far left) at the ghetto wall. They are members of a group of young people who bring food into the ghetto with the help of their non-Jewish neighbours.

⬆️ Lodz (Poland), 1941: Zgierska Street runs through the ghetto and divides it into two sections. The sections of the ghetto are closed off from the outside world with fences and walls. The Jewish inhabitants have to use a specially constructed bridge in order to cross the street.

⬅️ Lodz Ghetto, between 1941 and 1943: Hunger is ever present in the ghetto. Mendel Grossman, photographer for the Jewish ghetto administration, documents the everyday life of the inhabitants.

← ↓ ↓ Bielefeld (Westphalia), 13 December, 1941: Jewish inhabitants of the region of Rhineland and Westphalia at the railway station, just before deportation to Riga (today in Latvia); an official photograph for the "Kriegschronik" ("War Chronicle") of the city of Bielefeld, 1941.

↑ Lodz Ghetto 1941/42: Assembly point at Krawiecka Street. Waiting for the transport, probably to the Chelmno extermination camp. Photography by Mendel Grossman.

# 63

Chelmno, 1942:
Arrival of a deportation train from the Lodz Ghetto. At the Kolo railway station, the occupants had to transfer onto the open carriages of a narrow-gauge railway.

Siedlce, near Warsaw, 21-23 August, 1942: Deportation to the Treblinka extermination camp.

The corpses of two Jews who have been shot by Ukrainian auxiliaries of the SS.

↓ Warta, near Lodz (Poland), 1942: The sidelocks of the orthodox Jew, Hersz Lasowski, are cut off. Shortly afterwards, the German occupiers hang him, together with his father, Rabbi Eliasz Lasowski, and eight other Jews.

↑ ↗ The ravine at Sdolbunov (today in Ukraine), 14 October, 1942: Two members of a firing squad murder women from Misocz. The women had survived the previous mass shooting by German gendarmes and Ukrainian collaborators.

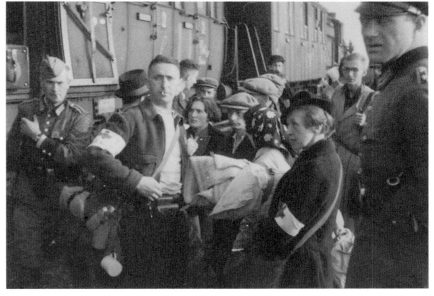

← ↙ ↓ Westerbork transit camp (Netherlands), probably end 1942: Deportation to the Auschwitz extermination camp. Photographs from an album that was made as a present for the camp commandant, Gemmeker.

➡ Skopje, March 1943: Deportation of Macedonian Jews to the Treblinka extermination camp. In spring 1941, Bulgaria had occupied large areas of Yugoslav Macedonia. In 1943, the occupying power delivered the Jewish population to the German Reich. In the foreground, on the left: Victor Nachnmias from Bitola.

↖ ↑ Salonika (Greece), 11 July, 1942: In baking heat, German occupying forces humiliate Jewish men on Eleftheria (Freedom) Square. The day has gone down in the history of the city as "Black Sabbath".

← Auschwitz-Birkenau extermination camp, 1942: Construction of Crematorium IV.

↑ ↗ The Krakow-Plaszow slave labour camp, 1943: Male and female prisoners in forced labour. Both pictures show the electrified camp fence and the tipper wagons on tracks. These had to be pushed manually.

→ Bershad, near Vinnitsa
(today in Ukraine), January 1943:
Jewish partisans: on the far left,
Moishe Shnajder; third from left,
Jankl Toles (squad leader); third
from right, Ladyshenskij (group
commander); second from right,
David Shor (platoon commander).

← Nalibocka forest, near Nowogrodek
(today in Belarus), summer 1944: Jewish
partisans in the "Bielski family camp". Named
after the commander, Tuia Bielski, the camp
formed a kind of Jewish community, with a
synagogue, court, workshops and school. It
served the partisans as a centre for supplies.

↑ Auschwitz-Birkenau, May 1944: Arrival of Hungarian Jews at the extermination camp. The four photographs come from an album made by the camp SS, which was found by a survivor, Lili Meier (née Jacob), in 1945. She was able to recognise herself and murdered members of her family on individual photographs.

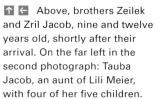

↑ ← Above, brothers Zeilek and Zril Jacob, nine and twelve years old, shortly after their arrival. On the far left in the second photograph: Tauba Jacob, an aunt of Lili Meier, with four of her five children.

↑ On the "Ramp" of the extermination camp. After arrival, an SS doctor decides who qualifies as "fit for work". All others are murdered straight away in the gas chambers.

Auschwitz, January 1945: Soviet soldiers with three survivors: Olga, Newenka and Oleg Mandic, family members of Anton Mandic, a former government minister in Yugoslavia. Still photo from a Soviet documentary.

Bergen-Belsen, April 1945, after liberation by the British Army: The site is strewn with the corpses of prisoners. To reduce the risk of an epidemic, numerous mass graves have to be prepared and the existing barracks burnt down. Among the dead are the few survivors.

Berlin-Charlottenburg, summer 1945: Arnold Blitz (left), a Dutch Jew and survivor of Sachsenhausen concentration camp, with his friend Toni Mast on a demonstrative walk in prisoner uniform on the Kurfürstendamm.

Warsaw, 1945: In the ruins of the city, Jewish survivors during a memorial march for the dead of the Warsaw Ghetto.

HUMAN LIFE AND STATISTICS
ON CALCULATING THE NUMBER OF JEWS MURDERED IN EUROPE UNDER NATIONAL SOCIALISM

In terms of a moral evaluation of this crime against humanity, it makes no sense to calculate the exact number of Jews murdered under National Socialism in Europe. However, historians, demographers and other scholars are committed to ascertaining this number for other reasons:

— First of all, it makes clear the dimensions of the mass murder. At no other time in history were one people persecuted across Europe with such intensity and with so many victims. In particular, the enormous number of children murdered underscores the singularity of the crime.

— In addition, statistics and figures give clues about events of which nothing else is known. On the basis of sources that became available only in the last few years in eastern Europe, it has become possible to conduct more finely differentiated local and regional research. One can ascertain the impact of the persecution on local and regional groups and on individuals as well. One can pinpoint locations from which Jews in individual communities were taken, and where and how these people met their deaths. Statistical material often forms the starting point for such refinement of research.

— Finally, a precise quantitative reconstruction of the crimes can help counteract the rampant falsification of history that this particular subject attracts.

It must be stressed from the outset, that the number of Jewish victims of National Socialist persecution extends beyond those who died before the end of the war. Many who survived under inhuman conditions were physically and mentally scarred for the rest of their lives.

Many challenges face scholars seeking to calculate the total number of Jewish victims of the National Socialist genocide. The first is the question of definition – of who is to be counted among the victims of the murder of European Jewry. Generally, all persons regarded as Jews by the perpetrators are counted among these victims, even if they did not see themselves as Jews. The victims therefore include converted and assimilated Jews, often people in occupied Europe, only some of whose ancestors were Jewish and in some cases, non-Jews who did not want to be separated from their Jewish partners and consequently met their deaths in the campaign against the Jews, particularly in eastern Europe. The fact that the definition of the victims by the perpetrators was different in each occupied area, remained a matter of dispute, and included even broader groups as the war continued. Jewish soldiers in the Polish, Yugoslav, and particularly in the Soviet armies, who suffered and died with their non-Jewish comrades under the miserable conditions of German prisoner-of-war camps, are to be regarded as victims of the "final solution", because they were deliberately given worse treatment – or murdered – because of their origin.

It is difficult to classify those deaths that, while occurring during the persecution, may be attributable to natural causes. How is one to calculate the natural mortality among Jews, which also took place from 1933 to 1945? Here one must consider the disproportionately high death rate in Germany from 1933 onward and in various other countries after they fell under German occupation, and discern its relevance. Finally, it remains unclear whether one should count those Jews as victims who died while fleeing the German onslaught, without directly coming within the grasp of Germany and her allies. Almost one million Jews of the Soviet Union fled the German invasion or were evacuated. Many died in flight or as a result of the terrible living conditions that also prevailed in unoccupied areas of the USSR; the loss of important agricultural areas to the Germans led to acute food shortages. However, those who died in the unoccupied areas generally are not counted as victims of the National Socialist persecution of the Jews. The same goes for Jews who died as a direct result of war, such as fallen soldiers, victims of air raids or of sieges. For example, during the blockade of Leningrad by the Wehrmacht – the city was sealed off for 900 days from 1941-1944 – tens of thousands of Jews died who never show up in the statistics.

SS-statistics, 31 March 1943: Report of the SS statistician, Korherr, who by then had listed millions of Jewish victims in Europe, bottom of page 9 and top of page 10.

At the same time, general methodological problems arise in calculating the number of victims. It is most important, in breaking down the numbers by country, to determine a common cut-off date, as borders and demarcation lines constantly shifted between 1938 and 1945.

Thus, a Polish Jew from Lodz lived within the territory of the German Reich in 1940. The situation in southeastern Europe was even less clear. Furthermore, it was not only borders that fluctuated – people also moved in every direction under the sun. Some of those who were persecuted, managed to flee at first; many were trapped later as the Germans' conquests caught up with them. For reasons of precision, then, calculations within individual countries must be based on uniform accounting principles, related either to place of origin, place of deportation, or place of death, in order to avoid double counting.

Although there were some clues about the total number of victims during the war – such as in conversations among perpetrators which became known – German authorities left behind no comprehensive calculation of the number of their victims before the capitulation in 1945. All that

E u r o p ä i s c h e   J u d e n b i l a n z .   Die Verminderung des Judentums in Europa dürfte damit bereits an 4 Millionen Köpfe betragen. Höhere Judenbestände zählen auf dem europ. Kontinent (neben Rußland mit etwa 4 Mill.) nur noch Ungarn (750 000) und Rumänien (302 000), vielleicht noch Frankreich. Berücksichtigt man neben dem angeführten Rückgang die jüdische Auswanderung und den jüdischen Sterbeüberschuß

-7-

10

in den außerdeutschen Staaten Mittel- und Westeuropas, aber auch die unbedingt vorkommenden Doppelzählungen infolge der jüdischen Fluktuation, dann dürfte die Verminderung des Judentums in Europa von 1937 bis Anfang 1943 auf 4 ½ Millionen zu schätzen sein. Dabei konnte von den Todesfällen der sowjet-russischen Juden in den besetzten Ostgebieten nur ein Teil erfaßt werden, während diejenigen im übrigen europäischen Rußland und an der Front überhaupt nicht enthalten sind. Dazu kommen die Wanderungsströme der Juden innerhalb Rußlands in den asiatischen Bereich hinüber. Auch der Wanderungsstrom der Juden aus den europäischen Ländern außerhalb des deutschen Einflußbereichs nach Übersee ist eine weitgehend unbekannte Größe.

Insgesamt dürfte das europäische Judentum seit 1933, also im ersten Jahrzehnt der nationalsozialistischen Machtentfaltung, bald die Hälfte seines Bestandes verloren haben. Davon ist wieder nur etwa die Hälfte, also ein Viertel des europäischen Gesamtbestandes von 1937, den anderen Erdteilen zugeflossen.

remained was an "interim report" of the SS up to the end of 1942, composed in coded language. Right after the end of the war, demographic estimates were made, comparing the Jewish population living in Europe before 1939 with information for 1945, and subtracting those who emigrated overseas, to come up with the number of those murdered, which was the difference. At the same time, detailed information was gathered from surviving relatives and acquaintances about individual victims of murder. This provided a collection of biographical data on several million people, which is far from complete (1). There is neither data on every single victim, nor is the person's fate known in each case. So it is important to carry out complicated individual investigations into local and regional crime locations, investigations which rest on numerous sources.

"Confessions of Mr. X", Budapest, November 1943 (conversation of Hungarian Zionists with a German entrepreneur, apparently Oskar Schindler): millions of Polish Jews exterminated, page 9.

These sources exist for individual European countries to quite varying degrees and are of varied quality. Thus they present quite diverse methodological challenges to the historian. Before the end of the war, the perpetrators deliberately burned large numbers of documents directly related to the murder: orders and reports about killings. Nevertheless, surviving German files on the theme of persecution of the Jews – if laid end to end – would take up many kilometres of shelves. The records for the German Reich, the Czech territories, western and northern Europe and Italy are comparatively rich. In almost all these areas, lists of names of victims survived or were relatively easy to reconstruct, using documents of the Jewish communities and the residency registration offices. Police and administrators, and also tax authorities, kept lists of Jews who died during the war in their homeland or who were deported. This was true not only for the German authorities, but also for Germany's allies, including Hungary and Vichy, the government of collaboration that administered unoccupied areas of France according to German instructions. In particular, the robbery of Jewish property led to an extensive production of files, which were not destroyed and which reveal information about the victims of the murder. Through a comparison with the names of survivors after 1945, recorded worldwide with relative accuracy, one could determine the number in these areas who were murdered. Only some of the persecuted Jews of southeast Europe are known by name. There are, however, deportation statistics. Here, too, a comparison with the number of survivors makes possible exact information about the dimensions of the murder. Similarly, the fates of individual deportation transports can be reconstructed. Wartime information often survived which, detailed conditions upon departure, upon crossing borders or upon arrival at the extermination centre, particularly in Auschwitz.

It is much more difficult to determine the number of victims from Poland, the Soviet Union or the Baltic states. Here, only a compilation of all information on each individual location can help, a very laborious procedure. One must first determine how many Jews were in a given location when the Germans arrived. It helps to have the last census of each country, which then must be extrapolated statistically to the time of the German invasion; also important are the registrations undertaken by the new occupying power, Jewish welfare organizations or the so-called Jewish councils (bodies controlled by the German occupiers and forced to represent the Jewish communities). While in Poland only about 10 per cent of the Jews managed to flee temporarily or in the long run from the German invasion, in the occupied areas of the Soviet Union and the Baltic about 30-40 percent were able to flee, with an increasing trend as one moved from west to east. Newly accessible Soviet documents contain information on escape, evacuation or forced deportation under Soviet aegis. Barely tapped until now as a source are the files of the Soviet registry offices, which, however, are not organized according to ethnic background. Information about local murder operations remains of decisive importance. For the first nine months of German rule in the Soviet areas — that is, up to March 1942 — the perpetrators left behind precise reports about their murder operations; for the period afterward, and for the Polish territories, the information is very fragmentary. Here, often scattered information must be drawn from the occupation administration, from local indigenous administrations, and occasionally also from records of German firms active in the occupied region. The knowledge of the Polish underground should also not be underestimated: they observed the mass murder relatively closely and reported on it. However, the overall dimensions of the murder operations, whether mass shootings or deportations to the concentration camps, can be reconstructed only with help of testimony from thousands of eye-witnesses. Jewish survivors often had their recollections recorded officially soon after the war, and those of German defendants and witnesses were taken down in court proceedings, particularly in the Federal Republic of Germany since the 1960s. While perpetrators tried, after the war, to minimize the number of victims, other witnesses often gave relatively precise figures. Little attention has been paid to reports from non-Jewish witnesses on the fate of Jews in their localities. In Poland, for example, two systematic inquiries were undertaken after the war, in which all local-government administrations were to provide precise information about the murder operations in their region. The witness statements contain rough estimates of the numbers of victims arising from recollections about the local city services, about documents that had been seen, and conversations overheard or conducted, or by eye-witnesses who saw Jews being taken away. Particularly in the latter case, the numbers often are a bit too high, because it is extremely difficult to estimate crowd size. However, this is somewhat compensated for by the fact that no reports whatsoever exist any longer for numerous murder operations.

The final means of reconstruction is the exhumation of mass graves, which the Soviet authorities especially undertook extensively from 1943. Of course, the counting of bodies was only done in smaller graves. When it came to mass graves from major shooting operations, estimates were based on the dimensions of the area, and generally are considered to be exaggerated. In many places, before retreating the perpetrators had the mass graves opened and the bodies burned in order to remove traces of the crime. This information therefore can be used only in combination with other sources.

By bringing together all this diverse information for each location, one gains a consistent picture, first for the towns and districts and then for an entire region under occupation. Because across-the-board information from the perpetrators about the numbers of victims is often already available, one arrives at an overview for an entire region and finally for whole territories under occupation, such as the General Government – the occupied parts of central and southern Poland – or the Reichskommissariat Ukraine. This collection of data from "bottom to top", from every Jewish community to the entire region where the persecution took place, leads to a reliable total.

Another source is the number of victims at concentration and extermination camps. While there still are fragments of camp records available for Auschwitz and Majdanek, this is not the case for the camps of the "Action Reinhardt" – that is, Belzec, Sobibor and Treblinka – where, by the end of 1943, the documents had been deliberately destroyed. Nevertheless, it is possible to reconstruct individual radio messages of camp authorities, because they were overheard and decoded by the British Secret Service. Thus, a relatively large percentage of prisoner reports from the concentration camps has been preserved. In Auschwitz itself, a prisoner, forced to work in the camp office, was able to note secretly the daily reports about arriving transports, including numbers of victims who were murdered immediately and not registered as prisoners. Also available are fragments of the so-called death registers, in which the deaths of registered prisoners were entered, but these contain only a small percentage of the dead. The reconstruction of prisoner deaths in the last months of war, when the camps were evacuated and the links between one area and another progressively disintegrated, proves especially difficult. Jews from numerous countries were marched out together with non-Jewish prisoners. Here, one is completely dependent on eye-witness reports, unless those who died during the evacuation marches were officially buried and thus registered locally. Altogether, an investigation of the camps is far from sufficient in order to determine the number of vic

DANZIGER VORPOSTEN

Einzelverkaufspreis 15 Rpf.

AMTLICHES ORGAN DER NSDAP UND VERKÜNDUNGSBLATT DES REICHSSTATTHALTERS UND SEINER BEHÖRDEN

Nummer 131 Sonnabend, den 13. Mai 1944 Jahrgang 14

Gewaltige Massen in Bereitschaft
Vor größter Anstrengung Moskaus
Voraussichtliche Zielsetzungen der kommenden Sowjetoffensive

Juda vor dem Fall
Von WILHELM LOEBSACK, Danzig

Danziger Vorposten, 13 May, 1944, newspaper article by Wilhelm Löbsack (NSDAP Gau Danzig, Nazi Party), who gave the number of Jews "eliminated" up to this point as five million.

tims. Historians report, based on more recently available sources, that fewer than half of all Jewish victims died in concentration and extermination camps; almost 40 per cent — far more than previously thought — were killed in mass shootings.

Meanwhile, in eastern Europe too, research into the fate of the Jews has become part of local history. Local and regional experts track down new details to fill in the "blank spots" in the landscape of mass murder. Within limits, and precisely because of the limited availability of sources and the methodological imponderables, the specific numbers for entire regions and the central extermination locations have been the subject of vigorous debate among historians. But there is no dispute regarding the overall dimensions of the murder. For reasons of scholarly honesty, therefore, one always should be aware that — considering the current state of research — while no exact number can be given, there is a verifiable range between the lowest and highest totals. Additional research that brings newly discovered sources to the surface will, however, lead to greater accuracy.

Of course, the number of victims is only one question among many in the investigation of this crime against humanity. More important always remains the question of why, and this concerns, above all, the politics and behaviour of the perpetrators and the reconstruction of the experiences and actions of the victims. Thus, the spotlight falls again on the individual, especially on those victims who could no longer give information after 1945.

4. Das Judentum hat weitere schwere Einbußen in anderen Räumen Europas zu verzeichnen. Die Kerngebiete jüdischer Zusammenballung, die wir in Polen, wie in Warschau oder Lublin fanden, sind heute ebenso neutralisiert, wie das zur Zeit mit den Siedlungen der 1½ Millionen Juden in Ungarn geschieht. Damit sind allein in diesen Ländern fünf Millionen Juden ausgeschaltet. In anderen europäischen Ländern verschärfen sich die seit langem getroffenen gesetzlichen Maßnahmen gegen das Judentum ebenfalls in steigendem Maße. Mit der Tätigkeit dieser Juden waren wesentliche Planungen und Hoffnungen des Weltjudentums verknüpft. „Sie sind das trojanische Pferd in der Festung des Feindes. Tausende in Europa lebende Juden sind der Hauptfaktor bei der Vernichtung unseres Feindes. Dort ist unsere wertvollste Hilfe für den Sieg", so äußerte sich Cajim Weizmann, Präsident der zionistischen Weltorganisation, in einer Rede am 28. 12. 1942 anläßlich des Weltkongresses in Neuyork. Diese Worte sind, um so bemerkenswerter, als damals bereits Ungarn mit uns verbündet und Weizmann der dortigen Judenfreunde trotzdem ganz sicher war.

---

(1) See the articles by Avner Shalev/Alexander Avraham and Eberhard Jäckel in this volume.

WRITING IN THE FACE OF DEATH
WRITINGS FROM THE GHETTOS AND CAMPS, THEIR AUTHORS, AND HOW THEY REACHED US

There are thousands of documents written by Jewish survivors of the persecution and Holocaust. Many of those who escaped death, felt a pressing duty to bear witness to crimes, which are of historic importance in their sheer magnitude. Most of these witnesses wrote down their memories in the decades following liberation, sometimes up to 50 years after the events, occasionally even later. A few compiled their reports during the Holocaust: in ghettos; in hiding; in concentration camps; even in extermination centres. Most of these writers did not survive. The focus here is on writings from the inferno itself, especially those fragments quoted in the "Information Centre" under the memorial.

What prompted people to risk their lives, often in the face of certain death, to record evidence of their existence: to write diaries, to collect documents, to start entire archives about this crime? Such acts alone, if discovered, could lead to immediate execution. In this situation, writing and documenting were the last remaining forms of human self-assurance, with an effect which went beyond one's imminent death. In the face of the National Socialists' absolute determination to kill, the authors did not see their own deaths as the greatest of catastrophes. Rather, the tragedy was the eradication of all reminders of Jewish existence and the removal of all traces of the crime of genocide. The idea of being killed and then deleted collectively from history and memory, is one of unparalleled horror, particularly considering the traditional Jewish link between religion, remembrance and the recording of history. Ritual remembrance of the history of the Jewish people and its martyrs is integral to Jewish religious observance. Only reports and documents can prevent a people from being eradicated from history without a trace.

At the same time, it was, for these authors, a question of bearing witness. They hoped that their testimony would, at some point in the future, bring them justice in a court of law. This prompted many of these Jews to write and collect testimony even during the Holocaust, at the greatest risk to their own lives, in order to act as witnesses against the murderers. They wrote for posterity and hoped to survive as a people in history, and thus to get justice. As Chaim Kaplan wrote in 1940 in his Warsaw diary: "Everyone who writes such reports risks his life, but that does not scare me off. I sense deeply the importance of this hour and my responsibility. I am aware that I am fulfilling a national duty, an historic duty that I cannot just shirk. (...) I am sure that providence sent me to fulfil this task. My chronicle will serve as source material for future historians." (1) Chaim Kaplan did not survive, but parts of his diary did. Documentation of the crimes was the only remaining way to fight them. With their testimony, the witnesses gave their lives value and purpose – even in death. In 1943, Herman Kruk, the librarian and chronicler of the Vilnius Ghetto who was murdered in 1944, wrote in a poem about his notes: "Drunk on the pen trembling in my hand, I record everything for future generations: A day will come when someone will find the leaves of horror I write and record." (2)

Those witnesses writing for posterity during the persecution were in a completely different situation from those authors who wrote memoirs after liberation. The former were living in the midst of a mass murder, whose extent and conclusion were unknown to them. Their ability to understand the experience was limited both in scope and time. With the constant risk of death hanging over them, they wrote in secret. Concern for the hiding and preservation of the manuscript was a part of its production. In writing, the possibility of discovery had to be taken into consideration and this led to a degree of self-censorship, so that one would not endanger oneself and others.

The difficulties of this task usually began with the extreme scarcity of paper and writing implements. In the ghettos and camps, writers used school notebooks, toilet paper, old boxes or even the empty pages and margins of printed books. They wrote in their numerous native tongues. Yiddish was most strongly represented in Poland. Written in the Hebrew alphabet, it offered the great advantage of not being immediately understood by Germans. Texts also have been found that were written in Polish, German, Greek, Dutch, French and many other European languages. Some active Zionists also wrote reports in Hebrew.

Style and character vary, depending on the age, level of education, purpose of the author and, above all, the circumstances in which he or she was writing. Many texts emphasize the role of being a witness, of delivering the largest possible amount of concrete information, even including documents. It is not, therefore, easy to speak of a definitive type of testimony. Sometimes a work takes the character of a chronicle, then that of a diary. But the transitions are always fluid. The classic diary, which records experiences with an inward look at oneself and one's environment, is rare when it comes to Holocaust testimony. True, sometimes emotions and hopes break through, despite the best efforts of the most resolute chroniclers — like Herman Kruk — to write factual reports. On 30 September, 1942, Kruk wrote in despair about the deportation of the Jews of Warsaw: "What is my life worth even if I remain alive? Whom to return to in my old home town of Warsaw? For what and for whom do I carry on this whole pursuit of life, enduring, holding out — for what?!" (3)

It was as difficult to write these reports as it was to make sure that they were handed down. We must assume that most testimonies were discovered and destroyed, at the very latest when their authors were deported to the death camps. Every single manuscript that survived is an exception. Most writings of those who did not survive were rediscovered after the war, either hidden or buried. Many have most likely never been found. In some cases, friends who escaped, or non-Jewish friends and acquaintances, smuggled reports out of ghettos and camps. There are even manuscripts from extermination camps that have survived: some reports were found buried in the grounds of Auschwitz-Birkenau, near the former crematoria. A few authors survived with their texts. One type of document in existence is the postcard thrown from the deportation train. Some were found and mailed to the addressee. Many of the texts that have survived are only fragments of the original, partly burned or decayed to the point of illegibility, because they were not found until decades later.

These texts were passed down in the most difficult circumstances. Even so, they did not always attract the interest that their authors had hoped they would. Many remained with relatives, while others sat, inaccessible, in archives. Publication was hampered by language, financial or political problems. In the former Soviet Union, for example, it was nearly impossible during the Cold War to publish an account of the murder of Russian Jews for ideological reasons. Numerous texts were written in Yiddish, and, after the Holocaust, there was a lack of competent translators to bring them to the attention of a wider readership. So while Herman Kruk's Vilnius chronicle was published in 1961 in Yiddish, it was not until 40 years later, in 2002, that it was published in English. But language was not the only problem. In Germany, as well as in the USA and Israel, interest in such texts was limited in the first years after the Holocaust. There was a focus on a few prominent examples of Holocaust testimony, such as the first, abridged version of Anne Frank's diary, published in 1947. By way of comparison, a diary from the Lodz Ghetto written in German by the Viennese writer Oskar Rosenfeld, who was murdered in Auschwitz in 1944, came out only 50 years later in Germany.

The largest and most astonishing documentation of National Socialist crimes was the underground archive in the Warsaw Ghetto. This extensive collection, created in total secrecy by the historian Dr. Emanuel Ringelblum (1900-1944) and numerous colleagues, is the only existing historical record compiled by a Jewish community about its own extermination. Material in Yiddish, Polish and German covers not only all aspects of life in the ghetto, but all available information on the murder of the Jews in Poland. The act of collecting these documents represented the pinnacle of intellectual and physical resistance. The archive also represented the greatest systematic attempt to record German crimes against the Jews, to make them known to the world, now and forever.

The archive project began in Ringelblum's home in November 1940, one week after the ghetto was cordoned off. The project was named Oneg Shabbat (Sabbath Joy) because its co-workers met at the end of every

Sabbath – on Saturday evening. The group used the most modern scholarly methods, carried out questionnaires and collected testimony on all aspects of ghetto life, including statistics, food ration cards, proclamations, underground newspapers, schoolbooks, diaries and photos. Ringelblum himself wrote a chronicle of the ghetto in the form of a diary (4).

The group Oneg Shabbat and its archive were a part of the underground movement of the ghetto. Its members managed to compile reports on the mass murders of Jews in Vilnius and at the extermination sites of Chelmno, Belzec, Sobibor and Treblinka. They got their information from postcards sent from other ghettos, from escapees from the death camps, from female couriers sent out of the ghetto and also from Polish helpers. Some of the material was published in the underground papers of the ghetto. Couriers transmitted this information to the Polish government-in-exile, based in London. In his diary entry of 10 June, 1942, Ringelblum, not without pride, writes: "In the last few weeks, English radio reported bestial crimes committed, among others, against the Polish Jews in Chelmno, Vilnius, Belzec (...) The Oneg Shabbat group has thus fulfilled its great historical task. It has told the world about our fate and, perhaps, saved hundreds of thousands of Polish Jews from extermination. That, however, remains to be seen. Who in our group will survive? Whom will fate choose to work on the material we have collected? One thing today is for sure: our efforts and sacrifice, our lives spent in constant anxiety, have not been for nothing." (5) Here it becomes quite clear how documenting the crimes and informing the world at large had become, for Ringelblum, the only purpose in a life, whose end he could foresee. His hope of rescuing Jews by informing the public proved tragically wrong.

After the destruction of the Warsaw Ghetto, Ringelblum went into hiding. He was found by German police on 7 March, 1944 and shot. The underground archive survived, hidden in metal boxes and milk churns, walled-in and buried under rubble. The German occupiers razed the Ghetto to the ground in 1943, after putting down the Jews' armed uprising. Nonetheless, most of the archive was recovered in 1946 and 1950. Today, it can be found in the Jewish Historical Institute in Warsaw. This unique material was carefully restored, but, to date, only part of it has been published.

Among the manuscripts rescued in the Ringelblum Archive was the dairy of Abraham Lewin (1893-1943). This Talmudist had, like Ringelblum, taught at the Jehudia Secondary School for Girls and was a member of the Oneg Shabbat group in the Warsaw Ghetto. He wrote about the group on 6 June, 1942: "We gather every Sabbath, a group of activists in the Jewish community, to discuss our diaries and writings. We want our sufferings, these 'birth-pangs of the Messiah', to be impressed upon the memories of future generations and on the memory of the whole world." (6) These words relate to the traditional Jewish religious belief that great suffering of the Jewish people is a sign of the coming of the Messiah. But, at the same time, the words also point to something else, that this suffering should not only be kept in the Jewish memory, like all other Jewish suffering in history. Rather, in its monstrosity, it must go down in world history.

Warsaw, December 1950:
Recovery and examination
of the hidden material
of the secret ghetto archive.

"(…) five small children, two to three years old, sit on a camp bed in the open from Monday to Thursday and cry and cry and scream incessantly – 'mama, mama, chce jeść!' ['Mama, Mama, I want something to eat!']. The soldiers shoot constantly and the shots silence the children for a short time."

Diary entry of Abraham Lewin (1893-1943), 11 September, 1942, Warsaw Ghetto.

To support this claim, Lewin made an intensive effort to document in his diary the worst phase in the story of the Warsaw Ghetto in the summer of 1942, when almost a quarter million Jews were deported to their deaths in Treblinka. The first part of the diary is missing. The remaining text covers March 1942 to 15 January, 1943. He reported constantly on the ceaseless crimes and horrors during the rounding up of victims, who were intentionally made submissive through hunger. The suffering of the children affected him deeply. From July 1942, he switched to writing in Hebrew rather than Yiddish, in anticipation of martyrdom. Through an escapee from Treblinka, the group Oneg Shabbat learned in August 1942 about the mass murders there: "This is without doubt the greatest crime ever committed in the whole of history." (7) In January 1943, Abraham Lewin was also deported to Treblinka. His diary survived him. It was published first in Yiddish and Polish. A Hebrew edition followed in 1969 and an English translation in 1988. Today, the original manuscript is partly faded and only legible with technical aids.

One testimony about the extermination of Polish Jews in the Oneg Shabbat collection was the transcript of an eyewitness report by Szlojme Fajner about the use of gas vans in the mass murder of Jews and Roma in Chelmno (8). Fajner, who was forced to throw earth over the dead in pits in January 1942 in Chelmno, managed to escape to the Warsaw Ghetto. After giving his testimony, which was recorded by Hersz Wasser, a colleague of Ringelblum, and his wife, Bluma, Fajner fled to Zamosc. He was captured there and deported to the Belzec extermination camp, where he was murdered. Similarly, a woman from the Kutno Ghetto reported in January 1942 about Chelmno as a killing site. Her frank postcard to relatives in the Warsaw Ghetto (9) found its way into the Ringelblum Archive.

It was not unusual for postcards to be thrown from trains during a deportation and put in the post by those who found them. Among them is the postcard written by Etty Hillesum (1914-1943) in a train going from the Dutch transit camp at Westerbork to Auschwitz in September 1943 (10). The student from Amsterdam, whose dairy and letters from Westerbork were later published in many languages, selflessly cared for the Dutch Jews interned in Westerbork. She tried to support others until she too was deported with her family. Her letters and diary chronicle the suffering in Westerbork.

Unlike Etty Hillesum, 12-year-old Judith Wischnjatskaja of Byten, in eastern Poland, knew full well what kind of death awaited her. A major in the Soviet army found the farewell letter from mother and daughter to Judith's father in the USA. Through him, the letter reached the Antifascist Jewish Committee in Moscow, which was systematically collecting testimony on the Holocaust to be published in a so-called "Black Book". But Stalinist censorship and a ban on the already finished work, stopped its publication. The Russian edition was first published in 1980 in Jerusalem, followed by a German translation in 1994 (11). The original farewell letter has, in the meantime, disappeared.

"After lunch the corpses from five vehicles were buried. From one vehicle a young woman was thrown out with a baby at her breast. It suckled its mother's milk and died. On this day we worked under the light from the searchlights until seven in the evening. Also on this day a vehicle drove so close to the pit that we heard the choked screams and desperate cries of the victims, as well as the pounding on the doors. Before work had finished, six of the pit workers were shot."

Report from Szlojme Fajner (unknown-1942), Chelmno extermination camp, 1942.

*"27 January, 1942, Kutno Ghetto
My dear ones! I have already written a card to you on the fate that has befallen us. They are taking us to Chelmno and gassing us. 25,000 Jews are lying there already. The slaughter goes on. 'Have you no pity for us?' Natan, the child, mother and I have escaped, no one else. I don't know what will become of us, I have no strength to live any more. If Aunt Bronia writes, write to her about everything. I send you warmest greetings, Fela"*

Postcard from the Kutno Ghetto, 1942.

"I am sitting on my rucksack in the middle of a loaded goods wagon. Father, mother and Mischa are several wagons distant. In the end, the departure came without warning. On sudden special orders from The Hague. We left the camp singing, father and mother strong and calm, Mischa as well. We will be travelling for three days (...) Etty"

Postcard from Etty Hillesum (1914-1943), thrown from a train during a deportation bound for Auschwitz-Birkenau, 1943.

| ² Говорят мертвые.

Это письмо я нашел в местечке Бытень Барановической области. Оно написано перед казнью Златой Вишнятской и двенадцатилетней Юнитой—мужу и отцу. Около 1800 евреев Бытени были убиты немцами.

Майор Владимир Демидов.

Мистеру Вишнет Оранж США
(Письмо по еврейски)
31 июля 42
Моему Мошкеле и всем моим дорогим!
25 июля у нас произошла ужасная резня, как и во всех других городах. Массовое убийство. Осталось 350 человек. 850 погибли от рук убийц черной смертью. Как щенков бросали в нужники, детей живых бросали в ямы. Много писать не буду. Я думаю что кто-нибудь случайно уцелеет, он расскажет о наших мучениях и о нашем кровавом конце. Нам пока удалось спастись, но на сколько?! Мы каждый день ждем смерти, и оплакаваем близких. Твоих, Мошкеле, уже нет. Но я им завидую. Кончаю, невозможно писать и не могу передать наших мучений. Будьте здоровы все. Единственное, что вы можете для нас сделать, это отомстить нашим убийцам. Мы кричим вам: отомстите! Целую вас крепко-крепко. Прощаюсь со всеми вами перед нашей смертью.

(приписка по польски) 3.
Дорогой отец! Прощаюсь с тобой перед смертью. Нам очень хочется жить, но пропало - не дают. Я так этой смерти боюсь, потому что малых детей бросают живыми в могилы. Прощайте навсегда. Целую тебя крепко, крепко.

Твоя И.

Поцелуй от Г.

"31 July 1942. – Dear father! I am saying goodbye to you before I die. We would so love to live, but they won't let us and we will die. I am so scared of this death, because the small children are thrown alive into the pit. Goodbye forever. I kiss you tenderly. Your J"

Note from 12-year-old Judith Wischnjatskaja under the letter from her mother, Slata, to her father. It was found by a Soviet soldier in Byten, near Baranowicze in eastern Poland. In Byten, German units shot more than 1,900 Jews. Copy in Russian; the original has been lost.

" (...) the rumours are terrifying. The Nazis are killing Jews in various ways. Some are sent to work camps, where they remain alive for one month at most. To hold out longer would be beyond human endurance. Some are shot, some burned, some poisoned by deadly gas ..."

Diary entry of Chaim A. Kaplan (1880-1942/43), Warsaw Ghetto, 1942.

In addition to the material from the Ringelblum Archive, other testimonies from the Warsaw Ghetto survived. Among them is a diary written in Hebrew by Chaim Kaplan (1880-1942/43), founder and director of a Hebrew private school in Warsaw. Kaplan came from Belarus, had attended a Talmud school and was a highly cultured intellectual. The diary covers the period from 1 September, 1939 to August 1942 and contains an extensive description of ghetto life and of the information that had reached him about the extermination of Polish Jewry (12). Increasingly, he recognized the hopelessness of the situation. On 26 July, 1942, during the massive deportation from the ghetto to the Treblinka extermination camp, he wrote: "Our only happiness is knowing that our days are numbered — that we do not have much time left to live under these conditions, and that, after our terrible suffering and wanderings, we will find the eternal rest that was denied us in life." (13) He, too, saw in his testimony a duty and a final purpose in life: "I know that the continuation of this diary up to the utter end of my physical and intellectual energy is an historic mission, in which I must not fail. My mind is still clear, my need to write has not been dampened, even if it is now five days since any real food has passed my lips." (14) On 4 August, 1942, the diary breaks off with these words: "When my life is ended – what will happen to my diary?" (15)

Kaplan was murdered in Treblinka, probably not long after penning these words. But shortly before, he had his diary smuggled out of the ghetto and entrusted to a Pole who worked with the Jewish underground. After liberation, this Pole gave part of Kaplan's diary to the Jewish Historical Institute in Warsaw and emigrated in 1962 to the USA, where he delivered another part of the diary to the American Hebrew scholar, Abraham Katsh. The latter published it for the first time in English in 1965, incomplete and abridged. Today there are numerous translations from the Hebrew, but there is no complete edition of the diary.

"Fall has come. 1 September.
September-resettlement with its horrors.
A separate chapter. Not particularly necessary
to mention here. If such a thing was possible,
what comes next? Why is there still war? Why is
there still hunger? Why is there still a world?"

Diary entry of Oskar Rosenfeld (1884-1944),
Lodz Ghetto, 1942.

Oskar Rosenfeld (1884-1944), born in Moravia, wrote his diary in German, in the Lodz Ghetto ("Litzmannstadt" to the National Socialist administration). Rosenfeld had studied in Vienna, had written for Zionist newspapers, co-founded the first Jewish theatre in Vienna, and published many works of prose. At the time of the "Anschluss", or annexation of Austria to the German Reich, in 1938, he fled to Prague, from where his wife was still able to emigrate. Rosenfeld, however, was deported in November 1941 to the Lodz Ghetto. From April 1940 onwards, the ghetto was sealed off with 160,000 Jews inside. In the autumn of 1941, the National Socialist authorities took in another 20,000 Jews from the old Reich and Prague. Rosenfeld worked in the official archive of the Jewish Ghetto administration. He wrote the official daily chronicle of the Jewish Council, the representative body that the Germans created and strictly monitored. This chronicle had to be written very carefully, given the German supervision of the ghetto and also that of Mordechai Rumkowski, the Jewish Council's autocratic president. Among other writings, Rosenfeld published short stories from the ghetto that, when read today, seem at first to trivialize the situation.

For Rosenfeld, writing and describing was always part of his life. Even in the ghetto, his notes were made, above all, with a view to giving them a literary treatment later. Although he wrote the ghetto chronicle under censorship, his diary contains notes, key words, first stabs at stories and even drafts of a screenplay that try to portray the reality of life in the ghetto. While doing so, his words increasingly dissolve after a few breathless sentences. His feelings and desperation about hunger, loneliness and constant fear of death, break every linguistic and literary form.

In January 1942, the gradual "resettlement" began of Lodz ghetto inhabitants to the Chelmno extermination camp. In the autumn, all children under the age of ten were deported, amidst dreadful scenes of terror. In this desperate situation comes Rosenfeld's cry: "Why is there still a world?" (16) The terrible hunger that the author continuously describes leads to more than 40,000 deaths. Rosenfeld, himself ill and weak, lived to mark his 60th birthday in May 1944. His prayer group (minyan) celebrates with speeches and little gifts. Just when Rosenfeld sensed that the end of the war and liberation was coming, the ghetto inhabitants were deported to Auschwitz in the summer of 1944 and murdered. The last entry in his diary is dated 28 July, 1944.

The Red Army liberated Lodz in January 1945. The few survivors of the ghetto rescued the many buried and hidden documents — Rosenfeld's diary was probably among them. In 1973, an Australian gave it to the Yad Vashem memorial in Israel with no clue as to how the manuscript had been rescued. The incomplete diary from February 1942 to July 1944 comprises ten notebooks. A further ten are filled with literary sketches of the ghetto, with quotes from the Bible and documents. Written in German, this diary was only published in 1994.

Another diary from the Lodz Ghetto is that of a young man. He wrote it from 5 May to 3 August, 1944, in the final phase of the ghetto's existence, when deadly hunger and fear of death due to constant deportations to extermination camps marked every moment. All we know of the author, whose name, background and age remain a mystery, is what he wrote about himself. He lived alone in the ghetto with his 12-year-old sister after their father starved to death. Obviously he was an educated young man, for he wrote the diary in four languages, switching between Yiddish, Hebrew, Polish and English. Because of the lack of paper, he wrote in the margins and blank pages of a French novel by François Coppée: "Les Vrais Riches" [True Riches], after which his diary was later named.

The young author wrote out of an emotional need: "I sense such an urgency to always break open my diary and pour out my bitter heart — oh, what we are going through, how terribly we suffer." (17) By writing, he tried

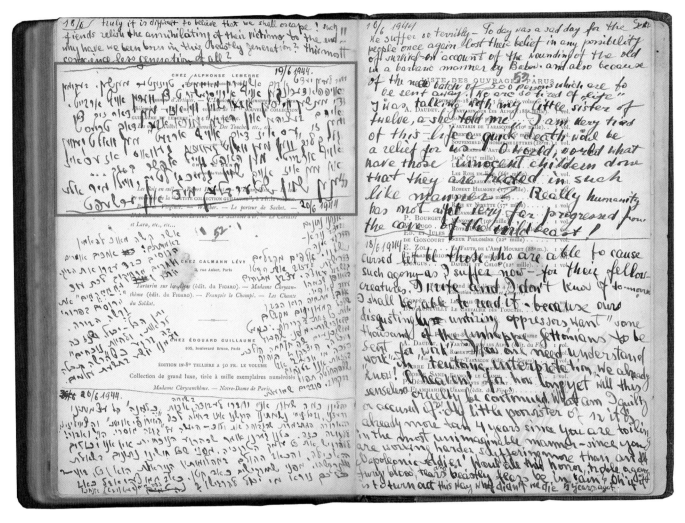

to relieve some of the terrible tension. His style and handwriting reflect the increasing agitation in a situation of starvation, where it seemed equally likely that one would be either murdered by the German occupiers or liberated by the Red Army. The author repeatedly runs into the limits of expression and what he is able to convey: "Even if I were to steal the muses of Homer, Shakespeare, Goethe and Dante: could I then describe what we suffer, what we feel, what we experience in our lives? (...) Can, in fact, poor human language take on the burden of depicting what a person in the ghetto in 1944 can bear?" (18) This text does not document thoughts and dreams for the future. Rather, it reflects the author's feelings. He broods in desperation over why the Germans continue to kill Jews, even during their retreat. And he asks: "Almighty God (...), how can you maintain such unscrupulous neutrality, to put it in modern terms, in the face of such unheard of horrors?" (19) The last entry is on 3 August, 1944, when the final deportation of the last 68,000 ghetto inhabitants is announced: "Oh God in Heaven, why did you create the Germans so that they could destroy humanity?" (20) The diary, written in four languages, was found in Auschwitz and given by a survivor to the Israeli memorial, Yad Vashem. It was first published in 1997 in a German translation.

"19.6.1944 – We are now going through a terrible time. Thousands of people are getting summonses – they will be sent to work. But everyone knows already what awaits them and they are afraid. And yet one consoles them: 'It really is for work!' One would be happy if one knew that it really is work. And then one hopes, maybe it really is (...) And one is also indifferent, because we are all tired and exhausted to death." (21)

"Les Vrais Riches", Lodz Ghetto, 1944.

"What kind of life would it be, even if I do survive? Who would I even find in my old home of Warsaw? Why and for whom this fight for life, bearing everything, always holding on – why?!"

Diary entry of Herman Kruk (1897-1944),
30 September, 1942, Vilnius Ghetto.

The writings of Herman Kruk (1897-1944) are more chronicle than diary. This librarian, memorialized in the dramatic work "Ghetto" by Israeli playwright Sobol, wrote an extensive chronicle of the ghetto in Vilnius. Kruk had fled ahead of the German invasion, leaving Warsaw for the Soviet-occupied city of Vilnius, which before the war had been home to a Jewish community with 60,000 members, which was extraordinary in cultural terms. As a political activist in the "Bund" – the General Jewish Workers Association in Russia, Lithuania and Poland founded in Vilnius in 1897 – Kruk was a socialist and anti-Zionist. Originally trained as a photographer, and almost completely self-taught, he promoted the cultural work of the Association for Jewish Workers in Warsaw and directed the headquarters of the Yiddish Libraries of Poland. When the German Army also occupied Lithuania in 1941, Kruk opened the extremely popular ghetto library, a few days after the creation of the Vilnius Ghetto in September 1941. In February 1942, he was forced by the Einsatzstab Rosenberg (literally "Action Staff Rosenberg"), which methodically plundered the libraries, archives and art galleries of European Jews, to prepare the archive of the Institute for Jewish Research (YIVO), founded in Vilnius in 1925, for transfer to Frankfurt am Main, location of the National Socialist "Institute for Research on the Jewish Question". In utter desperation, Kruk and his colleagues were able to save and hide a portion of the material.

Each day, Kruk dictated the ghetto chronicle in Yiddish in the library office. He always included additional documents like statistics, programmes, summonses or posters, so that at the same time he created an archive. In many ways his activities are similar to those of the Ringelblum group. True, Kruk wrote in secret, but also with the knowledge of the Jewish Council. His report was deliberately factual and filled with information. He seldom referred to himself. He too, had contacts with Jews outside Vilnius and learned from eye-witnesses about mass murders. When he heard about the deportation of most Jews from the Warsaw Ghetto, where he had many close relatives and friends, his desperation came to the surface. For whom and why should he still survive? "Where are the workers and masses for whom I used to struggle, suffer, and rejoice?" (22) It became an absolute necessity to write his chronicle. He called it "my chronicle – the hashish of my life in the ghetto" (23) and understood it as a "document of the horrors of our fearful time in the ghetto" for the post-liberation age. In a discussion about his own library reports, he described his motivations with modest pride: "For the future historian, this will certainly be a good contribution to research on the cultural activity and the psychology of the readers in the Vilnius Ghetto." (24)

In September 1943, the Vilnius Ghetto was liquidated. Kruk managed to bury his chronicle in a metal box in a cellar in the ghetto. He continued writing by hand in the Estonian concentration camps of Klooga and Lagedi, to which he was deported. On 18 September, 1944, the day before the Red Army liberated Lagedi, Kruk was shot there. But here as well, he had managed to bury his writings under the eyes of witnesses.

Kruk's daily reports from the ghetto and the camps cover the period from 5 September, 1939 to 17 September, 1944. They were recovered in 1944, albeit not in their entirety, by survivors who knew where they had been hidden. In Vilnius, the writer Abraham Sutzkever found the tin box broken open and its contents strewn about, so that pages were missing. The additional documents Kruk included were almost all lost. Even more problematic was the distribution of the saved manuscripts: the original is partly in the New York-based YIVO Institute, partly in Yad Vashem and partly in the Moreshet Institute in Israel. It was first published in Yiddish in 1961 and appeared only in 2002 in English, in a more or less complete edition. The reports take up a total of 700 pages.

While Kruk intended his chronicle as an objective representation arranged by theme, there is another diary from Vilnius that is completely different, though also written in Yiddish. The author, Yitskhok Rudashevski (1927-1943), was a sensitive, thoughtful and obviously very talented 14-year-old. He begins his diary in June 1941 with the German invasion, and manages to keep it going it until April 1943. He reports in a very personal and sometimes lyrical style about his life and studies in the ghetto, with deep concern for the fate of the people around him. He describes in devastating detail the massive manhunt for tens of thousands of people who, as he soon learned, were ultimately shot in Ponary, outside Vilnius. In addition, the diary shows a youthful joy in life and the great urge to study, as well as his faith in life after the ghetto.

Yitskhok was the son of a tailor and a typesetter, both of whom worked as forced labourers in the ghetto workshops. He attended the secondary school, which was set up with difficulty in the ghetto. He read a great deal and participated in literary and history discussion groups with other young people. He headed a group for creative writing and participated in a questionnaire on the life of ghetto inhabitants He wrote: "I consider that everything should be recorded and noted down, even the most gory, because everything will be taken into account." (25) He, too, was filled with the ethos of documentation. His dairy also testifies to his own development and artistic blossoming.

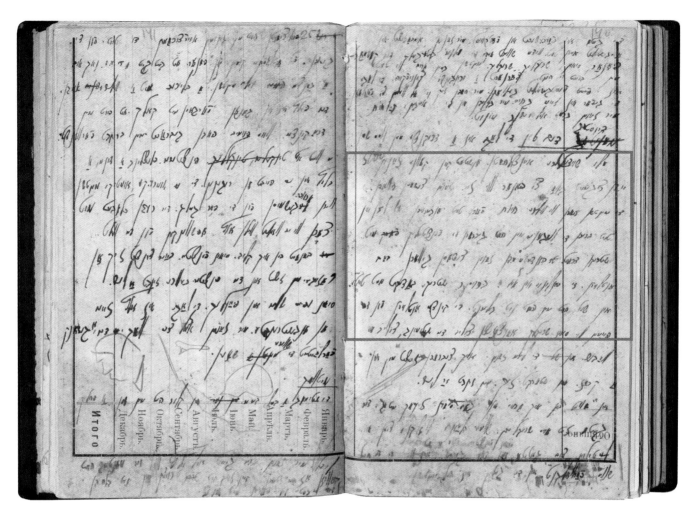

"Now we all know the terrible details. Instead of being sent to Kovno, 5,000 Jews were brought to Ponary and shot. Like wild animals before dying, the people began, in mortal fear, to break open the railway cars, they broke the small windows that had been secured with strong wire. Hundreds were shot as they tried to run away. A long stretch of the train tracks was strewn with bodies."

Diary entry of Yitskhok Rudashevski (1927-1943), 6 April, 1943, Vilna Ghetto.

The notes stop abruptly on 7 April, 1943. According to testimony from his female cousin, Yitskhok went into hiding with his family and his cousins during the violent liquidation of the ghetto at the end of September 1943. After two weeks hiding in the loft of a house, they were found by their German pursuers and shot in Ponary, as had been most of the Vilnius Jews before them. Yitskhok's cousin, Sore Voloshin, the only one able to flee, joined local partisans and returned to the city with them in July 1944, after its liberation by the Red Army. She found the diary hidden in the loft and gave it to the writer Abraham Sutzkever, who had often advised Yitskhok and who had survived as a partisan. Through him, the diary reached the YIVO Institute in New York. By 1953, Sutzkever already had published excerpts in Yiddish. The first Hebrew translation appeared in Israel in 1968, followed in 1973 by an English edition.

A 19-year-old Dane, Ralph Oppenhejm, born in 1924 in Copenhagen, recorded the daily life of the Theresienstadt Ghetto. He was a theatre student and son of a respected publisher. The family tried to flee to Sweden in a boat in 1943, as had more than 6,000 Danish Jews. But unlike the great majority of his Jewish compatriots, who succeeded in crossing over, he and his family were intercepted by the Germans and deported to Theresienstadt. Here, some 450 Danish Jews formed a privileged minority because the Danish government continued to show concern for its citizens and in the summer of 1944 even sent two officials to inspect the ghetto. The officials were tricked by the National Socialist authorities and did not recognize the true character of the ghetto camp. Nevertheless, the Danish Jews were spared transport to an extermination camp. Oppenhejm observed in April 1944 how files with lists of prisoners' names were burned. On 14 April, after intervention by the Danish and Swedish governments, citizens of these countries were permitted to leave the ghetto.

Oppenhejm took his notes with him and published them in 1945 in Copenhagen as a diary from Theresienstadt. This was his first book in a long career as an author. His published text was a literary reworking and fictionalization. He chose a woman to be the author of the "diary" and wrote numerous scenes in the form of a dialogue. In this version, the diary differs significantly from his texts written in the ghetto. The work was published in English, in German (1961) and in other languages (26).

The young partisan Gusta Draenger (1917-1943) wrote a manuscript in a Cracow Gestapo prison from January to April 1943 on strips of toilet paper. She called the notes "Justyna's Diary". She and her husband, Simon Draenger, were active leaders in the Zionist youth organization Akiba, which – together with other Zionist and communist groups – took up active resistance in spring 1942, in the face of the extermination of the Jews of Cracow. After fruitless attempts to operate in the forest as partisans, they began an armed struggle against the German occupiers in the centre of Cracow. The young men and women lived underground, both inside and outside the Cracow Ghetto, and carried out numerous attacks. On 22 December, 1942, the group attacked two coffee houses popular with members of the SS, killing 20 and wounding others. Most of the group was betrayed and arrested. Gusta Draenger gave herself up. She wanted to share the fate of her husband. The manuscript she wrote in the Cracow women's prison is not a diary, but rather a description of the young partisans and their life as a close-knit group of friends who became each other's family after their parents were murdered. Gusta Draenger used only pseudonyms, calling herself Justyna, and described the life of conspiracy with careful self-censorship. Her manuscript gives insights into the thoughts and motivations of young fighting women and men. After the murder of their families, they felt free to defend their honour, to avenge the deaths of their parents and to end their lives in armed struggle.

On 29 April, 1943, Gusta Draenger hid her manuscript in a tin box in the oven of her cell. On that day, she and her husband managed to escape the prison with other partisans. But they were rearrested in November. It is not known how they met their deaths. People who knew of its existence rescued the Polish manuscript from the cell. Today it is in the Ghetto Fighters House in Israel, near Haifa. It has been published in a somewhat abridged form in German (27).

The prisoners of the so-called "Sonderkommando" (literally "Special Detachment") at Auschwitz-Birkenau were the closest Jewish witnesses to the mass murder. The SS kept them isolated from other prisoners and forced them to drag the bodies from the gas chambers, to burn them and then to bury their ashes. As witnesses to this crime, they themselves were later killed. Many of these men recorded their testimony in this unimaginable situation and buried their notes near the crematoria, together with human ashes. From 1945 to 1980, a total of eight such documents were

"But why are they in such a hurry to erase the names? Are they afraid that the civilized world might get an idea of how many thousands they have killed? Are they trying to erase the traces of their crime? Yes, then they will also get rid of us few who still remain."

Diary entry of Ralph Oppenhejm (born 1924), Theresienstadt, 4 April, 1945.

"One does not need to be a revolutionary in order to bring oneself into mortal danger. It is simply enough to be oneself. It is sufficient to take one single step, and one falls into the treacherous trap set for Jews."

Notes of Gusta Davidson-Draenger (1917-1943), Cracow, 1943.

found, in bottles, jars and metal boxes. Damaged by dampness, some of the manuscripts are only partially legible. In one buried farewell letter to his wife, an unknown author wrote, "It is another world here, if you will; it is Hell, but Dante's Hell is outrageously funny in comparison to this reality, and we are the witnesses who are not permitted to live." (28)

"The compressed mass of people (...) was able, because of the great pressure of people (...) to hang in the air; for thirty hours it made it possible for them to remain upright. No conversation, no discussion (...) was held. All were only half out of their minds with tiredness and fatigue. This closeness pressed the [stamp] of exhaustion and weakness on all [and] bore [at the decisive] moment a victory over the spirit. One single time, the door of the wagon was opened, two police entered, who, in exchange for the wedding rings given to them by the women, allowed them to have a drink."

Notes of Lejb Langfus (ca. 1910-1944), written in the deportation train to Auschwitz-Birkenau, 1942.

"(...) directed gas inside (...) we carried the bodies of these (...) innocent women (...) who were brought to the ovens (...) and there put in an oven (...) and forced us to put it through a coarse sieve and later that was loaded into a car and spilled into the river which flowed nearby, and it covered up all traces. The dramas that my eyes have seen are indescribable. About 600,000 Jews from Hungary, French people, Poles (...)"

Notes of Marcel Nadjary (1917-1971), Auschwitz-Birkenau, probably written November 1944.

Lejb Langfus (ca 1910-1944) and Marcel Nadjary (1917-1971) were among those prisoners who, in expectation of their own death, left behind testimonies of indescribable crimes (29). Nadjary was an electrician from Salonika and arrived in Auschwitz in April 1944, where, after one month, he was assigned to the Sonderkommando. He is one of the few who survived this assignment, because in April 1945 the SS sent him to work in an armaments factory in Gusen, a satellite of Mauthausen concentration camp, from which he was liberated. His report in Greek about the Sonderkommando was found in 1980, in part of a buried thermos flask. Today, it is in a disintegrated condition and can be deciphered only in fragments.

Lejb Langfus came from the small Polish city of Makow Mazowiecki. At the end of 1942, he arrived in Auschwitz and was part of the Sonderkommando for almost two years, until he was killed in November 1944. Langfus was one of the most important chroniclers of the Sonderkommando and was a member of a resistance group. As a religious Jew who had studied Talmud, he sought comfort in his faith and assembled a group of Orthodox Jews who secretly held services with a Torah Scroll and also said prayers of mourning for those who had been murdered. His notes in Yiddish about the deportation and the work of the Sonderkommando, buried in a bottling jar, are also only partly decipherable. But many passages about what happened in the trains, the undressing rooms and the gas chambers, about the desperation and mortal fear, and about how the victims supported each other, remain intact. The testimonies of Langfus and Nadjary are in the archive at the Auschwitz memorial and have now been preserved as far as possible, using modern conservational methods.

Clearly, the notes from the ghettos and camps sprang from the writers' very strong inner need. The authors were under extreme psychological stress from hunger, violence, fear and the constant risk of death. Even so, they summoned the strength to write. Carried out in extremely humiliating conditions, this act of reporting was often the last chance for the writers to preserve their sense of personal worth and humanity and to express defiance. At the same time, they could relieve through their writing some of their psychological stress and, at least for a short time, exercise their minds. Above all, however, they saw their true purpose in preserving evidence of unimaginable crimes. They were very aware of this mission and tried, with hard-won objectivity, to compose eye-witness reports of daily events. It is true that feelings and thoughts often interrupt the objective tone of the chronicler. At the same time, many writers despaired of ever being able to put into words these dreadful events.

It was clear that the victory of the Allies over National Socialist Germany was approaching, but most of these writers knew they were unlikely to survive. In this situation, they were motivated by an ethical and historical drive to testify for posterity and so deliver the perpetrators to their judges. By writing, they linked themselves with a future, just world, and this gave meaning to their lives beyond their own deaths. One can see this as part of the Jewish tradition to deliver historical remembrance of the deeds and the suffering of the Jewish people. But, at the same time, it can be seen as a political legacy for future generations of humanity.

(1) Abraham I. Katsh (ed.), *Buch der Agonie. Das Warschauer Tagebuch des Chaim A. Kaplan* (Frankfurt, 1965) p. 124.

(2) Herman Kruk, *The Last Days of the Jerusalem of Lithuania. Chronicles from the Vilna Ghetto and the Camps 1939-1944*, ed. by Benjamin Harshav, (New Haven, London, 2002), Endpaper.

(3) ibid., p. 371.

(4) Emanuel Ringelblum, *Notes from the Warsaw Ghetto* (New York, 1974).

(5) Josef Wulf, *Vom Leben, Kampf und Tod im Ghetto Warschau* (Bonn, 1963), p.12.

(6) Abraham Lewin, *A Cup of Tears. A Diary of the Warsaw Ghetto* (Oxford, 1989), p. 120.

(7) ibid., p. 170, entry of 28 August 1942.

(8) Ruta Sakowska, *Die zweite Etappe ist der Tod. NS Ausrottungspolitik gegen die polnischen Juden, gesehen mit den Augen der Opfer. Ein historischer Essay und ausgewählte Dokumente aus dem "Ringelblumarchiv" 1941-1943* (Berlin, 1993), pp. 174-179.

(9) ibid., p. 156.

(10) Etty Hillesum, *Letters from Westerbork* (New York, 1986), p. 146.

(11) Published in German in: Wassili Grossman/Ilja Ehrenburg (eds.), *Schwarzbuch. Der Genozid an den sowjetischen Juden* (Reinbek, 1994), p. 370.

(12) loc. cit., *Buch der Agonie*, p. 356.

(13) ibid., p. 384.

(14) ibid., p. 385.

(15) ibid., p. 404.

(16) Oskar Rosenfeld, *Wozu noch Welt. Aufzeichnungen aus dem Ghetto Lodz* (Frankfurt, 1994), p. 195.

(17) *Les Vrais Riches. Notizen am Rand. Ein Tagebuch aus dem Ghetto Lodz (May-August 1944)*, ed. by Hanno Loewy/Andrzej Bodek (Leipzig, 1997), p. 79.

(18) ibid., p. 44f.

(19) ibid., p. 59.

(20) ibid., p. 100.

(21) ibid. p. 52 of the facsimile.

(22) loc. cit., *Last Days*, p. 371, entry of 30 September 1942.

(23) ibid., p. 324, entry of 9 July 1942.

(24) ibid., p. 469, entry of 3 March 1943.

(25) Yitskhok Rudashevski, *Diary of the Vilna Ghetto, June 1941-April 1943* (Tel Aviv, 1979), p. 84.

(26) Ralph Oppenhejm, *An der Genze des Lebens. Theresienstädter Tagebuch* (Hamburg, 1961).

(27) Jochen Kast/Bernd Siegler/Peter Zinke (eds.), *Das Tagebuch der Partisanin Justyna. Jüdischer Widerstand in Krakau* (Berlin, 1999).

(28) *Inmitten des grauenvollen Verbrechens. Handschriften von Mitgliedern des Sonderkommandos. Letter written by Chaim Hermann, 6 November 1944.* Staatliches Museum Auschwitz-Birkenau (ed.), (Oswiecim, 1996), p. 263.

(29) ibid., p. 121 and 271; Eric Fiedler/Barbara Siebert/Andreas Kilian, *Zeugen aus der Todeszone. Das Jüdische Sonderkommando in Auschwitz* (Lüneburg, 2002), p. 380 and 382.

IMAGES OF LIFE AND DESTRUCTION
THE FATES OF JEWISH FAMILIES 1900-1945

At the living room table in the Pilsudski Street in Lodz; in front of the parents' shop on a village road of Uttenheim in Alsace; at a banquet in Amsterdam; on the terrace of a house in Belgrade – relatives gather to preserve a moment of mutual family life. Four photos – four families in different parts of Europe and – it is visible at first glance – with different cultural and social backgrounds: bourgeois or rural, prosperous or poor.

Almost all those depicted would become victims of the German policies of persecution and murder of European Jewry between 1941 and 1945. Through an indirect route or by chance, their family portraits survived – buried, hidden by non-Jewish friends or slipped into the hastily packed bags of surviving relatives. The survival of these documents is a rare exception. Usually such mementos were destroyed together with the people they represented. Almost no private possessions remain for most of those murdered in the Holocaust. Letters, photos, diaries disappeared when flats were cleared out after their inhabitants had been removed; or they were taken from deportees upon arrival in the camps. Severe punishment awaited those found with personal possessions in the concentration camps.

The photos and documents seen here not only permit a glimpse at a few life stories. They also testify to the diversity of Jewish everyday life in Europe in the first third of the 20th century. This rich variety of Jewish cultures, and its destruction after 1933, form the central focus of the Room of Family Histories in the Information Centre at Berlin's Memorial to the Murdered Jews of Europe. Of the 15 family histories depicted there, four stories will be told here in more detail.

Lodz – 58, Pilsudski Street

The family patriarch sits at the right-hand side of the table. Shmuel David Grossman's appearance reveals that he is an orthodox, chassidic Jew: he has a long beard, wears a traditional skullcap, and is dressed in a long black coat and high boots. On the other end of the table sits the mother, Chaya Ruda Grossman. She hides her hair under a sheytl, a wig. Married orthodox Jewesses do not go out with their heads uncovered. Between the two are their children: Rushka and Faiga, the daughters, and their son, Mendel, then just starting out as a painter and photographer. The photograph probably was taken with his camera, perhaps using the automatic shutter. There is nothing imposing and stiff about the photograph; rather, it has a spontaneous and friendly feel. The family does not pose in some middle-class salon. On the right side of the photograph one can see a bed. The father sits calmly at the table, his legs crossed.

The Grossman parents with their children Rushka, Mendel and Faiga.

The Grossmans had lived in Lodz for some 20 years. Like hundreds of thousands of others, they moved there from the countryside and built a new life in the city. The parents came from central Poland near Lodz, the area that fell under the control of the Russian czars after 1815 and remained so until the First World War. Shmuel David was born in 1882 in Gorzkowice, a village south of Lodz; Chaya was born in 1887 in Lowicz, a city halfway between Lodz and Warsaw. In both towns, Jews made up a significant part of the population as a whole. Chaya and Shmuel David grew up in traditional Jewish environments: Lowicz and Gorzkowice were typical shtetls. It is not known how and when Shmuel David and Chaya Ruda met or were introduced to one another. After all, their birthplaces were more than 70 kilometres apart. Perhaps relatives or a shadchen – matchmaker – arranged the marriage. Many other details of their daily lives remain unclear. Apparently the Grossmans lived for a time in Gorzkowice and for a time in Lowicz, for they brought children into the world in both places. Then, about 1915, they decided to move to Lodz.

The 'Manchester of the East' was the centre of the textile and clothing industry in Poland, and the Grossmans were among those involved in this trade. Shmuel David Grossman supported his family as a clothing dealer. When his daughters were old enough, they began to sew clothing, which their father sold. More than three quarters of the Jews of Lodz did similar work. They were self-employed, assuming full business risks.

But for Shmuel David, business was not the central focus of his life, but rather, as a pious chassidic Jew, it was prayer and the study of religious texts. "The main task was learning", his son-in-law remembered. The religious renewal movement of Chassidism gained wide support in the early nineteenth century among the Jews in Galicia, Volhynia and Bukovina (today Poland and Ukraine). Many saw in the movement a way to escape a world which offered no consolation. The original idea of Chassidism was the connection between piety and affirmation of life, between performing good deeds and changing oneself. Shmuel David belonged to the Zychliner Chassidim, one of numerous chassidic sects, which traced its origin to the town of Zychlin. Despite the strict religious nature of their lives, Shmuel David and Chaya Grossman allowed their children relatively broad freedom in choosing their own paths through life. Above all, this applied to their son.

Shmuel David Grossman studying religious texts (photo by Mendel Grossman).

Shmuel David Grossman with
his grandson, Yankush.

Mendel studied with the Lodz artist, Hersh Zvi Schillis, who survived the war and later worked in Israel. In order to contribute to the family's finances, Mendel trained as a photography teacher and also learned how to retouch photos. At the end of the 1930s the family grew: daughter Faiga married Shimon Frajtag, and they had a son, Yankush. His uncle Mendel recorded the growing up of the boy in numerous photographs. Child portraits were one of Mendel's main themes at the time. He prepared a photo series on child poverty in Lodz for the Jewish organization TOZ, Towarzystwo Obrony Zdrowia – Society for the Protection of Health.

At the same time, Mendel entered Yiddish literary avant-garde circles in Lodz. Together with two previously unknown young artists, Julek Levin and Pinchas Schwarz, he received a contract to illustrate with photomontages, a new volume of poetry by the well-known author and theatre director, Moshe Broderson. The book came out shortly before the German attack on Poland of 1 September, 1939. The start of German rule over Lodz some weeks later brought to a violent end the free development of Jewish culture and the hopeful early careers of artists of Mendel Grossman's generation.

Uttenheim in Alsace, in front of Benjamin Bloch's Spice Shop

The children came from Strasbourg and from across the Rhine to visit their elderly parents. They had a photo taken in front of the old, somewhat crooked family house. Above them hung the sign advertising the

The Dreifuss (left front) and Bloch families in front of the house of grandfather Benjamin Bloch, in Uttenheim in Alsace. On the building hangs a small sign with the words: "Benjamin Bloch – Spice Dealer".

spice shop of their father, Benjamin Bloch. With pipe in hand, he sat amongst his family. His daughter Léonie and cigar-smoking son-in-law, Leopold Dreifuss, took their place at the far left. Léonie and Leopold lived in Altdorf, a community on the Baden side of the Rhine. At the time the photo was taken, about 1912, the river was not a border, because both banks were part of the German Reich. The Bloch and Dreifuss families were among the established Jewish families who had lived in the Upper Rhine region for generations. Sitting on the motherly lap is the little daughter Alice, her image somewhat blurred; between the knees of his proud father is Siegfried (also known as Fritz), wearing a sailor suit, in the fashion of the day. The choice of first name shows the national feeling of the parents. In this they did not differ from the great majority of German Jews.

Even after 1918, when Uttenheim once again belonged to France and Altdorf remained part of Germany, nothing much changed for the family. The Altdorfers stayed in touch with the Alsatians. They shared a rural life.

Their everyday lives were marked by close contact with Christian neighbours. In southwestern Germany, Hesse, Franconia, Alsace and northern Switzerland, there were several hundred such villages and small towns with significant Jewish populations. But these were not "shtetls" in the eastern European sense. Unlike in Poland, Jews in these communities seldom comprised more than a quarter of the population. Generally, the minority and the majority got along well. Neighbours were close and helped one another; children played together; women had their daily gossip; and Catholic and Jewish veterans met in the Altdorf Soldiers Association. Despite this closeness, there was no intermarriage. Unions between Catholics and Protestants were also rare.

Leopold Dreifuss (front, with legs crossed) in 1916, as a German soldier during World War I.

Leopold Dreifuss owned a kosher butcher shop in Altdorf. Leopold's butcher business was small, and reflected old-fashioned village circumstances. The shop was located in one room of the house. Léonie Bloch helped with sales. The Jewish religion prescribes that livestock must be slaughtered with one cut of the knife and then drained of blood. The meat is only kosher if this is carried out by a trained slaughterer. Leopold did not have this training, so a relative with the necessary licence performed the task. Catholics also bought meat in the Dreifuss shop. Leopold and Léonie could not have made a living with Jewish customers alone. In 1875, when Leopold Dreifuss was born, there were 283 Jews living in the village, about a fifth of the entire population. In 1925 there were only 68 Altdorf Jews. Most Jews who left the community moved to larger cities in the region, such as Freiburg, Mannheim or Frankfurt/Main, where there was a Jewish community rich in tradition. More than a few made the long journey to America. The village offered a sufficient livelihood only to a few. Most Jews living in the countryside worked in the modestly profitable livestock trade. In order to give their son, Fritz, better employment opportunities, his parents sent him to the secondary school in the nearby district town from 1918 to 1922. He subsequently completed a sales apprenticeship with a Jewish ironmonger. In 1930, he found a job on the other side of the border, in Strasbourg. Alice helped at home. In official records she appears as "house daughter". In 1931, at the height of the global economic crisis, she reached her coming of age.

Leopold Dreifuss (centre, with peaked cap), with his children Fritz, left, and Alice (second from left), in front of the butcher shop in Altdorf. The shop was located next to the synagogue.

Alice Dreifuss in a "Fasching" (Carnival) costume, 1928.

Sara Demajo (second from left) with a circle of friends having a coffee and a smoke, Belgrade, 1904.

On a Veranda in Belgrade

In the historic photo of the Demajo family of Belgrade, those pictured are smoking as well. And here it was the women who indulged in the pleasures of tobacco. With it, they sipped coffee from small cups. Second from right, Sara Demajo sat on the veranda surrounded by friends. When she was born as Sara Arueti in Belgrade in 1868, Serbia was officially still a part of the Ottoman Empire. Turkish traditions in the Balkans did not only consist of enjoyment of coffee and tobacco. The Ottoman heritage also included the many Muslim and Jewish communities in the Balkans. Orthodox and Catholic Christians, Muslims and Jews lived closely together. In the fifteenth century, the Ottoman sultans had allowed Sara Arueti's ancestors to settle in their empire. The Aruetis and thousands of others had fled Spain, whose Catholic rulers ordered the expulsion of the Jewish population in 1492. The Spanish-Jewish refugees, "Sephardim", kept their traditions for more than 400 years. Sara Arueti's everyday language was Judeo-Spanish, called Ladino, a mixture of elements from Spanish and Hebrew.

A Demajo family picnic, Arueti and Elkalai, Belgrade, 1924.

Sara Demajo with her daughters and grandchildren, Belgrade, 1937.

Sara was married to Shmayahu Demajo, who was also Sephardic. He came from a modest background. His father worked as a porter at the Danube harbour in Belgrade, and he himself was a house painter. The couple had three daughters and one son. In 1915 Shmayahu Demajo fell in battle as a Serbian soldier in the First World War. The youngest daughter was then only seven. Sara now had to support the family on her own. As she had done before the death of her husband, Sara worked as a domestic servant for families in Belgrade. She is remembered in her family as a hard-working woman with tremendous discipline.

Sara may not have been a very religious Jewess, but she observed the most important holidays. For the generation of her children and grand-children, who worked as shopkeepers, skilled workers and civil servants in Belgrade, the religious and cultural heritage receded into the background. They were completely integrated in the Serbian urban society of Belgrade. One of Sara's daughters and one niece married non-Jews. Connections with the Sephardic community in Belgrade, which in 1930 had some 8,000 members, were rather loose. Newborn boys in the family were circumcised, but they had no Bar Mitzvahs at the age of 13. Religious knowledge was similarly limited. The grandson, Rafael Pijade, born in 1916, remembered that he no longer understood the meaning of the expression, "Next year in Jerusalem", repeated at each family Passover celebration.

Amsterdam, Hotel Hiegentlich in the Oude Hoogstraat

The fourth family photo originated somewhat later than the others. It was taken in August 1940, in the banquet hall of the Hotel Hiegentlich in Amsterdam. The family had come to cel-ebrate the wedding of Louis Peereboom and Lena Brilleman. The mood appears optimistic and joyful, even if unwarranted by the situation outside. Three months earlier, the Netherlands had been occu-pied by the Wehrmacht and placed under a German "Reich Kommissar". But the occu-piers were still holding back and seldom intervened in public life.

Photo of the wedding party of Louis Peereboom and Lena Brilleman. At the left side of the table are the parents of the groom, Vrouwtje and Josef Peereboom.

The 27-year-old groom, Louis Peereboom, was overflowing with joy in life. He had met his future brother-in-law, Nico Gerri-tse, a jazz musician, while working for the wholesale textile trading firm, Schönberg. Louis organized gigs for Nico's band in the Workers' Friends Circle, in the guildhall in the Roetenstraat in Amsterdam; he put up posters and took care of tickets. Louis was also an enthusiastic boxer. Until he married Lena, Louis had lived at home. The Peereboom flat was in the centre of the city's historic Jewish quarter. Louis' parents, Josef Peereboom and Vrouwtje Peereboom, née Saksioni, came from old Amsterdam Jewish families. The Saksionis traced themselves back to Sephardic immigrants from Spain and Portugal. Like Belgrade, Amsterdam had a long Sephardic tradition. Since the early seventeenth century, refugees from the Iberian Peninsula had been allowed to practise their faith openly here. Later, many Jews came to Amsterdam from Germany and Poland as well, among them the Peereboom ancestors.

Josef and Vrouwtje Peereboom with their daughter Louisa and son-in-law Nico Gerritse, Zandvoort, around 1935.

The family patriarch, Josef, had worked since he was 20 years old for the Joachimsthal Publishing Company. The firm published the 'Nieuw Israe-lietisch Weekblad' (New Israelite Weekly) and also ran a bookshop where one could purchase religious articles and Jewish literature. Josef worked in the advertising department of the newspaper. The relationships with the publishing family and the company were close. The Peereboom's flat

Vrouwtje Peereboom with her daughter, Louisa, in front of the King's Palace in Amsterdam (about 1935).

was directly above the newspaper office. On Friday afternoons, when the bookshop and print shop closed at 3:30 p.m., Josef Peereboom and the publisher Joachimsthal drank a few glasses of Genever, a Dutch gin together. Then the Sabbath began in the Peereboom family. The children especially enjoyed this, and not only because of the good food, but because they were allowed to stay up late. It was cosy being together with the large family circle, and the day felt quite different from the rest of the week, since guests often came to visit, particularly from the mother's large family.

The Peerebooms were not well-off, but they led a materially secure existence. In this they differed from many other residents of the rather poor Jewish quarter. Josef Peereboom maintained many contacts with neighbours, for whom he set up "putting-aside books", savings books that enabled them to buy what they needed for the major Jewish holidays. On Thursday afternoons, he did the books for the poor, on Sunday those for the better off.

Diverse Jewish Cultures in Europe

Yellowed, torn and crumpled photos, images less from everyday life than from holidays, taken with obvious care to capture the fleeting moment: thus we encounter Jewish families from various regions of Europe. What is it that linked these people from areas so distant from one another, from such different social strata, with different language, different citizenship and different occupations? For most of those pictured here, it was their Jewish faith and membership in a local Jewish community that unites them. But they would also be linked by their common fate as victims of persecution and genocide. They died of hunger and illness in the ghetto, in mass shootings or after deportations lasting several days and taking them across Europe to a German extermination camp in occupied Poland.

The mass murder destroyed countless lives and brought unprecedented suffering to millions. It lends a uniform colour to our perception of the lives which were destroyed – just as the black and white photographs show silhouettes and shadows, but would not allow us to sense the colours. Their shared fate suggests a cultural uniformity of European Jewry. The richness and diversity of European Jewish cultures before the National Socialists rose to power in Germany and extended their murderous rule over nearly the entire European continent, thus recede into the background.

The origins of European Jewish communities lay in the Mediterranean, in the early communities of the Diaspora, in what today are Turkey, Greece, Italy, southern France and the area south of the Pyrenees. The first of the two great cultures of European Jewry unfolded on the Iberian Peninsula. "Sfarad", from which the term "Sephardim" comes, means nothing other than "Spain" in Hebrew. The Sephardic culture produced religious and scholarly authorities, whose achievements included taking up and developing further the distinguished traditions of the Jewish exile in Babylon (roughly from the sixth century before the Common Era to the seventh century after the Common Era). It was marked by an intensive intellectual exchange with Christianity and Islam.

The expulsion of the Jews from Spain in 1492 (the same year that Columbus discovered America) and from Portugal in 1497 brought the Sephardic culture of the Iberian Peninsula to a sudden end, but at the same time led to the establishment of numerous new Jewish communities. The Iberian refugees settled as traders in major port cities such as Amsterdam, Hamburg and Bordeaux or, like the ancestors of Sara Demajo, took up the invitation of the Ottoman Sultans. So a Sephardic culture arose across a large swathe from the North Sea to southern France, Italy, the Balkans and Turkey, all the way to the Middle East, maintaining a separate identity from the eastern European and central European Jews.

The latter, the "Ashkenazim", developed their identity through a long history of migration. There is evidence that Jewish communities existed on the Rhine from the tenth century. These early central European Jewish settlements long preserved consciousness of a cultural link to the Mediterranean, at least until the High Middle Ages. Yet, they developed their own tradition of scholarship, passed along in the writings of the "Pious of Germany". This first blossoming of religious mysticism in the twelfth and thirteenth centuries in Germany (in Hebrew: "Ashkenas"), as well as the later migrations through eastern Europe, contributed to a self-understanding as a group of its own, as Ashkenazi Jewry.

These migrations were prompted by the pogroms during the period of the Crusades and the expulsions from German cities in the fourteenth and fifteenth centuries. At first there was some settlement in the trading centres of Bohemia, Hungary and western central Poland. This developed into the most extensive and compact Jewish settlement in European history – that of Poland. Gradually, Ashkenazi scholars began to distance themselves from the Spanish Jewish tradition, which they previously had seen as a model.

Ashkenazi Jews far outnumbered the Sephardim. Around 1930, there were not more than a few hundred thousand Sephardic Jews in Europe (including Istanbul), as opposed to about eight million Ashkenazis, though there were also many communities, particularly in western Europe and in the Balkans, where they lived among one another.

○ Ashkenazi communities with at least 20,000 members.
● Most important Sephardic communities.
○ Other Jewish communities mentioned in text.

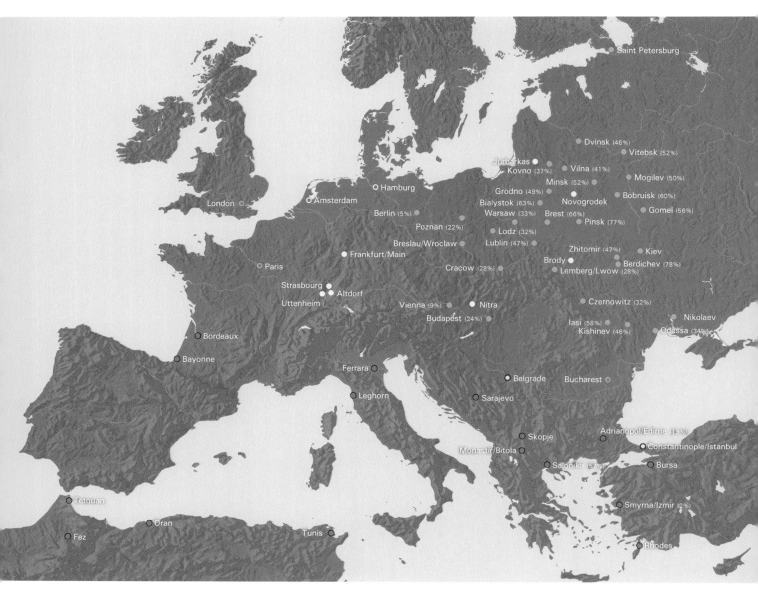

The numbers in parentheses give the percentage of Jews in the total population.

Two phenomena linked Europe's two great Jewish cultural traditions. Firstly, the Jews of both eastern Europe and of the Mediterranean preserved the language of their origin in the Middle Ages – as Yiddish was the mother tongue for the Ashkenazi Jews in eastern Europe, so Ladino constituted a linguistic niche for the Sephardic communities of the eastern Mediterranean. Secondly, both Ashkenazim and Sephardim maintained Hebrew in a nearly original form as the language of prayer, of religious writings and of Jewish legal teachings. Thus there remained, even if only for a numerically small elite, a possibility for communication across borders.

Maps Ashkenazim - Sephardim

Particularly in the cultures of eastern and southeastern Europe, many languages overlapped in a single area. The marketplace made it advantageous for Jewish merchants to learn the languages of their customers. Furthermore, it also was necessary to know the language of the local administration. So Shmuel David Grossman, in addition to speaking Yiddish, certainly spoke Polish in the streets of Lodz, and Sara Demajo most likely spoke Serbo-Croat with her customers while speaking Ladino at home or with co-religionists. In Altdorf and in the southern German rural communities, on the other hand, Jewish livestock dealers spoke the local Alemannish dialect of their Christian neighbours and used only a few relics of Yiddish, while the rural Christian population had adopted numerous Yiddish expressions into their everyday speech.

Hungarian and German business card of Jewish watchmaker Adolf Abraham Antmann from the city of Nitra, which was home to Slovakians, Hungarians and Germans. Until 1918, Nitra was part of Austrio-Hungary, and afterwards became part of Czechoslovakia.

Ashkenazi and Sephardic Jews shared yet another, fundamental historical experience. Though in many localities, particularly in eastern Europe, they comprised a majority of the population, they did not advance to the status of a majority society with full legal rights. Emancipation, which was first granted to the Sephardic Jews of southern France as a result of the French Revolution and the Declaration of the Rights of Man in 1789, brought about the formal recognition of legal equality for individual Jews. From west to east, in the course of the nineteenth century, many European states followed the model of revolutionary France, after stubborn struggle. At the same time, the Jewish communities thereby lost a substantial chance for collective self-determination.

In the legal sense, the Jews of the Russian Empire were the farthest behind. As elsewhere in eastern Europe, up to 1914, in cities large and small, an extremely rich and manifold Jewish society had developed, in which diverse religious and political strands competed with one another. There were networks of charitable associations, self-help institutions from establishments for caring for the ill and organizations providing credit to volunteer fire departments (together with non-Jews). However, Russian Jews attained full equality only after the 1917 Revolution.

A Jewish fireman, Moshe Kagan, from the Polish city of Nowogrodek (today in Belarus). Moshe Kagan was a saddler and volunteered in the fire brigade in his free time.

Cultural Identity and Migration

What role did the expression of these differing Jewish cultures and traditions play in the everyday lives of the Peerebooms, the Grossmans, the Demajos and the Dreifuss-Blochs? Certainly they were a part of a shared communal identity, as well as the basis for a distancing from Jews from other cultural traditions. The Jews in Lodz in Poland, of course, knew that a German Jew probably regarded himself as member of a superior, i.e. German culture. The Sephardic and Ashkenazi Jews who lived

together in cities like Hamburg, London or Istanbul (Constantinople), preserved their own identities in that they maintained separate synagogues and cemeteries and discouraged marriage between members of the two groups. And finally, the pejorative term "Ostjude" [east Jew] used in German-speaking areas, took on increasing importance against the backdrop of the huge migrations of the late nineteenth and early twentieth centuries. This frequent verbal and social distancing prompted a response from the writer Joseph Roth, who himself came from eastern Europe and grew up speaking German, like most of the Jews from his Galician home town of Brody. In 1927 he wrote: "Almost all Jews were western Jews before they came to Poland and Russia. And all Jews were once "Ostjuden" [for "east Jews"] before some of them became western Jews. And half of all Jews who refer to the east with contempt or disdain had grandfathers who came from Tarnopol. And even if their grandfathers did not come from Tarnopol, it is only by chance that their ancestors did not have to flee to Tarnopol."

Interior of the Portuguese
Synagogue in Amsterdam.

All the family histories presented here can be described as part of this complex structure of voluntary change of residence and peaceful settlement on one hand and expulsion and flight on the other – it is merely a question of how far back we go into the past to discover the traces of migration and flight. This is how rural German Jewry, of which the Dreifuss-Bloch family were members, came into existence, as a result of the expulsions from the cities in the High Middle Ages. Through the generations it developed its own imprint in the villages and towns of Baden, Bavaria and Hesse. The beginnings of Sephardic Jewry in parts of the Ottoman Empire can also be traced back to this time. Here, too,

Amsterdam, around 1899: The storefront of the New Israelite Weekly. Front left at the door: the young apprentice Josef Peereboom.

the origins of most communities lay in the expulsion from Spain, while the example of Belgrade – with its several hundred years of unbroken Jewish presence – illustrates the comparably pragmatic attitude of both the state administration and the Christian-Orthodox population in the new home. The case of the Sephardim of Amsterdam was different. The conditions of their flight led to a particular dynamic in the development of this new community: many of them had had themselves baptised in the hope of averting expulsion from the Iberian Peninsula, and lived for quite some time as Christians (the so-called Marranos). Even if they returned to their old faith in Holland, they were familiar with Christianity. In their new environment marked by religious tolerance – the Calvinist Amsterdam of the sixteenth and seventeenth centuries – this led to an intense level of interchange between Jews and non-Jews, such as was seldom found in Europe. The closeness marked by mutual respect is certainly one of the reasons why the Jews in Amsterdam became, both linguistically and socially, an integral part of their new home. Nevertheless, they preserved their cultural independence, as is shown by the existence of a Jewish press, in which Josef Peereboom worked.

In Lodz, by contrast, within three generations an industrial metropolis of the first rank had emerged, and also one of the largest Jewish communities on the European continent. Countless Jews who had left the countryside to find better means of living in the metropolitan area had contributed towards this extraordinary growth. This migration was accompanied by phenomena exhibited in all European industrial centres: precarious living conditions for workers and craftsmen, widespread poverty and social conflict, also between Christians and Jews. The tension-filled decades of extreme growth accelerated social change among all

The New Synagogue and the Great Synagogue in Amsterdam, where Ashkenazi Jews attended services.

residents of Lodz: Poles, Jews and Germans. The development can be seen in the relationship between the Grossman father and son: here, the bearded tradesman, who in all photographs is wearing traditional garments, and there, the young urban-dweller who would not have been out of place in Berlin or Paris. In addition, with the introduction of general

Young members of the Zionist Betar movement in the small Lithuanian city of Jurbarkas, at a meeting with their group leader Moshe Krelitz (centre). Zionism had been the dominant political force in Jurbarkas since the 1920s: 62 percent of Jewish voters in the region supported Zionist parties in the Lithuanian parliamentary elections. As a result of rising anti-Semitism in Lithuania after 1930, the movement became even stronger.

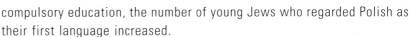

compulsory education, the number of young Jews who regarded Polish as their first language increased.

Boryslav (Poland, today Ukraine), 1941: Members of the youth group of the Zionist movement Hashomer-Hatzair ("Guardians of Zion"). In the background is a drilling derrick. Boryslav was a centre of Polish oil production.

The political, economic and cultural progress deeply affected the various European Jewish communities. Unlike in the Middle Ages or in the age of enlightenment, the great majority of them could not and usually no longer wished to isolate themselves from these developments, even if the most integrated communities continued to maintain separate religious and social institutions. Generally, religious affiliations seemed to diminish in importance. Then, the far-reaching consequences of the First World War shook traditional values and customary routes all over Europe. It led to the creation or reconstruction of states, to the Russian Revolution, to the spread of parliamentary democracy. In 1917, with the Balfour-Declaration, the United Kingdom recognized the right, in principle, of Jews to their own state in the British Mandate of Palestine and thus gave great impetus to political Zionism. Zionist groups of various orientations gained support, not least among Jewish youth in Poland, Lithuania and other eastern European countries. It seemed that a new epoch had begun. Few supposed that the legal equality of Jews would be thrown into question and that the prejudices that continued to exist would find expression in discriminatory legislation.

Hatred of Jews and Antisemitism

What importance did these prejudices possess in the years after the First World War? The Christian-based religious hatred of Jews that had dominated for centuries lost some influence, even if this view of the world continued to exist in legends and stereotypes, particularly in rural areas. The medieval idea of the religiously motivated killing of a Christian by Jews still prompted a trial in Kiev in 1911. Only after court proceedings had dragged on for two years was the accused, Mendel Beilis, released. Within the European tradition of hostility to Jews, Christian motifs and ideas had receded from the close of the nineteenth century. Their place was taken by new ideologies. Already, in the middle of the century, the French philosopher Arthur Gobineau (1816-1882) had developed his pseudo-scientific concept of the differences between what he called human "races". In short, it formed an essential prerequisite for racist ideologies, which derived their claim to rule the colonized peoples of Africa and Asia from the supposed superiority of a "white" race. In Europe, this gave the hatred of Jews a new, ideological dress. The contrast thus constructed between the "Aryan" and "Semitic" peoples became a basis for the rise of antisemitism as a political ideology. The centre of this development was the German Empire in the 1870s and 1880s, yet the ideology quickly gained a foothold and produced its own local variations in other European countries. In France, this development helped the punishment and banning of the Jewish military officer, Alfred Dreyfus, find public acceptance (subsequently withdrawn); in Russia it accompanied the hate-driven pogroms in the south of the Empire in 1881-1882. It proved particularly dangerous in places where many cultures co-existed and where Jews were blamed for social or political conflicts and antagonisms – i.e. precisely in eastern Europe. A direct line led from the defamation of Polish Jews by the Prussian historian Heinrich von Treitschke, who, in 1879, coined the phrase "The Jews are our misfortune", to the propaganda of National Socialist Propaganda Minister Joseph Goebbels, who had a banner bearing these words displayed in the Berlin "Sport Palace" before inciting the Germans in February 1943 to "total war".

Did the Grossmans, the Demajos, the Peerebooms or the Dreifuss-Blochs think much about these enmities, their causes and consequences, before the impending disaster was heralded with the rise of National Socialism and the ensuing discrimination set in train against German Jews? Without doubt, the memory of past persecutions remained alive among all Jews of Europe, and anti-Jewish positions played a more or less prominent role in the politics and society of their home countries during the period between the world wars.

Judenfeindliche Hetzer

verwenden aus dunkler Quelle stammende Mittel, um durch Verbreitung von plumpen Schmähschriften die Bevölkerung zu täuschen und aufzuhetzen.

Eine Feigheit

ist es, wenn man **bei Nacht und Nebel** unbefugter Weise Häuser, Türen und Fenster, ja sogar das Gotteshaus, mit Schmähschriften verschandelt und nicht den kleinen Mut aufbringt, diese Hetzschriften **mit der Angabe des Herausgebers** zu versehen. Für eine **gute** Sache kann man mit **offenem Visier** kämpfen. Warum also so „namenlos", so feige?

Eine Gemeinheit

ist es, lügnerischer Weise durch die Anrede „**Genossen**" den Eindruck zu erwecken, als käme ein solcher Wisch aus den Kreisen der „Genossen", während die ganze Hetze von rechts ausgeht und die „Genossen" ködern will. Man **lügt,** weil man sich schwach fühlt, und Stärke, die aus den links stehenden Massen kommt, vortäuschen will!

Ein Verbrechen

begeht, „wer in einer den öffentlichen Frieden gefährdenden Weise verschiedene Klassen der Bevölkerung zu Gewalttätigkeiten gegen einander öffentlich anreizt" (§. 130 St.G.B.), ein Verbrechen, das heute zehnmal schwer wiegt, wo wir im Innern friedlich aufbauen müssen, um nach Außen weiter Ansehen und Stärke zu erlangen.

Feige, gemein und verbrecherisch

handeln die „namenlosen" Hetzer. Sie sind schlimme Schädlinge; sie stellen ihre **eigenen Interessen** über das Wohl der Gesamtheit!

Mitbürger!

Merkt ihr nicht, daß die antisemitische Hetze euch **mißbrauchen** will?
Merkt ihr nicht, daß es gewisse „enge Kreise", die sonst stolz auf euch herabsahen, sind, die sich nun auf einmal euch anbiedern wollen, um mit eurer Hilfe — sie selbst sind winzig klein und schwach, haben aber große Mittel! — auf die Juden einzuschlagen?
Warum diese Wandlung?
Sie haben schwere politische Schuld auf sich geladen, sie fürchten die Strafe dafür! Da rufen diese schlauen Diebe auf der Flucht: „Haltet den Dieb". Sie suchen einen

Sündenbock,

auf den sie den allgemeinen Grimm von sich abwenden können: wer eignet sich besser als Sündenbock, wie der Jude? Die russische Zarenregierung hat dieses Mittel so oft angewandt. Warum sollten ihre Geistesverwandten nicht von ihr lernen?
Und kann man durch Verbreitung hetzerischer Lügen unaufgeklärte Volkskreise mit sich reißen: wird man da nicht politisch für sich **im Trüben einen guten Fischfang machen können?** So denken die „engen Kreise"; um ihren Fischfang zu fördern, ist ihnen das verächtlichste Mittel gerade gut genug!
Welches sind denn ihre **Vorwürfe gegen die Juden?**

„Sie haben sich im Kriege gedrückt."

Auch die Tausende von Juden, die in glühender Begeisterung als Freiwillige zur Fahne geeilt sind, die Tausende, die für ihr deutsches Vaterland den Heldentod gestorben, die durch den Krieg zum Krüppel geworden sind, die Tausende, die für ihre Tapferkeit ausgezeichnet, die, obwohl man es ihnen wahrlich nicht leicht machte, Offiziere wurden, die treulich bis zum Schlusse für ihr Vaterland kämpften? An die Laterne mit ihnen, antwortet die Schmähschrift.

„Sie haben unsere Niederlage verschuldet."

Die Juden, nicht die Uebermacht der Feinde, der Mangel an Mannschafts- und Materialersatz, die Aushungerung, die Absperrung von allen Rohstoffen, die falsche Politik eben der „engen" Kreise, die heute ihr „Kreuziget" rufen!!
Wissen die Hetzer nicht, daß Ludendorff Waffenstillstand binnen 24 Stunden verlangte, sonst drohe der militärische Zusammenbruch? Sie wissen das alles, aber es paßt ihnen nicht in den Kram, fördert ihre Zwecke nicht; darum: Der Jude wird verbrannt!

„Sie haben sich im Kriege bereichert."

Und Landwirtschaft und Schwerindustrie, beide fast „judenrein", sind wohl verarmt? Nein: am allermeisten haben sie durch die Kriegskonjunktur verdient.
Haben etwa die christlichen Kaufleute bankerott gemacht?

An appeal from the Baden-Baden branch of the "Central Association of German Citizens of the Jewish Faith", against antisemitic propaganda, about 1920. The Central Association was founded in 1893 in the German Empire, at the peak of antisemitic agitation, in order to fight against anti-Jewish activities. Almost simultaneously, a parallel organization was formed in Baden, the "Union of Baden Israelites", which later joined the Central Association. Many of those Jews who lived in the countryside belonged to this group. In their flyer, the local branch of the Central Association in the spa town Baden-Baden took up the issue of common antisemitic stereotypes and refuted them. This argumentation focused on a characteristic trait of antisemitism: the combination of diverse, sometimes contradictory accusations against Jews. At issue here was the participation of Jews in World War I. Although the number of Jewish soldiers in German troop associations – Leopold Dreifuss was one of them – represented the percentage of Jews in the total population, antisemites continually tried to suggest the opposite.

(334/1343. 16.9.1919)

Die **Wahrheit** ist: Der Landwirt, der Industrielle, der Kaufmann, sie **alle** haben infolge der Kriegsverhältnisse reichlich verdient, Christen genau so wie Juden; nur an den ganz grossen Gewinnen hatten die Juden keinen Anteil, die blieben der ganz „judenreinen" Schwerindustrie vorbehalten.

Und schließlich:

„Sie sind eben Juden und keine Deutschen."

Will man denen den Namen „Deutscher" versagen, die nicht den Nachweis reiner Abstammung von den Schwaben, Franken oder anderer germanischer Völkerschaften erbringen können, wahrlich: Die „Deutschen" hätten in der Republik Birkenfeld Platz!

Sind nicht zahllose Italiener und Franzosen, Polen und Masuren und deren Mischlinge längst gute Deutsche geworden? Ist nicht unser grenzenloser Schmerz der, daß uns der Friedensschluß so viele **dieser** Deutschen, vor allem im Osten, raubt? Waren die Posadowsky und Podbielski, die Verdy du Vernois (deutscher Kriegsminister) und François schlechtere Deutsche als die anderen?

Wohnten nicht die Juden schon bald tausend Jahre in Deutschland, das sie, soweit man es ihnen gestattete, als ihr Vaterland liebten, als die französischen Emigranten nach Deutschland kamen, und wer wollte diesen guten Bürgern, trotz ihrer französischen Namen, ihr Deutschtum bestreiten!

Deshalb: hinweg mit all diesen **erbärmlichen Spiegelfechtereien! Ehre** dem, der im Kriege treu seinen Mann gestanden, der sich nicht in unerlaubter Weise bereichert hat, der sein politisches Wirken heute nicht zu bereuen hat **Schmach und Schande** aber über alle politischen Schädlinge, Drückeberger, Wucherer und Schieber,

mögen sie Christen, Juden oder Heiden sein!

Nicht Glaube und Abstammung scheidet zwischen gut und böse, nützlich und schädlich, sondern das moralische, politische und wirtschaftliche Verhalten

jedes Einzelnen.

Schon vor dem Kriege war es üble Gewohnheit, zu schreien:

„Die Juden haben's getan,"

wenn irgend **ein** Jude sich verging. Ist's im Kriege uns Deutschen nicht ebenso gegangen?

Beging irgend **ein** Deutscher oder **ein** deutscher Soldat ein Verbrechen, gleich schrie das ganze Ausland: **die** Deutschen sind Verbrecher, Barbaren! Haben wir uns nicht aufs schärfste gegen solchen Wahnsinn gewehrt? Und sollten wir uns nicht schämen, die **gleiche verruchte Methode** gegen die eigenen jüdischen Mitbürger anzuwenden? Nur **gewissenlose Schädlinge** an der Volksgesamtheit können so handeln.

Mitbürger!

Auch mit kleinen und kleinlichen Mitteln wollen die Hetzer wirken. Laßt euch nicht durch den Hinweis auf die verhältnismäßig große Zahl **jüdischer Kurgäste in Baden-Baden** aufreizen!

„Da sieht man's", rufen die Hetzer. „**Die** Juden haben das Geld verdient und verprassen nun im Bade". Warum sieht man hier so viele Juden? Schon im Frieden, heute in gesteigertem Maße, haben die Juden zahlreiche Badeorte an der See, im Harz, auch anderorts wegen der dort hervortretenden judenfeindlichen Strömungen gemieden; man ging deshalb nach der Schweiz, Tirol, dem Auslande. Das ist jetzt verschlossen. Im Musterlande Baden glaubten sie vor Anpöbelungen sicher zu sein. **Deshalb** strömten die Gäste jüdischen Glaubens in Baden und dessen Perle Baden-Baden zusammen!!

Fragt die Wirte, die Kaufleute, die Behörden, ob sie auf die jüdischen Gäste verzichten wollen?! Laßt die Flugblattmänner weiter hetzen und ihr werdet sehen, wie die Juden künftig auch

Baden-Baden meiden

werden, wie sie Borkum und andere antisemitische Badeorte meiden!

Die Hetzer selbst werden den Schaden nicht haben. Wer sind sie denn? **Meist Leute, die von auswärts kommen, die ihr Gastrecht in Baden mißbrauchen und denen das demokratische** Süddeutschland überhaupt ein Dorn im Auge ist.

Welches sind sonach die Wirkungen der Hetze?

Herabminderung des deutschen Ansehens im Auslande.
Schwächung unserer inneren Kraft und Geschlossenheit.
Schädigung der Interessen der Gesamtbevölkerung, bis herab zu den Interessen der Gemeinden und der Einzelnen.

Bekämpft deshalb diese aus dem Verborgenen heraus hetzenden Schädlinge. Die Augen sind euch geöffnet!

Ihr dient damit nicht nur

dem Nutzen des Vaterlandes,
sondern auch der
Gerechtigkeit.

Der Vorstand des Centralvereins deutscher Staatsbürger jüdischen Glaubens
Ortsgruppe Baden-Baden.

Ernst Kölblin, Hofbuchdruckerei, Baden-Baden.

GLA O 277

So the Peerebooms, living in the tolerant climate of the Netherlands, with its long and secure democratic tradition, were rarely confronted with direct anti-Jewish hostility; nor were there any remarkable antisemitic events in Belgrade before and after the First World War. In 1889, Serbia, under pressure from western European states, had recognized the legal equality of its Jewish citizens, and from that point on this was no longer called into question.

However, in Poland, which re-emerged as a state after the First World War, the traditional hostility of the Church towards the Jews remained active, and political antisemitism was part of the ideological equipment of the conservative parties. With its re-establishment, the Polish state promised the minorities in the country – including the Germans and the Jews – legal protection. This was the precondition for the international recognition of the country. Precisely because of this, in public debate, right-wing political groups regarded the signing of the treaties concerning minorities as a restriction of national sovereignty. Antisemites placed the blame for this especially on the Jews.

In 1935, the Polish State President Josef Pilsudski died. He had supported a vision of the Polish state, which went beyond these cultural boundaries and he had enjoyed great esteem. After 1935, the nationalist right took an increasingly antisemitic turn. There were isolated instances of pogrom-like violence. The local parliaments established after the First World War also served as a stage for inter-cultural conflicts. In Lodz, coexistence faced particular challenges, as the city was home to some 350,000 Catholic Poles, 200,000 Jews and 50,000 Germans. For each group there were numerous political parties. The Jewish minority, too, was politically diverse. For the generation of Mendel Grossmann, that is for those born about 1910, the division into Orthodox (the Agudath Israel Party), Jewish Socialists (General Jewish Workers League called "Bund") and Zionists went without saying. Despite these numerous divisions, there was also cooperation, not least between the representatives of the different population groups. If representatives of the Polish National Democrats, whose ideological foundations included antisemitic positions, introduced motions directed against the interests of the Lodz Jews (usually this concerned the use of funds for schools or social institutions), as a rule these were rejected not only by the Jewish deputies, but also by the Polish and German Social Democrats.

Similarly, in the Baden homeland of Leopold Dreifuss, there were recurring waves of anti-Jewish agitation. Leopold was still a child when political antisemitism took shape in Berlin about 1880. By 1881, antisemitic pamphlets surfaced in south Baden. As a young man, Leopold experienced the rise of these forces into a political movement. Although in the elections to the Reichstag it did not gain a foothold in Catholic Altdorf, it had more success in some Protestant villages nearby. But the rapid rise was followed by decline. The Grand Duke of Baden and his bureaucracy, and the Jews themselves, joined to ward off the Antisemites. Jewish villagers did not shrink from disrupting or breaking up meetings. It was not until about 30 years later that politically driven hatred of Jews returned in the form of racist ("völkisch") parties and, ultimately, the NSDAP. In all the elections after 1929 the National Socialists achieved growing support. In Altdorf itself the Catholic Centre Party still retained a majority, but in some neighbouring villages the NSDAP won more than 77 percent of the votes cast in the Reichstag elections of November 1932. In Baden and elsewhere in Germany attacks against Jews and Jewish institutions increased. On 30 January 1933, Reich President Paul von Hindenburg named Adolf Hitler Reich Chancellor.

Depriving the Jews in Germany of their Rights

The path towards depriving the Jews of their rights and excluding them from German society began immediately after Hitler's appointment and continued through numerous individual measures, laws and incidents. Among these were the economic boycott and exclusion from professions (April 1933), the Nuremberg Laws of 15 September, 1935, which presented a legal basis for racially justified exclusion; and the expulsion of some 17,000 Polish Jews from Germany (28 October, 1938) – to name but a few.

When in reaction to the expulsion of Polish Jews from Germany, Herschel Grynszpan, a Jewish youth of Polish background, shot the German embassy official vom Rath in Paris, the National Socialist government used the occasion to unleash an unprecedented wave of violence against German Jews on the night of 9-10 November, 1938. Tens of thousands of Jewish men were arrested and taken to concentration camps; the majority of synagogues in Germany and Austria, which by then had been annexed to the German Reich, went up in flames; countless shops were destroyed.

These developments were viewed with great attention and anxiety by Jews in neighbouring countries. In Poland, the increasingly aggressive exclusion of Jews and denial of their rights led to a call for a boycott, urged primarily by Jewish parties and parliamentary deputies. As early as March 1933, the Lodz City Council took up a motion from the Socialist Bund, dealing with the persecution of Jews in Germany. But the boycott movement was unable to influence subsequent developments, in part because of the lack of official Polish support. Up to the summer of 1939, the right-wing Polish government cherished the hope of finding political accommodation with National Socialist Germany. Yet, at the same time, preparations already were under way for the German-Soviet secret agreement and with it, the decisive steps towards the German attack on Poland. With the German invasion of Poland on 1 September, 1939, the Second World War began.

The Lodz Ghetto

Only a few days after the start of the war, the Wehrmacht reached Lodz. The city and the newly created 'Warthegau' (administrative district) were incorporated into the 'Greater German Reich' and thus separated from the largest part of German occupied Poland, the so-called General Government. The persecution of Jewish and Catholic Polish inhabitants began immediately. The speed of events overwhelmed the Jews of Lodz, who were forced to wear armbands and to place their businesses in the hands of trustees. In addition, they were exposed to the attacks of German soldiers and members of the German minority. In February 1940, the German administration ordered that all the Jews move into one section of Lodz. Together with more than 100,000 others, the Grossmans had to leave their flat and move into the poorest district, Baluty, which would later become the Ghetto. There was now barely a chance for escape. Like all the other Jews of Lodz, the Grossmans were registered officially according to their religion. Flight from the Warthegau into the General Government was hardly pos-

A weakened Shmuel David Grossman at prayer in the Ghetto flat. He wore a prayer shawl and phylacteries.

sible. In May, a fence was erected around the Ghetto, which was guarded constantly. The seven members of the Grossman family lived in one small flat. Their daily life was characterised by forced labour in the Ghetto factories, which increasingly exhausted them, especially because the provision of food was completely insufficient. Work assignments were coordinated by the 'Judenrat', or Jewish Council, appointed by the Germans. Its chairman, Chaim Rumkowski, held the view that high productivity in the Ghetto factories would protect Ghetto residents from further persecution. With the slogan "Our only way is through work", he legitimized

Faiga Frajtag and her son Yankush in the Ghetto flat. Malnutrition meant that Ghetto inhabitants always felt cold. In winter, when not at their assigned forced labour, they usually remained in bed because there was not enough fuel for heating.

his strategy of accepting the increasingly extreme measures of the occupier. Here, Rumkowski also asserted himself against the broad resistance of conspiratorial Jewish opposition groups and unions (who organized strikes), relying on the Jewish police set up by the occupying power. At the same time, Rumkowski pushed the idea, both to the German administration and to the Ghetto population, that the 'Work Camp Ghetto Lodz" could not be dispensed with, and he placed great emphasis on professionally documenting the activity of the Jewish Council. Some friends of Mendel Grossman worked in a 'statistical department', creating portfolios with photographs of Ghetto facilities and economic figures. They succeeded in getting Mendel employed as a photographer and retoucher. Mendel still owned a camera. He went beyond the narrow limits of his assigned duties and photographed the starving and the dead, as well as illegal gatherings. His work was part of the self-assertion of the Ghetto inhabitants in the face of humiliation by the occupiers.

Shmuel David and Chaya Ruda Grossman partaking of a meagre meal in their ghetto flat.

Altdorf - Berlin

Although they had been stripped of many basic rights, German Jews still had more room for manoeuvre at the start of the war than did the Jews in occupied Poland. German Jews were still not forced to wear an identifying badge in public. To a limited degree it still was possible for them to move within Germany or to emigrate. Before the war, Leopold and Léonie Dreifuss had tried to move to France, where their son Fritz already lived. They came to this decision primarily because of the experiences connected with the pogrom of November 1938, particularly Leopold's several weeks of internment at the Dachau concentration camp. The family's plans to emigrate failed. Only the mother, Léonie, was permitted to enter France, since she originated from Alsace; Leopold and Alice were turned back. They did not want to stay in Altdorf, and they decided to move to Berlin, where a relative lived. They hoped to avoid attacks in the anonymity of the large city and, besides, there was still an active Jewish community in Berlin in 1939 with about 80,000 members. Leopold and Alice moved into the centre of the city, a few houses away from the New Synagogue. By then Leopold was 65 and had diabetes. Alice took care of him. They received a monthly sum from a relative. But when this relative managed to immigrate to Uruguay in 1940, the tax office confiscated her property and stopped the payments. Only after a legal representative intervened was the support continued, but only for Leopold. Alice, who by then was a forced labourer in the Siemens-Schuckert factory, was considered gainfully employed and not eligible for support. Her daily routine, which frequently began at 4 o'clock in the morning, was characterized by shift work.

Leopold Dreifuss and his daughter, Alice, probably in Berlin (1939-1942).

Léonie Dreifuss with her son Fritz in Strasbourg, around 1940.

Léonie and Fritz Dreifuss had to leave Strasbourg after the Germans entered, and at this point they lived for a time with other relatives in the unoccupied part of France. The family suffered from being torn apart. Alice wrote: "If only we had the chance to return soon to the family circle. Couldn't you do something, or must we do something about it? Write to us about it. The longing for you could not be greater." In another passage she expressed: "You surely can understand the homesickness for the good old days in Altdf. [Altdorf] and wish to dear God to hope that He allows us again to experience a similar existence in health and peace. Amen."

Police Raid in Amsterdam

For nine months, from September 1939 until June 1940, it appeared as if the neutral Netherlands would remain undisturbed by the consequences of the war. But then the Wehrmacht arrived here, too. The first anti-Jewish regulations came into force. For the Peerebooms, little changed at first; the 'New Israelite Weekly' was able to continue as the 'Jewish Weekly', while all other Jewish newspapers were banned. Then, in February 1941, events overwhelmed them. Domestic right-wing radicals attacked Jews in Amsterdam and wreaked havoc in the Jewish quarter. The incident was just a link in the chain of similar or even more brutal attacks in areas of German occupation, from Paris to Antwerp to Warsaw, as well as in Lvov, Kovno and Riga. As a rule, the local perpetrators had close connections with the German occupation forces, which had a great interest in escalating the persecution. Apparently "wild" attacks on Jews were to provide an excuse for the introduction of even more radical discriminating regulations, all the way to forcible relocation into the newly created ghettos. In Amsterdam, the perpetrators encountered resistance from both Jews and non-Jews. There was one death. The SS and police closed off the district. They carried out a raid and arbitrarily arrested hundreds of Jewish men. Six Jews were murdered. The general public was shocked and in some larger cities, workers went on strike. Unimpressed by the protests, the Germans deported 389 young men to the German concentration camp of Buchenwald at the end of February. The Peerebooms were affected by this deportation, because among those arrested were Louis Peereboom and his brother-in-law, Nico Gerritse. Both were visiting their parents

Broken shop windows of the "New Israelite Weekly", in February 1941.

Februari 1941
Ingegooide ramen N.I.W.
Jodenbreestr. 63
(Joachimsthal)

when the police raid took place. Most of those arrested were later taken from Buchenwald to the Mauthausen camp near Linz. Nico Gerritse died there in July 1941. Louis Peereboom survived in the camp only for a few months; he died on 13 October, 1941 under circumstances unknown. For the Dutch Jews, the events of February 1941 had far-reaching consequences. In Amsterdam as well a Jewish Council was set up which had to implement the decisions of the occupation authorities. The 'Jewish Weekly' became the bulletin that printed official announcements, which appeared to guarantee the safety of the remaining family members.

Mass Shootings in Serbia

In the summer of 1940, the German sphere of control already extended from Poland to the Atlantic. Yugoslavia was spared from war for the time being and, in comparison to most other Jewish communities, the Jews in Belgrade were doing well. Sara Demajo's grandchildren were beginning to build lives of their own. The eldest, Rafael, finished his study of medicine in 1940; his sister Lili-Luna was about to marry the Jewish lawyer, Moshe Varon. But despite the apparent normality, the Jews of Belgrade had reason for serious concern. The Yugoslav government was pursuing a course of rapprochement with Germany. In October 1940 two anti-Jewish laws were passed, limiting study at university and choice of occupation. Whoever had access to funds, tried to flee to Turkey, where there were large Sephardic Jewish communities, or they tried to find a way to get into the USA. The family of Sara Demajo was not able to do either. Sara's daughter, Rivka, and son-in-law decided, however, to move elsewhere within Yugoslavia. Sara followed them to Skopje, near the Greek and Bulgarian border. In Skopje, Lili-Luna and Moshe Varon married. At their wedding, more than 300 relatives met for the last time.

In April 1941, German troops occupied a large portion of the Balkans. On Hitler's order, the Yugoslav state was "smashed to pieces". Skopje fell under Bulgarian occupation, Belgrade under German occupation. Yugoslavia, once one of the few areas in Europe in which Jews were not threatened with life and limb, now turned into the extreme opposite. In the autumn of 1941, the German occupiers turned to comprehensive mass murder in the Serbian part of the country. The starting point of this escalation was the persecution of Serbian partisans, who had fought against the Germans since the country had been occupied. The Wehrmacht leadership in Belgrade reacted to the resistance with the arrest of hostages, primarily Jews, and had them murdered after renewed attacks. On 10 October, 1941 the German Army raised the arrest quota. At the same time they had all Jewish men, and a certain number of other civilians, arrested where they had garrisons. The shootings were now directed systematically against Jewish men and men from the Roma minority. By the end of November, about 5,000 Jewish men had been murdered in Serbia. Among them were Sara Demajo's son, Chaim, and nearly all the other men of the Demajo and Arueti families. Their wives and daughters were taken with the other Jewish women to a camp on the fairgrounds (Sajmiste) of Belgrade. Their subsequent fate was closely linked with developments in other areas occupied by the German Reich.

Autumn 1941: Genocide Begins

The second half of 1941 marks the transition to the genocide of European Jewry. The centre of the crime was, from July 1941, in the occupied Soviet Union. There, the 'SS Einsatzgruppen', or Mobile Killing Squads, turned to the mass shooting of Jewish men shortly after the invasion. As of late summer, they also murdered women and children. At the same time, the German leaders continued their policy of persecution in other occupied areas and within the Reich. As of September 1941, the Jews in the German Reich had to wear the yellow star as identification. On Hitler's orders, the systematic deportation of German, Austrian and Czech Jews to the occupied Soviet and Polish areas began in October 1941. Most transports led to existing ghettos, which were unprepared for the increase in population. Local representatives of the German occupying forces reacted in various ways, sometimes with more crimes. In Riga, thousands of local Jews were shot before trains arrived from Germany. In Lodz, the new arrivals – 20,000 people – at first were housed within the Ghetto. But the conditions there were already catastrophic and now became even worse. The German administrative offices took no measures to relieve the situation. On the contrary, since the summer of 1941 they had been preoccupied with planning the mass murder of the Ghetto inhabitants. North of Lodz, in Chelmno, they set up a camp with approval from Berlin, to which a so-called gas van would be driven. Rebuilt lorries of this type already had been used by the SS to murder handicapped people. The victims were forced into the airtight van, into which the exhaust fumes were directed. December 1941 saw the first mass murders of Jews using motor exhaust fumes. Soon thereafter, the SS used the same method in numerous locations in the Soviet Union.

In March 1942, the Berlin Reich Security Main Office sent one such van to Belgrade. Every day, except Sundays, the van took off from the camp. When the driver reached the Save Bridge, at the entrance to the city of Belgrade, he would flip a switch and thus divert the exhaust fumes into the van. He would then drive a further 15 kilometres, up to the southern border of the city of Belgrade, where the bodies of the suffocated victims were unloaded and buried. By May 1942, nearly all inhabitants of Sajmiste had been killed, including all those members of the Demajo family who had lived in Belgrade.

Deportations Across Europe

In the spring of 1942, while the mass crimes continued in the occupied Soviet Union and in Serbia, the German leadership extended its murder programme to the more than 3.3 million Polish Jews. In addition to Chelmno, there were now two more centres of death – Auschwitz and Belzec – located on Polish territory. Three more were under construction: Treblinka and Sobibor in the spring of 1942, Majdanek in the summer of 1942. The newly built camps included fixed gas chambers, in which people were murdered with motor exhaust fumes or poison gas.

Plans had long been underway to murder Jews from other regions occupied by or dependent on Germany. Not everywhere was the criminal plan carried out so smoothly as in Poland, whose political structures had been destroyed and whose elites for the most part had been killed. Particularly in western Europe the German leadership was compelled to negotiate with collaborating governments in order to achieve their goal.

This was all carried out under the strictest secrecy and thus without the knowledge of the victims. But one thing could not be overlooked, even by the non-Jewish population: the extreme radicalization of the persecution in late spring and early summer of 1942. In the beginning of May 1942, all the Jews of the Netherlands – including the Peerebooms – were forced to wear a yellow star. In June, they had to give up their bicycles and they were not permitted to use public transport. Shopping was allowed for only two hours per day and there was a curfew from eight in the evening until six in the morning. Thus robbed of their freedom, the Jewish community of the Netherlands awaited the next measures of the occupier.

On 5 July, 4,000 Jews received a summons to report for a "Work Deployment in Germany". Few followed the order. The German police responded with raids. In a special edition, the 'Jewish Weekly' published the renewed summons to gather at the assembly point. At the same time,

Excerpt from a private 8-millimetre film by Max Peereboom (1942). The picture shows his wife (right) at her sewing.

the German administration published the threat that those arrested in the raids would be sent to a concentration camp if the quota for the work deployment were not met. This time, many people reported. The first transports left the Netherlands for Auschwitz. There, a large proportion of those arriving were classified as not "capable of work" and murdered immediately. In early September 1942, the oldest son, Max Peereboom, his wife and their children, also received their deportation order. To the very end, Max used his 8 mm film camera. The pictures he took are the last evidence of the young family. None of them survived the deportation.

The End of Hope

The transports now regularly leaving all occupied countries put the remaining members of the Grossman, Peereboom, Demajo and Dreifuss-Bloch families in a constant state of fear. Léonie and Fritz Dreifuss were in great danger in southern France after the Wehrmacht arrived there, too, in 1942. Along with the relatives of the Bloch family, they now had to prepare for a life in hiding. Sara Demajo and her relatives were aware that they remained safe in occupied Skopje only as long as the Bulgarian occupiers did not give in to the pressure of their German allies to deliver up their Jewish population.

Amsterdam, about 1942: Simon Peereboom with his wife, Roosje, in front of the Jewish Community House. On Roosje's dress, the yellow star that Jews of the Netherlands were forced to wear is particularly visible. The sign on the entryway reads: "Stars sold out". The Jewish population was forced to pay for this identification themselves.

The situation in Berlin, Amsterdam and Lodz was even more dangerous. In July 1942, Leopold Dreifuss was forced to provide a "declaration of property". This measure preceded each deportation. On 28 July, 1942, he had to board a train for the Theresienstadt ghetto camp in Bohemia, to which the German leadership mainly brought the elderly and veterans of the First World War. Contrary to propaganda that spoke of a "Model Jewish Settlement", the camp was completely overcrowded and its inhabitants chronically hungry. Leopold Dreifuss died there in February 1944 at the age of 78, not knowing the fate of his daughter Alice.

In Berlin, in mid-1942 there were still tens of thousands of Jews, most of them working as slave labourers in the armaments factories. As with those people in the ghettos and forced labour camps in Poland, they drew their will to live from the expectation that the German war economy would not dispense with their work. However, in the first half of 1943, hope was destroyed for many of these people. In early January, Alice Dreifuss received the summons to prepare for transport. On 12 January she and at least 1,000 others – possibly more than 1,200 Jews from Berlin – boarded a transport to Auschwitz. According to the records of the camp, only 127 men from the transport were given the tattooed identification numbers. The rest were murdered in the gas chambers immediately after arrival.

The Demajo and Peereboom families, too, became victims of persecution in the spring of 1943. In March 1943, the German leadership had achieved its goal in the Balkans. They now prepared deportations from Salonika in Greece and from the Bulgarian zone of occupation. The Jews of Skopje were locked up in a tobacco factory. Sara Demajo's grandson, Rafael Pijade, who worked as a doctor, was able to have his parents released. But he could not save his grandmother. Together with thousands of others, Sara Demajo was taken on a journey of several days to the Treblinka extermination camp in occupied Poland and was murdered there immediately.

Josef Peereboom, his wife and their remaining children, Louisa and Simon, received a summons in early June 1943 to prepare for transport. Until then, Josef Peereboom's work for the 'Jewish Weekly' had protected the family; now, however, the protective stamp on their identity cards was cancelled. Simon managed to flee. He was later imprisoned, but survived. The other family members died soon after the deportation, in the gas chambers of the Sobibor extermination camp in occupied Poland.

The Liquidation of the Lodz Ghetto

After the violent liquidation of the ghettos of Warsaw, Vilnius, Bialystok and Bedzin-Sosnowiec in the spring and summer of 1943 and the murder of their inhabitants in the extermination camps, Lodz – with 70,000 inhabitants – was the last large ghetto remaining in occupied Poland. Mendel Grossman and his sisters Rushka and Faiga as well as Faiga's son, Yankush, were still alive. The other family members had fallen victim to the inhumane living conditions. Faiga's husband, Shimon Frajtag, collapsed and died in the flat on the evening of 15 March, 1942 after returning from forced labour. In July 1942, the parents, Shmuel David and Chaya Ruda, died in quick succession, as a result of systematic malnutrition. Mendel continued his photographic work. He saw his

Lodz, about 1942: Mendel Grossman documented a deportation from the Ghetto.

life's mission in documenting the crimes of the German occupiers. Regardless of the price, risking to his own life, he documented the stages of extermination, photographing the deportations of 1942 to Chelmno. Equally important to him was to document the political underground organizations, particularly among Jewish youth. These organizations were based on the broad, diverse spectrum of Jewish political forces that had existed in Poland before the war. They opposed the strategy of the Jewish Council, which sought to ensure the continued existence of the ghetto by handing over its inhabitants.

Lodz, about 1942: Mendel Grossman (kneeling) photographed a deportation. The photographer of this scene was probably one of Mendel Grossman's friends.

In the meantime, a struggle over the continued existence of the Lodz Ghetto had begun between the Berlin SS leadership and those authorities who profited from the Ghetto factories. SS-Reichsführer Himmler was pressing for the murder of all Jews still living within the German sphere of influence, including the forced labourers. Himmler won in the end. In July 1944, the liquidation of the Ghetto began. Because the inhabitants were not prepared to come voluntarily to the assembly point, the SS rounded them up. Again, trains headed for Chelmno and Auschwitz. Faiga and Yankush Frajtag were among those deported. Mendel and his sister Rushka were held back from the deportation and eventually were sent to perform forced labour within the German Reich. Before he left, Mendel managed to hide his collection of about 10,000 photographs in the Ghetto. He was deported to forced labour in a satellite camp of the Sachsenhausen concentration camp in Königs Wusterhausen (near Berlin), and then to Sachsenhausen itself. Shortly before the liberation, Mendel Grossman died on a death march from Sachsenhausen in the direction of Mecklenburg. The exact location of his death is not known.

Life After the Holocaust

In the summer of 1945, Rushka Grossman returned briefly to Lodz, the only member of her family to survive the deportations after the liquidation of the Lodz Ghetto. Friends gave her the hidden negatives of her brother's photographs. Léonie Dreifuss, who had survived with her relatives in southern France, resettled near her old home. She spent the end of her life in Strasbourg, where a renewed Jewish community was established and even grew due to immigration. Rafael Pijade, Sara Demajo's grandson, moved with his parents from Bulgaria back to Serbia, where he worked for several decades as a doctor. Simon Peereboom was taken in January 1945 in an open railway car from Auschwitz to Prague and from there deported to the Buchenwald concentration camp, where he was liberated by American soldiers in April 1945. He returned to live in Amsterdam.

Of those surviving members of the Peereboom, Demajo, Dreifuss and Grossman families, Simon Peereboom was the only one who resettled in his former home city. Léonie Dreifuss returned to the region of the Upper Rhine, but for her it was out of the question to return to Altdorf, from which the last Jewish inhabitants had been deported in October 1940. Rushka Grossman soon left Poland, as did most of the other 330,000 Jews who had escaped the genocide. Christian neighbours had often occupied their flats and houses and confronted the returnees with open hostility that many times turned into outright violence. The attempt to establish new Jewish communities in the former German areas of Silesia was abandoned due to the increasing hostility towards Jews exhibited by the ruling Workers Party.

The survivors had two goals above all: the USA and Palestine, where in 1948 the State of Israel was founded. Even before the state was established, Rushka Grossman moved to the British Mandate. Rafael Pijade decided to move to Israel in 1964, later than the great majority of Jews from Belgrade. The prospect of being for the first time part of the majority society, as in Israel, or of being a citizen of a country like the USA, that promised a new life for all newcomers, held great attraction for many survivors of the Holocaust.

Rushka Grossman, Léonie Dreifuss, Rafael Pijade and Simon Peereboom each made a new beginning, each in their own way. For all four, it was a life marked by survival, by the loss of their loved ones. The diverse Jewish cultures to which they had belonged were destroyed by the mass murder which Germany had launched. With their lovingly preserved family documents, and through their readiness to bear witness, these people do, however, convey to us the memory of their lost families and of the pain they suffered.

Bibliography

Haim Hillel Ben-Sasson (ed.), *A History of the Jewish People* (Cambridge, Mass., 1976).

Heiko Haumann, *History of East European Jews* (Budapest, New York, 2002).

Victor Karady, *Jews of Europe in the Modern Era: A Socio-Historical Outline* (Budapest, New York, 2004).

Elke-Vera Kotowski/Julius H. Schoeps/Hilltrud Wallenborn (eds.), *Handbuch der Geschichte der Juden in Europa*, 2 vols. (Darmstadt, 2001).

The citation was translated from Joseph Roth, *Juden auf Wanderschaft* (Berlin 1927), p. 23; English translation: Joseph Roth, *Wandering Jews* (New York, 2001).

The maps are based on: Nicholas de Lange, *Atlas of the Jewish World* (Oxford, 1984) and Paul Robert Magocsi, *Historical Atlas of Central Europe. From the Early Fifth Century to the Present* (Washington, 2002).

THE IMPORTANCE OF NAMES

Memorials are among the earliest artistic creations of humankind. The oldest and most common form, today as yesterday, is the gravestone. Its purpose is to remind one of a dead person and, therefore, it usually records the name, often with additional information. From time immemorial, there have also been monuments dedicated to the memory of large numbers of dead, particularly those who died together in an unusual event. The latter include the famous Spartan memorial for those who fell in the battle of Thermopylae (480 BC); it bears the classic inscription: "Strangers, go to Sparta, tell them there that you saw us lying here, as the law commanded."

This type of war memorial is part of a tradition, of which there are thousands of examples. It can take the form of a grave marker in a soldier's cemetery or a blank monument recording only names and found at particular sites, most commonly in cemeteries located in the communities where the dead once lived. Central memorials of this type, commemorating war dead, exist in almost all countries. They include the Arc de Triomphe in Paris, the Arlington Cemetery in Washington DC, the war memorial near the Kremlin in Moscow, and so on. One of the more recent ones is the memorial in Washington for the American soldiers who died in the Vietnam War, which, incidentally, names every one of them.

Almost none of the Jews of Europe murdered in World War II have their own grave. They were buried hurriedly or burned, and the pits into which they were shot or thrown were concealed as far as possible. Thus, only blank memorials could be created on which to record the names of the dead. Such monuments are common, increasingly in Germany, at sites from which Jews were deported. They are also located in national capitals, to represent an entire country. For example, an early memorial from 1958 in the Pinkas Synagogue in Prague records 77,297 names. In contrast, memorials at killing sites, in the extermination camps and execution areas, rarely bear names.

An early attempt to collect all the names of victims from throughout Europe was undertaken in Israel after the end of the war and before the founding of the Jewish state. It was the original and most important task assigned to the memorial "Yad Vashem" in Jerusalem, upon its foundation in 1953. It was a difficult job. In most cases the perpetrators had not recorded the names of their victims. Initially, survivors were asked to submit "Pages of Testimony" naming victims they had known, including dates of birth and death, names of their parents, as well as the place and cause of their death. This was not possible in all cases. Nevertheless, this information forms the main element of today's database. Later, other sources were tapped. As a result, about three million names are now known, representing little more than half the total of those murdered. These names are in Yad Vashem – some in books and some in a database – in the so-called "Hall of Names". In keeping with an old Jewish tradition, the names of the dead are read aloud on certain occasions, such as the annual day of remembrance for the Shoah.

The Berlin "Memorial to the Murdered Jews of Europe" takes on a similar, but appropriately modified task in Germany. One of the first prize-winning proposals for the memorial was to inscribe as many names as

The memorial site at Belzec, 2005, "The Niche", or Wall of Names.

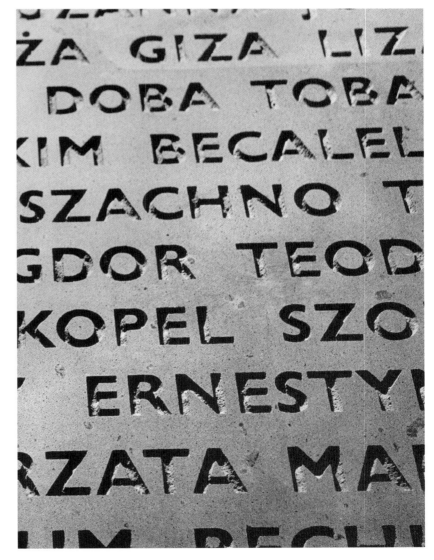

possible on the site itself. That idea being rejected, the database in the "Information Centre" is now to contain a collection of those names that are known, with brief biographical data. This is, in a sense, the heart of the memorial. One can interpret it as a blank gravestone, a cenotaph. But here in Germany too, the names of the victims will be recorded.

This is why it was of particular importance that, in 1999, Yad Vashem agreed to the request of the initiators of the memorial to make its collection of names available for the project. The Foundation for the "Memorial to the Murdered Jews of Europe" was able to use the database exclusively for research in preparing the display of names in Room 3 of the Information Centre. Never before had another institution been granted permission to use it. The belief was that the names of the murdered Jews of Europe should be gathered in two prominent places: in the land of the victims and in the land of the perpetrators. The original database remains where it was created, in Israel. In Berlin there is, so to speak, a window through which the visitor can look at the entire database. In addition to making this database exhibit possible, Yad Vashem took up the challenge of modern technology and made its collection of names available worldwide on the Internet. Since November of 2004, anyone can use the database for research at home. But the combination of multi-media installation and database in the Information Centre of the Berlin memorial remains unique.

Berlin-Steglitz, 2005,
"A memorial at the former Synagogue
House Wolfenstein": The names, dates of birth,
and addresses of Jews deported from
Berlin-Steglitz, on polished, high-grade steel.

The Information Centre is also joining in with the task of helping to find the approximately three million missing names. As in Jerusalem, visitors who know a name that is not yet recorded are encouraged to share it. They will receive a questionnaire to fill out. If the name can be verified, it will be added to the database. The expectation is that those visitors travelling to Berlin will come from other places than those who go to Jerusalem, in particular from eastern Europe, from where most of the missing names come. In this way, the memorial will contribute to completing the collection of names. Even if it cannot be completely achieved, the goal is to record as many names as possible.

Nearly all the names of the murdered Jews of western Europe are known and have been published. In the Netherlands, the "War Graves Foundation" ("Oorlogsgravenstichting") collected the names of fallen Dutch soldiers early on and published them during 1972 in 41 volumes; it also includes the names of some 102,000 Jews who were deported from the Netherlands and murdered. By 1952, a book was published that included the names of 739 murdered Jews from the islands of Rhodes and Kos. In France, in 1978, Serge Klarsfeld published "The Memorial to the Deportation of the Jews of France" ("Le Mémorial de la Déportation des Juifs en France"), which, following many revisions, now contains 76,000 names. Belgium followed in 1982 with "The Memorial to the Deportation of the Jews of Belgium" ("Mémorial de la Déportation des Juifs de Belgique"), which named 25,475 deportees, of whom 1,335 survived. In 1986, Oskar Mendelsohn published the names of 739 murdered Jews of Norway in his book "Jewish History of Norway" ("Jødenes historie i Norge").

That same year, the German "Bundesarchiv" (the national archive) published, actually at the request of Yad Vashem, a two-volume "Memorial Book" ("Gedenkbuch") with the subtitle "Victims of the Persecution of Jews under the National Socialist Dictatorship in Germany 1933-1945" ("Opfer der Verfolgung der Juden unter der nationalsozialistischen Gewaltherrschaft in Deutschland 1933-1945"), which contained 128,091 names. However, it only applied to West Germany and Berlin; a revision to include former East Germany and the former eastern areas of Germany is under preparation. The complete memorial book will contain more than 160,000 names.

The greatest gaps exist in eastern Europe, which had by far the largest number of victims. Of about six million murdered Jews, up to 165,000 came from Germany, which made up between two and three percent of the total. Another 280,000 – about five per cent – came from the other western European countries (the Netherlands, France, Austria, Belgium, Italy, Luxembourg, Norway and Denmark). About one million, or 16 to 17 percent, came from Hungary, Romania, Czechoslovakia, Yugoslavia, Greece and Albania. For Poland, however, the total number of murdered

Berlin-Steglitz, 2005: "A memorial at the former Synagogue House Wolfenstein".

Jews is estimated at three million, perhaps somewhat more; and for the former Soviet Union (including Estonia, Latvia and Lithuania) about 1.3 million, so that the numbers for these countries equal more than 70 percent of the total. Even if the information is somewhat inexact in its detail, and thus in percentages, there is no doubt that the murder of European Jewry was predominantly a murder of eastern European Jews. This fact has not sufficiently penetrated public awareness, particularly among Germans. It is one of the particular tasks of the memorial to illustrate this dimension in particular.

Initially, lists of names were also collected in the Soviet Union, but the victims were usually described not as Jews, but as Soviet citizens. Most memorials in the Soviet Union and its satellite states did not give names. Closer research was generally not permitted or was prevented. Now there is no longer an official obstacle. In some countries, such as Lithuania, the systematic collection of names is already under way, and other countries may follow. So many decades after the war, this task will be more difficult to carry out than in western Europe. But it must be attempted, and particularly with support from the Berlin memorial.

Here, names will not only be saved in a database, but a steadily augmented, representative sample of names will be presented, both visibly and audibly, reflecting in numbers the percentages of victims from each country – so eastern Europe stands out. Individual names will be projected continuously onto the four walls of the "Room of Names". At the same time, visitors will hear short biographical sketches of the people named here, sketches that show that the victims were individuals with their own fates and life stories. The Foundation for the "Memorial to the Murdered Jews of Europe", with the support of the "Society for the Promotion of the Memorial", is putting tremendous efforts into this project. Information in the pages of testimony from Yad Vashem, some of which are more than 50 years old, will be compared with the results of new historical research and supplemented. In the last few years in particular, some studies and reference works have been published that describe the murderous operations in eastern Europe in detail. This material makes it easier to describe individual fates more accurately. That is why in a few cases, the individual life stories that visitors will hear in the "Room of Names" may deviate from the information in the Yad Vashem database.

The reading of each biography lasts about 20-30 seconds in German and English, separated by a pause of five seconds. Since the visitor usually only lingers a few minutes, and would thus only hear and see a few biographies, they will be told that it would take about six years and eight months to read all the names in this way. Although the readings and projections will be repeated at certain intervals, there will be an effort to include as many names as possible. When federal funds run out in the second half of 2005, the continued collection of names will be supported through a fundraising drive by the "Society for the Promotion of the Memorial". Even so, the addition of names will require great effort, as well as support, from visitors.

The memorial will certainly be a reminder of the unprecedented process of the murder of European Jewry. Never before had a state decided to wipe out as thoroughly as possible, a group of people that the state identified as Jews, including the elderly, women, children and infants. It was a decision carried out using the apparatus of the state and its instruments of power in such a way that members of this group were not only killed wherever they could be found, but also, in many cases, they were brought to institutions built for the purpose of murder, mostly over great distances. Obviously, human history is marred by endless cruelty, but never before had a persecution of this nature occurred. Traditional antisemites had contented themselves with persecuting the Jews in their own country, expelling them and also killing them. Among the unique aspects of the German mass murder was that it was not only directed at German Jews, but against all Jews within the German sphere of power and influence, so that by far most victims were foreigners.

This memorial, in addition to serving as a general reminder, will also name the dead. Numbers and statistics are insufficient. There is an old saying: "Only one whose name is forgotten is truly dead." To ensure that the murdered Jews are not left nameless: that is the memorial's other significant task.

Paris, 2004, The Wall of Names
at the Mémorial de la Shoah /CDJC.

"UNTO EVERY PERSON THERE IS A NAME"

THE DOCUMENTATION OF HOLOCAUST VICTIMS' NAMES BY YAD VASHEM

The destruction of the ghetto of the old town of Kowel began on 19 August, 1942. The Jews were assembled in the Great Synagogue. They were kept there for several days, without food or water, before being taken to the cemetery where they were shot. The prisoners, knowing their end was near, left inscriptions on the walls of the synagogue – a kind of last testament (1). "Farewell my beautiful world, in the last hours of my life. Your friend, Hannah Avrech", reads one of these inscriptions.

Hannah Avrech wanted to be remembered, and to convey her love of life to future generations. Anyone who wants to learn more about Hannah Avrech can find a "Page of Testimony" in the Hall of Names at Yad Vashem. Pages of Testimony are forms that have been collected at Yad Vashem since its inception, containing biographical information on those who perished in the Holocaust and filled out by friends and relatives.

One of the synagogues in Kowel.

The Page of Testimony commemorating Hannah tells us that she was born in the town of Wierzbnik, to Menachem Mendel and Sara Feige Tenenbaum. Hannah was a teacher by profession, and lived in the town of Kowel with her husband Yosef and their two children. She was 34 years old when she was murdered and forcibly parted from the world she loved so much.

Yad Vashem collects and assembles documentation from all possible sources in order to put together the fullest picture of the events of the Holocaust. Consequently, more information can be found about the Avrech family and the Kowel community. There is a photograph showing Hannah's husband with the other teachers of the "Tarbut Hebrew Grammar School" in the town. One file contains information on his last moments. In the trial of Erich Kassnen and Fritz Manthei for the murder of the Kowel Jews, held in Oldenburg, Germany, in the mid 1960s, survivors of the massacre carried out in the cemetery on 2 June, 1942, gave evidence. According to them, Avrech called out defiantly to Manthei, the German police officer, that even if they killed all the Jews, the defeat of Germany was near. Manthei shot and killed him on the spot (2).

How should we remember Hannah Avrech and her family? Decades after she and her family were murdered, what do we hope will remain of her, other than the old inscription on the wall? Why are we interested in the story of a Jewish woman who lived in another country, in a different time, someone with whom we have no family connection?

Imparting memory, expressed by the command "Zachor!" (Hebrew for "remember!"), is a major component of Jewish tradition. Uniquely, in Jewish tradition, the commandment to remember and pass on historic memory to the next generation became a religious obligation, which served the purpose of reinforcing faith. This is observed in ceremonies, religious rituals and festivals of historic significance, by which the story of forma-tive events in the history of the people of Israel are preserved and passed on (3). In the Middle Ages, in response to the disas-ters that befell the Jewish people, an additional element was added in the form of composing Slichot (prayers of atone-ment) and mourning rituals. Mourning was expressed in prayer and study, fast days and spiritual creativity. However, no pattern was set for memorializing the names of individuals by the community. Religious customs made it the responsi-bility of the family to commemorate the names of the departed, and there was no form of commemoration by the community as a whole. Despite the fact that Judaism attributes great significance to a person's name in all the incidents and persecutions throughout the long history of the Jewish people, it is only the events that are remembered and not the people and their names.

A photo portrait of Hannah Avrech, nee Tennenbaum, 1908-1942.

After the Holocaust, the deep-seated Jewish tradition of remembrance faced an enormous challenge. Existing patterns of commemoration and mourning were called into question due to the unprecedented scale of the disaster, the depth of the trauma, the fact that the centre of Jewish life in Europe had been destroyed, the confrontation with the ultimate evil, the vast fracture that had shattered relations between Jews and the rest

Her husband, Yosef Avrech (far left) with teachers from the "Tarbut Hebrew Grammar School".

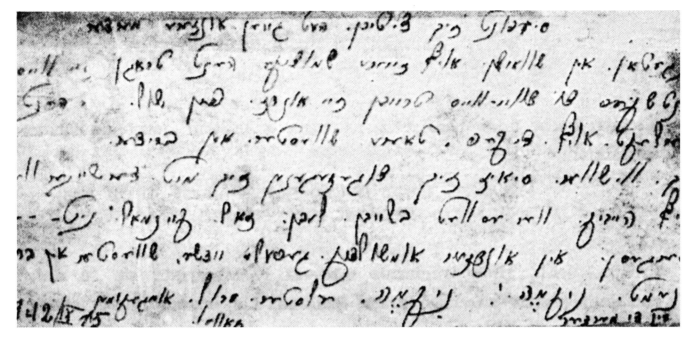

Last words, written on the wall of a synagogue in Kowel, transcribed after the war.

of the world – a fracture undermining the fundamental universal values on which human society rested and defying the principles of religious belief, the meaningless nature of the murder and the difficult questions it prompts with regard to human nature. The frameworks established by Jewish tradition in the past were intended to give meaning to the events which they commemorated. In view of the totality of the Holocaust and the inability to give religious or any other meaning to this event, it was impossible to make use of existing commemorative frameworks. On the other hand, the need to remember cried out to heaven.

Interestingly, from the very beginning, alongside the need to document the event itself, arose the need to collect the names of the victims – to register every single name. In line with Hannah's request to be remembered, the motif of perpetuating the names was prominent among the first ideas for commemorating the Holocaust in the land of Israel.

The first proposals to establish a memorial centre for the Holocaust were brought up during the war, when the first news of the systematic murder of European Jewry began to filter through. Mordechai Shenhavi, a member of Kibbutz Mishmar HaEmek who drew up the first plans for a Holocaust memorial back in 1942, proposed, among other things, to gather the names of the victims in a Hall of Remembrance (4). The name Shenhavi chose for his memorial project was eventually adopted. It was the Hebrew phrase "Yad Vashem" [a Monument and a Name], taken from the book of Isaiah in the Bible: "Even unto them will I give in my house and within my walls a monument and a name that shall not be cut off." (5) This name enfolds within itself the two dimensions of remembrance: the "monument" – the site itself – the physical place where all the commemoration and documentation efforts are centered, and the "name" – giving name in perpetuity to the individuals who were killed. Thus, recording the victims' names was a central component from the outset. Coming full circle, sixty years later, it is the software created by a high tech company from Mishmar HaEmek, incidentally also the kibbutz of the man who initiated the foundation of Yad Vashem, that forms the basis of the computerized names database and of all of Yad Vashem's vast repositories.

With the end of the war, the commemoration efforts were joined by survivors who, immediately on liberation, began to document their stories. They began writing testimonies, collecting documents and names, writing Yizkor (memorial) books for their lost communities.

After the establishment of the State of Israel, planning began for a state authority that would undertake to commemorate the Holocaust. Entrusted with the major task of perpetuating the memory of the Holocaust, the Yad Vashem Remembrance Authority was established in 1953 by a special law passed in the Knesset. Today, all the components of remembrance are gathered in one place, on the Mount of Remembrance in Jerusalem: the gathering of documentation in the archives and library, scientific research into the Holocaust period, educational activities in Israel and around the world, commemoration of the acts of Righteous Among the Nations, who saved Jewish lives during the Holocaust, outreach activities and commemoration ceremonies, and a museum complex for millions of visitors. Over the years, the Mount of Remembrance has become a multi-dimensional campus. This is the place where the public at large, and in particular Holocaust survivors, can come to mourn and commune with the victims; it serves as a centre and a symbol around which Holocaust commemoration is focused, and it has become a universal landmark and a warning beacon against racism.

The law under which Yad Vashem was established makes special mention of the gathering of names. The state of Israel wished to assume responsibility for perpetuating the memory of the Holocaust or "to gather to the homeland the memory of all those members of the Jewish people who fell and gave their lives (...)", as it is stated in the law (6). Thus, the law provided for granting Holocaust victims commemorative citizenship of the state of Israel. Professor Ben Zion Dinur, who was Minister of Education and the first chairman of the Yad Vashem Directorate, outlined the vision in 1956: "If we wish to live and to bequeath life to our offspring, if we believe that we are to pave the way to the future, then we must first of all not forget and make record. This is not the duty of individuals — it is a national duty. It is a human duty. It is the continuation of the war against Hitler and all those who want his acts to be forgotten (...) They wished to scatter the ashes over the seas (...) to disperse, to fragment their memory. And the opposite of dispersal and fragmentation is collection and gathering in. We want to collect the name of every single one of the six million (...) because if they were not able in life to come to the land of Israel and join their people, at least their names will live on here (...)". (7)

Entrusted with this mission, Yad Vashem launched a national campaign from 1955 to 1957 to gather Pages of Testimony in Israel. Special registration offices were opened in the main towns, and public announcements were issued through the media for people to come forward and register their families and friends who had perished. A door-to-door campaign was launched in the main localities of Israel. By the end of 1957, the campaign had yielded 600,000 Pages of Testimony with about 800,000 names (children under the age of 18 were registered on the same page as their parents). However, many names remained unaccounted for. For example: the orthodox religious sector of the population remained virtually uncanvassed; entire communities and families that had been wiped out left no one to register their names.

One third of the Jewish people had been murdered during the Holocaust. The mourning process continues to this day. At the end of the 1940s, there was hardly a home in Israel, which had not lost someone. Many European Jews had immigrated to Israel only a few years prior to World War II. They left parents, brothers and sisters behind who were lost in the Holocaust. In the first years of the existence of the State of Israel, survivors comprised a third of the population. In the absence of graves, there was no physical place where they could commune with their loss. In most cases, there was not even a family member left to eulogize and remember the dead. Recording the names in the Pages of Testimony filled a need to establish a memorial for their murdered loved ones of whom no trace was left. Others were not able or did not want to deal with the pain. The survivors turned their faces to the future and put all their energies into building new lives. Many of them chose not to record the names, which necessitated looking back into the abyss, and coping once again with the absolute loss of their family. In view of the magnitude of destruction and the fact that entire families and communities were

רשות־זכרון לשואה ולגבורה. ירושלים

דף־עד   2236042

לרשום חללי השואה והגבורה

ירושלים, רחוב בן־יהודה 12

	בעברית	1. שם המשפחה
Awruch (Tenenbaum)	בשפת ארץ המוצא (באותיות לטיניות)	
CHANIU	בעברית	2. שם פרטי בשפת ארץ המוצא (באותיות לטיניות)
		3. שם האב
		4. שם האם
	1908	5. תאריך הלידה
Wierzbnik, Polania		6. מקום וארץ הלידה (גם באותיות לטיניות)
Kowel		7. מקום המגורים הקבוע (גם באותיות לטיניות)
		8. המקצוע
		9. הנתינות לפני הכבוש הנאצי
		10. מקומות המגורים במלחמה (גם באותיות לטיניות)
Kowel		11. מקום המות, הזמן והנסיבות (המקום גם באותיות לטיניות)
	נשוי/מספר הילדים 2 דרוג	12. מצב משפחתי
		13. שם האשה ושם משפחתה לפני הנישואין
	גילה	
	גילו	שם הבעל

חוק זכרון השואה והגבורה —

יד ושם

תשי"ג 1953

קובע בסעיף מס' 2

תפקידו של יד־ושם הוא לאסוף אל
המולדת את זכרם של כל אלה
מבני העם היהודי, שנפלו ומסרו
את נפשם. נלחמו ומרדו באויב
הנאצי ובעוזריו, ולהציב שם וזכר
להם, לקהילות, לארגונים ולמוסדות
שנחרבו בגלל השתייכותם עם
היהודי, ולמטרה זו יהא מוסמך —

... (4) להעניק לבני העם היהודי
שהושמדו ונפלו בימי השואה והמרי
אזרחות־זכרון של מדינת ישראל
לאות היאספם אל עמם. ...

(ספר החוקים מס' 132
י"ז אלול תשי"ג (28.8.53

14. שמות הילדים עד גיל 18 שנספו (מעל לגיל זה רושמים "דף־עד" מיוחד)	גיל	המקום והזמן שנספו

ה ע ר ה !   את הילדים יש לרשום ב"דף־העד" של אחד ההורים אך לא יותר מפעם אחת.

אני _____ הגר ב (כתובת מלאה) _____ ת. 2.3
קרוב/ה מכר/ה _____ של חנה אברך (טענטום)
מצהיר/ה בזה כי העדות שמסרתי כאן על פרטיה היא נכונה ואמיתית, לפי מיטב ידיעתי והכרתי.
אני מבקש/ת להעניק לנ"ל אזרחות־זכרון מטעם מדינת ישראל.
מקום ותאריך _____ חתימה _____
חתימת הפוקד _____

אזרחות־זכרון הוענקה	
מספר №	

לידיעת ־האגף המדעי־ בירושלים, רחוב בן־יהודה 12

הייתי בזמן המלחמה במחנה (הסגר, עבודה, השמדה וכו') _____		בגיטו _____
במחתרת _____	ביערות _____	וכו' _____
חתימת העד _____	כתבתו _____	ואני מוכן למסור עדות על כך.

The "Page of Testimony" for Hannah Avrech, filled out and signed by her brother-in-law, Moshe Bagani, on 11 February, 1957 (10 Adar I, 5717), in Bnei Brak, Israel.

annihilated, terrible difficulty faced those who were forced to fill out dozens of Pages of Testimony – one for each person who had been murdered. Some of the survivors turned to the task only years later, others were not aware of the possibility, or were unable to muster up the strength to do it to this very day. Many names, known only to the people of that period, have been lost in this way, and more disappear every day and every hour, together with the generation that went through those events.

Over the years, the collection of Pages of Testimony continued at a pace of some 15,000 pages per year, a rate that doubled following the fall of the Iron Curtain, when Jews from Eastern Europe had the opportunity to contribute. New campaigns to collect Pages of Testimony were launched in 1999, yielding some 400,000 new forms, and in 2004, when Yad Vashem uploaded its repository onto the Internet.

The actual Pages of Testimony are preserved at Yad Vashem. Originally housed in a "Room of Names" in the administration building, they were transferred in 1977 to a "Hall of Names". In 2005, the Hall of Names, with the Pages of Testimony, was moved to its present location within the new Holocaust History Museum.

The computerization of the Pages of Testimony and of victims' names from archival lists began in 1992, and revolutionized access to the database, as well as the processing and retrieval of information. The computerization campaign was given an enormous boost by the Volcker Commission, which was charged with identifying Holocaust victims among the owners of dormant Swiss bank accounts. In order to produce a digitized list of Holocaust victims which could be compared to the list of bank account holders, the Volcker Commission turned to Yad Vashem, whose Hall of Names held the largest collection of Holocaust victims' names. In an enormous technological and organizational effort – in cooperation with Tadiran Technologies (now IBM) and Manpower Israel – the repository of some two million Pages of Testimony was scanned and digitized within five months in 1999. Another million digitized names from archival lists were integrated into the system.

The next step was to make this repository widely accessible. When the Yad Vashem Central Database of Holocaust Victims was uploaded onto the Internet – with applications developed by Idea Ltd. and IBM Israel – it contained some 3.4 million name records documenting about three million individuals (the same person may be documented in more than one Page of Testimony, as well as in lists). It is an ongoing process. The collection of Pages of Testimony continues, and millions of names that appear in a wide variety of historical documents still need to be recorded and integrated. Fellow institutions involved in documentation and commemoration of victims have joined this effort and have contributed their computerized lists to the repository. Due to the enormity and totality of the destruction perpetrated by Nazi Germany, there will probably never be a complete list of all its victims, but Yad Vashem experts estimate that a concerted effort to digitize all existing information may yield at least some information on perhaps five million of the victims.

One of the main challenges in the computerization process was to create intelligent knowledge tools and data retrieval systems. It was clear that it would be possible to retrieve information effectively, only if the system was able to retrieve information regardless of the original language in which the forms were filled in (forms written in Hebrew, Latin and Cyrillic characters), the different spelling of names (Schwartz / Shwarz / Szwartz, etc.), the existence of variants on the same name in different languages or of nicknames (Sandor is Alexander in Hungarian, Leib is the Yiddish version of Leo, etc.), or the changes in name of geographic places as political borders shifted. The city of Klausenburg is called Cluj in Romanian and Kolozsvar in Hungarian.

Over the years, the simple notebook in which the different forms of each name were noted was replaced by a highly sophisticated system of computerized indices. When the database was uploaded onto the Internet, the index of first names contained 4,305 basic names with 101,000 spelling variants, diminutives, endearments and associated names in different languages; the family names index had 90,049 basic names with 282,238 spelling variants; and the geographic index comprised 43,739 names of locations and an additional 51,000 variants. Thus, a family member in Israel today can retrieve information about his grandfather Zvi from Bratislava, even if Zvi was registered by someone in another country, at another time and in a different language, who recorded him as Hirsch (the German equivalent of Zvi) from Pressburg (the German name for Bratislava).

The task of collecting the names developed over the years, and the enlistment of advanced technologies opened up new possibilities for the commemoration of Holocaust victims. In addition, over time there have been changes in our perception of the Holocaust and the place accorded to the Holocaust in our collective identity. Paradoxically, interest in the Holocaust has increased as we have moved further away in time from the event itself. The complex processes of inter-generational transition and the fundamental changes in attitudes and awareness of the Holocaust in Israel, in the Jewish world and in the West have led to an increasing focus on the individual fate and the human dimension of the story. It is the very distance in time that generated our need to abandon abstract definitions and to try to draw closer to the human aspects – to identify with the victims and touch their lives.

Yad Vashem, Jerusalem 2003:
Memorial event of Israeli youth associations
in "The Valley of the Communities".

One of the expressions of this trend is the reading of names in ceremonies called "Unto every person there is a name« – taken from the first line of a poem by the Israeli poet, Zelda. This project for perpetuating the names of Holocaust victims by reading out their names in public on Holocaust Memorial Day has been taking place since 1989. The fact that the reading of the names has spread to many places around the world shows that it responds to a genuine need. It expresses a desire to identify with the individual – the need for an intimate and direct contact between those who remember and those who are remembered.

We can also see here a line spreading out into other areas of remembrance around the world. When describing the rationale behind the Washington Vietnam Veterans Memorial, Maya Ying Lin, planner of the site, said that her intention was "showing the war as a series of individual human sacrifices and giving each name a special place in history... The names would become the memorial«. (8)

Reading out names has, indeed, become an accepted motif in the commemoration of other tragic events. Focusing on the individual, however, takes on special significance beside the unique totality of the Holocaust, because of its objective being the elimination of all traces, both of the victims and of the murder itself. In an attempt to deal with the uniqueness of the Holocaust, the individual can be a key to our ability to identify with the story. Connecting with the story of Hannah Avrech through the Page of Testimony, through her last words left on the synagogue wall, has an experiential dimension, which in turn can be the starting point for an educational journey into the world before the Holocaust, into the victim's existence and struggle to survive. Accepting responsibility for commemorating the individual victims – the commitment to remember Hannah Avrech, to redeem her human image and to build up a picture of her life and death – gradually changes the pattern of commemoration and contains the seeds of a new tradition.

Modern technologies present us with a new challenge in realizing the vision with which Yad Vashem started out. They give us the ability "to ensure the establishment of a memorial for every person in Israel (…) and to bring our slain brethren to us and to the next generations«, as Professor Ben-Zion Dinur said, when he presented the Yad Vashem Law to the Knesset in 1953 (9). On the groundwork of documentation laid by the founders, we are adding an additional and new tier – the processing of the material and making it accessible to the general public. Enlisting technology in the service of memory, we are putting the names onto the Internet and disseminating the information. To the ongoing documentation of the names, we have added a dimension of active remembrance, in which the database becomes a source of identification contributing to the shaping of the younger generation's identity. We have set ourselves the task of gathering existing information on every victim, on every destroyed community, and of bringing them into every home, every classroom, and every community.

We are in the process of making a breakthrough, of creating a new model for commemoration and remembrance. By means of the Pages of Testimony and the stories that accompany them, we are turning the abstract number of six million victims into something tangible, into something that can be touched – even by those who are far away in time and geography. It is a dialectic process, in which we translate the collective into individuals to enable us to identify and remember, and then go on to remember the collective through the individuals. We turn the gathering and reading of names into remembrance that is shaping identity. By remembering and identifying with the victims, we tug on the broken thread that connects us with the past and try to rebuild its continuity.

1   *Polish Communities Register*, Vol. 5 (Yad Vashem, 1990), p. 164.

2   Yad Vashem Archives *TR-10/1001*, pp. 66-67.

3   Yosef Haim Yerushalmi, *Zachor* [Hebrew] (Am Oved, 1982), p. 27.

4   Ronnie Stauber, *A Lesson for the Generation* [Hebrew]
    (Yad Yitzhak Ben Zvi and the Ben Gurion Heritage Center, 2000).

5   *Isaiah 56:5.*

6   *Martyrs' and Heroes' Remembrance* (Yad Vashem) Law, 5713 – 1953, Article 2.

7   *Yad Vashem News*, January 1956.

8   *Vietnam Veterans Memorial brochure* –
    www.nps.gov/nama/graphics/vietnam_back2.pdf

9   Ben-Zion Dinur, *Zachor* [Hebrew] (Yad Vashem, 1958), p. 85.

STRATEGIES OF TERROR
PLACES OF PERSECUTION AND EXTERMINATION

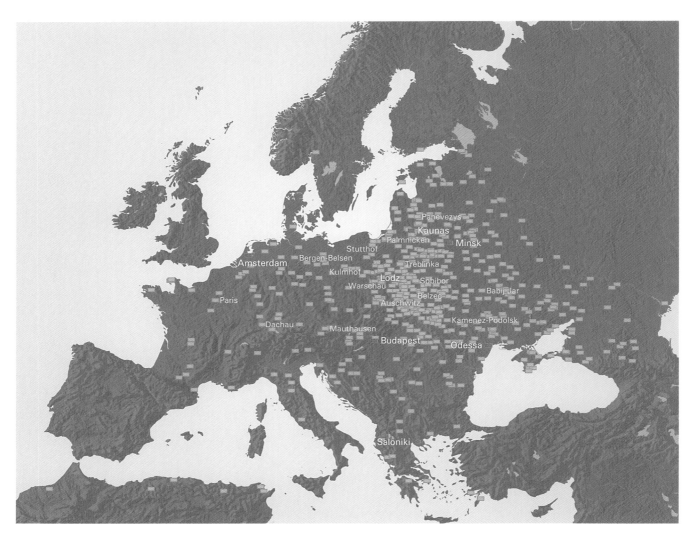

The persecution and extermination of European
Jewry happened in thousands of places. In this
text, seven cities represent the Holocaust:

Amsterdam is the largest city in the Kingdom
of the Netherlands. At the time of the invasion
by the German Wehrmacht in May 1940, 75,000
Jews lived there, more than 50 percent of the
country's entire Jewish population.

Budapest, the capital of Hungary, on the Danube, also counted Jews among its population from the 12th century. Between the world wars, approximately 200,000 of the 450,000 Jews in Hungary lived in this city.

Kovno, at the junction of the Neris and Nemunas rivers, was the temporary capital of independent Lithuania from 1920 until 1939. Some 40,000 Jews – a quarter of the city's population – lived here.

Lodz, the second largest Polish city, was famous for its textile industry and called the "Manchester of the East". At the outbreak of war in September 1939, about a third of its 672,000 residents were Jewish.

Minsk was the capital of the former Soviet Republic of Byelorussia. At the end of the 1930s, almost 71,000 Jews lived in Minsk – about 30 percent of its inhabitants. Most Minsk Jews were employed as labourers and office workers.

Odessa, the famous port on the Black Sea, is located in south-west Ukraine. At the start of the 20th century, it was, after Warsaw, the most important centre of Jewish literature and of Zionism in the Russian Empire. Before World War II, 180,000 Jews lived here.

Salonika was the centre of Greek Sephardic Jewry. Jews driven from Spain and Portugal had found a new home here in the early 16th century. With 50,000 Jewish inhabitants, Salonika was home to about 70 percent of all Greek Jews.

On 1 September, 1939, the German Wehrmacht marches into Poland. The start of the war enables the National Socialist dictatorship to "radicalize" its policy of persecution of the Jews. The invasion of Poland becomes a model for future expansions and for the occupation regime in the East as a whole. On the eighth day of the campaign, German troops reach Lodz. Immediately after the city is taken, the first outrages against the Jewish population begin. After the annexation of Lodz into the German

Forced evacuation in the ghetto district of Lodz in spring 1940. From the end of 1939, Jews had to identify themselves by wearing a yellow star.

Reich on 7 October, 1939, as part of the newly created administrative district of Warthegau, the military administration issues a decree, forbidding Jews from working in the textile trade. Very many Jews therefore lose the means to support themselves. At the same time, the occupying power introduces open terror: on 9 November, the first of many public executions takes place in Lodz; two days later the synagogues are set on fire. In addition, Jews are forced to wear an identification mark. On 8 February, 1940, the forced resettlement of the Lodz Jews, who number over 160,000, into a poor district of the city, the so-called "ghetto", begins. In early May 1940, this area is sealed off and surrounded by barbed wire. Living conditions worsen rapidly: daily life is characterized by starvation and epidemics. In spite of these conditions, the Jewish administration tries to organize a social life. For a time, the ghetto is conceived as a transit camp, from which those interned in the General Government, the part of Poland occupied by the German Reich, are to be deported. As this plan proves unworkable, the German administration turns the Lodz Ghetto into a large work camp.

In May 1940, German soldiers occupy the Netherlands. There are 75,000 Jews living in Amsterdam. A civil administration dominated by the SS soon launches anti-Jewish measures. In October 1940, Jewish shops are registered; a month later, Jewish public servants are suspended from their jobs. In early February 1941, Dutch National Socialists force their way into the Jewish district of Amsterdam, beat up Jews and set fire to synagogues. The events in the Netherlands are a link in a long chain of terrible destruction in various European cities, starting with the pogrom night of November 1938 in the German Reich and continuing at Easter and in August 1940, in Warsaw and Paris, where local fascist groups incite attacks on Jews. Those responsible for these acts are in close contact with the Reich Security Main Office in Berlin.

In Amsterdam, however, the perpetrators run into opposition from workers and from Jewish residents of the district. As a result, the German occupation administration seals off the area and moves the non-Jewish residents out. As a "reprisal", it also deports 400 Jews for extermination through hard labour, in the quarries of the Mauthausen concentration camp near Linz. By way of reaction, strikes are called in Amsterdam and other cities. The strikes are broken only through the introduction of martial law and the threat of heavy fines by the commander-in-chief of the German Wehrmacht in the Netherlands. In the days that follow, the German authorities systematically pursue the process of concentrating Dutch Jews into confined areas and reducing their freedom of movement. In January 1941, the German Reich Commissioner introduces mandatory registration of Jews; this is followed in July with the addition of the "J" to Jewish identity passes. In the autumn of 1941, the registration of all Jews is completed. As of May 1942, Jews in the Netherlands are forced to wear a yellow star, which they must purchase themselves. Thus confined, the Jewish community of Amsterdam helplessly awaits further developments.

At dawn on 22 June, 1941, German units, sometimes accompanied by troops allied to the Reich, cross the border of the Soviet Union. From the beginning, this campaign is planned as a "war of extermination against Jewish Bolshevism". Two days after the start of the military action, the Wehrmacht marches into the Lithuanian city of Kovno. There – after the hurried retreat of the Red Army, which had annexed Lithuania in 1940 – the German soldiers encounter a pronounced anti-Jewish mood among the Catholic Lithuanian residents of the city. The situation escalates. Beginning on 25 June, 1941, Lithuanian "partisans" unleash brutal riots against the Jewish population, in the presence of German soldiers, the SS and citizens of Kovno and with even less restraint than was the case in Warsaw, Paris and Amsterdam. Within three days, between 800 and

The "Jewish quarter" of Amsterdam. As of May 1942, the Jews of the Netherlands also had to wear a star, such as the man in the foreground on the left.

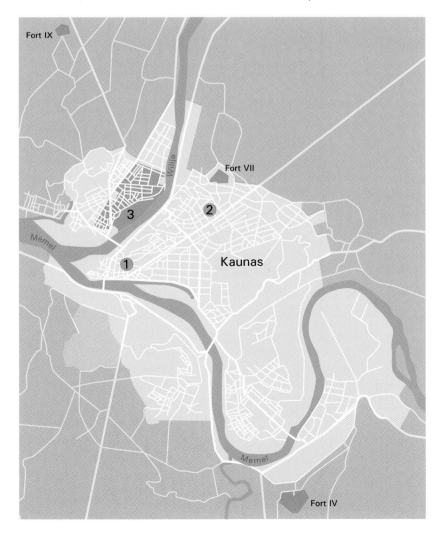

1 – Old Town
2 – Site of the massacre at the "Lietukis" garages.
3 – Ghetto. Surrounding the city are old defensive structures, the Forts. Here, SS personnel and Lithuanian auxiliaries carry out mass shootings of Jews, beginning at the end of June 1941.

The massacre at the "Lietukis" garages in the centre of Kovno, 27 June, 1941.

1,000 people are killed. The SS integrates the local readiness for violence against Jews into its own measures. Everywhere on the front in the summer of 1941, SS-Einsatzgruppen (mobile killing squads) of the Security Police and Security Service follow the German army. They kill primarily Jews behind the front lines – particularly in the part of eastern Poland that had been occupied by the Soviet Union in 1939, as well as in Byelorussia and the Ukraine, traditional areas of Jewish settlement. In Kovno, under orders from SS-Einsatzgruppe A, the 12th Lithuanian "Schutzmannschaft" (Protective Detachment) battalion carries out mass shootings – above all in Fort VII and Fort IX, previously defensive fortifications. By the beginning of August, more than 8,000 Jews, mostly men, have been murdered. The "radicalization" is executed rapidly; vague orders from Berlin are interpreted unambiguously by the SS units on the ground. The transition to genocide occurs here in Lithuania. By the middle of August 1941, Jewish children, women and men are being murdered indiscriminately. In Panevezys, on 23 August, the balance sheet of murder reads as follows: "1,312 male Jews, 4,602 female Jews, 1,603 Jewish children". Up until the end of the year, a German-Lithuanian SS-Rollkommando (SS Raiding Squad) hits region after region in Lithuania. The Jewish communities of entire villages and cities are eradicated. Except for the residents of three ghettos – Vilnius, Kaunas and Shiauliai – the Jews of Lithuania, about 137,000 people in all, have been murdered by December 1941. In the Kovno Ghetto, where 30,000 people have been enclosed behind barbed wire in a tiny area since 10 July, only some 15,000 people remain alive at this point, following additional shootings and starvation.

The SS commandos wreak havoc across the occupied Soviet region, growing ever more radical and systematic. At Kamenets-Podolsk, in the Ukraine, the SS and police leader has 23,600 Jews shot from 26 to 28 August, 1941. In the ravine at Babi Yar, near Kiev, members of SS-Einsatzkommando 4a murder, by their own accounts, a total of 33,371 Jews on 29 and 30 September, 1941, Yom Kippur, the holiest day of the Jewish year. On 16 October, 1941, Romanian troops allied to the German Reich capture Odessa on the Black Sea. The city becomes the headquarters for the governor of the Romanian area of occupation in the Ukraine. By this time, there are still between 80,000 and 90,000 Odessa Jews, who have not managed to flee. On 22 October, they have to register. That very eve-

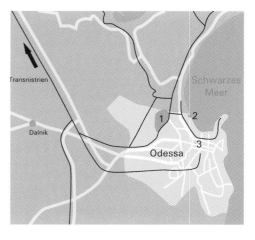

1 – Ghetto
2 – Location of massacre in the harbour
3 – Military headquarters

The harbour of Odessa, autumn 1941.

ning, a bomb explodes in the military headquarters. 60 members of the German and Romanian military die. In "reprisal" ,Jews are shot in the streets and hundreds are hanged in public gardens and parks. On 23 October, the Romanians shoot between 10,000 and 23,000 Jews throughout the port area of Odessa, pour petrol on both dead and wounded and set them on fire. In addition, every Jewish family of the city must hand over someone as a hostage. These 500 to 2,000 men, women and children are immediately shot in a well shaft by 20 members of SS-Sonderkommando (Special Commando) 11b. In the days that follow, Romanian units murder an additional 16,000 Jews in anti-tank ditches near Dalnik, just outside Odessa. The 35,000 Jews still remaining in the city are herded into two ghettos in November 1941. Many die of illness and exhaustion. In January and February 1942, the Romanian police and military deport almost 19,300 Jews to Transnistria, the area of Ukraine occupied by Romania. Odessa is subsequently pronounced "free of Jews".

110

Der Befehlshaber der Sicherheitspolizei u. des SD   Kauen, am 1.Dezember 1941
              Einsatzkommando 3

                                    5 Ausfertigungen!
                                    4.Ausfertigung.

Gesamtaufstellung der im Bereich des EK.3 bis zum 1.Dez.1941
durchgeführten Exekutionen.

Übernahme der sicherheitspolizeilichen Aufgaben in Litauen
durch das Einsatzkommando 3 am 2.Juli 1941.
     (Das Gebiet Wilna wurde am 9.Aug.41, das Gebiet Schaul.
2.Okt.41 vom EK.3 übernommen. Wilna wurde bis zu diesem Zei.
vom EK.9 und Schaulen vom EK.2 bearbeitet.)

     Auf meine Anordnung und meinen Befehl durch die
     lit.Partisanen durchgeführten Exekutionen:

4.7.41	Kauen - Fort VII -	416 Juden, 47 Jüdinnen	463
6.7.41	Kauen - Fort VII -	Juden	2 514

Nach Aufstellung eines Rollkommandos unter Führung
von SS-Ostuf.Hamann und 8 - 10 bewährten Männern
des EK.3 wurden nachfolgende Aktionen in Zusammen-
arbeit mit den lit.Partisanen durchgeführt:

7.41	Mariampole	Juden	32
7.41	"	14 " und 5 komm.Funktionäre	19
.7.41	Girkalinei	komm.Funktionäre	6
9.7.41	Wendziogala	32 Juden, 2 Jüdinnen, 1 Litauerin, 2 lit.Komm., 1 russ.Kommunist	38
9.7.41	Kauen - Fort VII -	21 Juden, 3 Jüdinnen	24
.7.41	Mariampole	21 " , 1 russ. 9 lit.Komm.	31
.7.41	Babtei	8 komm.Funktionäre (6 davon Juden)	8
.7.41	Mariampole	39 Juden, 14 Jüdinnen	53
9.7.41	Kauen - Fort VII -	17 " , 2 " , 4 lit.Komm., 2 komm.Litauerinnen, 1 deutsch.K.	26
1.7.41	Panevezys	59 Juden, 11 Jüdinnen, 1 Litauerin, 1 Pole, 22 lit.Komm., 9 russ.Komm.	103
22.7.41	"	1 Jude	1
23.7.41	Kedainiai	83 Juden, 12 Jüdinnen, 14 russ.Komm. 15 lit.Komm., 1 russ.O-Politruk.	125
25.7.41	Mariampole	90 Juden, 13 Jüdinnen	103
28.7.41	Panevezys	234 " , 15 " , 19 russ.Komm., 20 lit.Kommunisten	288

                                    Übertrag: 3 834

Report on the mass murder in Lithuania of 1 December, 1941 by the Commander-in-Chief of the SS
Security Police and the Security Service in Kovno, SS-Standartenführer (SS-Colonel) Dr. Karl Jäger.

Blatt 3.

		–Übertrag:	16 152
22.8.41	Aglona	Geisteskranke: 269 Männer, 227 Frauen, 48 Kinder	544
23.8.41	Panevezys	1312 Juden, 4602 Jüdinnen, 1609 Judenkinder	7 523
18.bis 22.8.41	Kr.Rassiniai	466 Juden, 440 Jüdinnen, 1020 Judenkinder	1 926
25.8.41	Obeliai	112 Juden, 627 Jüdinnen, 421 Judenkinder	1 160
25.und 26.8.41	Seduva	230 Juden, 275 Jüdinnen, 159 Judenkinder	664
26.8.41	Zarasai	767 Juden, 1113 Jüdinnen, 1 lit.Kom. 687 Judenkinder, 1 russ.Kommunistin	2 569
26.8.41	Pasvalys	402 Juden, 738 Jüdinnen, 209 Judenkinder	1 349
26.8.41	Kaisiadorys	alle Juden,Jüdinnen u.J.-Kinder	1 911
27.8.41	Prienai	" " " " "	1 078
27.8.41	Dagda und Kraslawa	212 Juden, 4 russ.Kr.-Gefangene	216
27.8.41	Joniskis	47 Juden, 165 Jüdinnen, 143 Judenkinder	355
28.8.41	Wilkia	76 Juden, 192 Jüdinnen, 134 Judenkinder	402
28.8.41	Kedainiai	710 Juden, 767 Jüdinnen, 599 Judenkinder	2 076
29.8.41	Rumsiskis u. Ziezmariai	20 Juden, 567 Jüdinnen, 197 Judenkinder	784
29.8.41	Utena und Moletai	582 Juden, 1731 Jüdinnen, 1469 Judenkinder	3 782
13.bis 31.8.41	Alytus und Umgebung	233 Juden	233

Monat September:

1.9.41	Mariampole	1763 Juden, 1812 Jüdinnen, 1404 Judenkinder, 109 Geistes- kranke, 1 deutsche Staatsangehörige, die mit einem Juden verheiratet war, 1 Russin	5 090
		–Übertrag:	47 814

Across Lithuania, the SS-Raiding Squad Hamann murder hundreds, sometimes thousands of Jews every day in the summer of 1941.

113a

Blatt 5.

-Übertrag: 66 159

Monat Oktober:

2.10.41 Zagare   633 Juden, 1107 Jüdinn.,496 J.-Ki. 2 236
                    (beim Abführen dieser Juden ent-
                    stand eine Meuterei, die jedoch
                    sofort niedergeschlagen wurde.Da-
                    bei wurden 150 Juden sofort er-
                    schossen. 7 Partisanen wurd.verletzt)

4.10.41 Kauen-F.IX- 315 Juden,712 Jüdinn.,818 J.-Kind. 1 845
                    (Strafaktion weil im Ghetto auf
                    einen deutsch.Polizisten geschos-
                    sen wurde)

29.10.41 Kauen-F.IX- 2007 Juden, 2920 Jüdinnen,   9 200
                    4273 Judenkinder
                    (Säuberung des Ghettos von über-
                    flüssigen Juden)

Monat November:

3.11.41 Lazdijai   485 Juden,511 Jüdinn.,539 J.-Kind. 1 535
15.11.41 Wilkowiski   36 "   48   "   31   "   115
25.11.41 Kauen-F.IX- 1159 " 1600   "   175   "   2 934
                    (Umsiedler aus Berlin, München u.
                                    Frankfurt a.M.)

29.11.41   "   "   693 " 1155   "   152   "   2 000
                    (Umsiedler aus Wien u.Breslau)

29.11.41   "   "   17 Juden, 1 Jüdin, die gegen die
                    Ghettogesetze verstossen hatten,
                    1 R.-Deutscher, der zum jüdischen
                    Glauben übergetreten war und eine
                    Rabinerschule besucht hatte, dann
                    15 Terroristen der Kalinin-Gruppe   34

Teilkommando des EK.3
in Dünaburg in der Zeit
vom 13.7.-21.8.41:
                    9012 Juden, Jüdinnen und Judenkinder, 9 585
                    573 aktive Kommunisten

Teilkommando des EK.3
in Wilna:

12.8.bis
1.9.41 Wilna-Stadt 425 Juden, 19 Jüdinnen, 8 Kommunist.   461
                    9 Kommunistinnen

2.9.41   "   "   864 Juden, 2019 Jüdinnen,
                    817 Judenkinder
                    (Sonderaktion, weil von Juden auf
                    deutsche Soldaten geschossen wurde)   3 700

                    -Übertrag: 99 804

One of the main locations of genocide is Fort IX in Kovno. As early as July 1941, Jewish children and women are shot here.

```
                    Blatt 6.

                    -Übertrag:                                    99 8o4

12.9.41  Wilna-Stadt   993 Juden,167o Jüdinn.771 J.-Kind.         3 334
17.9.41    "      "    337   "      687   "     247      "         1 271
                       und 4 lit.Kommunisten
2o.9.41  Nemencing     128 Juden, 176 Jüdinn. 99        "            4o3
22.9.41  Novo-Wilejka  468   "  ,  495   "     196      "         1 159
24.9.41  Riesa         512   "     744   "     511      "         1 767
25.9.41  Jahiunai      215   "     229   "     131      "           575
27.9.41  Eysisky       989   "    1636   "     821      "         3 446
 .9.41   Trakei        366   "     483   "     597      "         1 446
4.1o.41  Wilna-Stadt   432   "    1115   "     436      "         1 983
6.1o.41  Semiliski     213   "     359   "     39o      "           962
9.1o.41  Svenciany    1169   "    184o   "     717      "         3 726
16.1o.41 Wilna-Stadt   382   "     5o7   "     257      "         1 146
21.1o.41   "      "    718   "    1o63   "     586      "         2 367
25.1o.41   "      "     -     "    1766   "     812      "         2 578
27.1o.41   "      "    946   "     184   "      73      "         1 2o3
3o.1o.41   "      "    382   "     789   "     362      "         1 533
6.11.41    "      "    34o   "     749   "     252      "         1 341
19.11.41   "      "     76   "      77   "      18      "           171
19.11.41   "      "      6 Kriegsgefangene, 8 Polen                  14
2o.11.41   "      "      3          "                                 3
25.11.41   "      "      9 Juden, 46 Jüdinnen, 8 J.-Kinder,          64
                        1 Pole wegen Waffenbesitz u.Besitz
                        von anderem Kriegsgerät


Teilkommando des EK.3
      in Minsk
vom 28.9.-17.1o.41:

      Pleschnitza,
      Bicholin,
      Scak,
      Bober,
      Uzda          62o Juden,1285 Jüdinnen,1126 J.-Kind.
                     und 19 Kommunisten                            3 o5o
                                                                  ─────────
                                                                  133 346

   Vor Übernahme der sicherheitspol.Aufgaben durch das EK.3,    4 ooo
Juden durch Progrome und Exekutionen - ausschliesslich von
Partisanen - liquidiert.
                                                                  ─────────
                                              Sa.                137 346
```

On 1 December 1941, SS-Colonel Jäger reports more than 137,000 murdered individuals in Lithuania, most of them Jews.

At the end of June 1941, German troops march into Minsk, in Byelorussia. On 19 July, the local field commander's headquarters orders that a ghetto be set up in the nearly destroyed city. Between 50,000 and 60,000 Jews are herded into two square kilometres. The majority are crammed into one or two-storey wooden houses. By late summer 1941, the supply situation in Minsk has worsened dramatically. At the same time, German plans are to deport Jews from the Reich that autumn into the already overcrowded ghetto – also to Riga and to Kovno. The local German authorities solve the problem they created – too little food and too little room – in a brutal manner: in November and December, units of the SS Security Police, together with auxiliary police, shoot more than 13,600 Jews, in keeping with a set quota. In November 1941, 7,000 German, Austrian and Czech Jews arrive in Minsk, with at least another 17,000 arriving between then and mid-1942. They are restricted to their own section of the ghetto. In the summer of 1942, the SS carries out additional mass murders in Minsk: between 28 and 31 July, mainly in the Maly Trostenets extermination camp, 10,000 Byelorussian and German Jews are shot, or asphyxiated in gas vans.

A warning sign at the Maly Trostenets extermination camp. Photographed by the Extraordinary State Commission of the Soviet Union, which in July 1944, shortly after the liberation of Minsk, already begins investigating the National Socialist crimes at the camp.

On top of this, from late 1941 and in the course of 1942, the Berlin administration deports to the Lodz Ghetto some 20,000 German, Austrian, Czech and Luxembourg Jews, plus another 18,500 Jews from cities and villages in the Warthegau and 5,000 Sinti from Burgenland, seized as Gypsies. The conditions created by the occupation administration – overcrowding, hunger, disease – become ever more unbearable. As in Minsk, the authorities combat these conditions with racial violence. Just as transports are arriving from the west, the SS begins on 16 January, 1942 to deport the Lodz Ghetto's inhabitants to Chelmno (Kulmhof), the first

Deportation from the Lodz Ghetto, June-August 1942. Jewish policemen are forced to supervise the deportation.

camp established for the systematic extermination of Jews. The victims are brought by train to Kolo, where they must climb into open freight cars. In Chelmno, they are forced to undress in the ground floor of a villa, apparently in order to wash. SS personnel then lead them to a ramp in the cellar, at the end of which a lorry waits. During the journey to the nearby forest of Rzuchow, the engine's exhaust fumes are channelled into the windowless back of the lorry. The people inside suffocate in agony. Jewish forced labourers bury the bodies in mass graves in the forest.

The Chelmno extermination camp is run by members of the SS Special Commando Lange, which already in the early summer of 1940 had murdered 2,000 psychiatric patients in Soldau, East Prussia, in the same manner. The ongoing costs of the Special Commando and the running of Chelmno had to be met by the German administration of the Lodz Ghetto. During 1942, more than 70,000 Polish Jews and 15,000 Jews from the German Reich, as well as up to 4,300 Austrian Sinti from the Lodz Ghetto, are murdered in Chelmno. By the spring of 1943, almost the entire Jewish population of the Warthegau is killed there.

While the mass murder with gas vans is taking place in Chelmno, the SS and Police Leader for the Lublin district, Odilo Globocnik, has three extermination complexes built with stationary gas chambers in remote forests in Poland: Belzec, Treblinka and Sobibor. "Action Reinhardt" is the name given to the systematic extermination of Jews in the General Government using motor exhaust fumes. The murder takes between 20 and 30 minutes. From March to October 1942, between 450,000 and 600,000 Jews, mostly from Galicia, die in Belzec: 230,000 are from Lvov (Lemberg) and its environs, another 130,000 from the Cracow area. In Sobibor, from May 1942 to June 1943, the SS murder approximately 250,000 Polish, German, Dutch, French, Lithuanian and Byelorussian Jews. In Treblinka, between July 1942 and May 1943, some 2,000 Sinti and Roma are murdered, as well as 800,000 to 900,000 Jews, almost exclusively from Poland, including 330,000 Jews from Warsaw – once home to the largest Jewish community in Europe. The property of the victims is sent to the German Reich for "utilization". Not one of those murdered at Chelmno, Belzec, Sobibor and Treblinka – from the smallest baby to the most elderly – is registered by name; the transport lists give only estimated figures.

Kolo railway station, 1942: here deportees from the Lodz Ghetto board open freight cars that transport them to the Chelmno (Kulmhof) extermination camp.

Deportation from the Warsaw Ghetto, July-September 1942, to the gas chambers of Treblinka.

Westerbork transit camp, probably 1942. Photograph from an album prepared for the commander of the camp, Gemmeker.

By the end of March 1941, the SS have set up a "Central Office for Jewish Emigration" in Amsterdam. From the point of view of those responsible, there is not the slightest doubt at this point about a "territorial final solution to the Jewish question". Only the numbers are debated. On 22 June, 1942, Adolf Eichmann, the officer in charge of Jewish affairs at the Reich Security Main Office, informs the foreign ministry in Berlin that an agreement has been reached with the German national railway regarding the transport to Auschwitz of 100,000 Jews from the Netherlands, Belgium and the occupied areas of France. For the Netherlands, the number is set at 40,000. Eight days later comes the decree that Jews may only shop between 3 p.m. and 5 p.m.; they may not use public transportation; and they must remain indoors from 8 p.m. to 6 a.m. Beginning on 5 July, 1942, 4,000 Jews living mostly in Amsterdam receive a summons to report to the Headquarters for Jewish Emigration for possible participation in a "work detachment in Germany". Most of those who receive the summons do not respond. To apply pressure, German Ordnungspolizei (Order Police) conduct round-ups in Amsterdam's Jewish quarter and arrest 540 Jewish women and men. The Central Office threatens to deport them to a concentration camp, if the 4,000 Jews continue to disobey orders. The memory of the victims sent to their deaths in Mauthausen in the spring of 1941 is powerful. Consequently, some 1,600 Jews report for registration in the following days. They are sent first to the Westerbork transit camp, not far from the German border, where lists of names for transport are complied. Beginning in the middle of July 1942, the first trains filled with Dutch Jews leave Westerbork for the East. Time and again, raids are conducted to round up Jews for deportation. Throughout February 1943 – with a four-week break for Christmas – there are 52 transports, carrying a total of 46,455 children, women and men; 42,915 are sent directly to Auschwitz-Birkenau, the rest to labour camps.

As a ransom for most of the Jews drafted into forced labour in July 1942, the Jewish community of Salonika is forced to sell its 500-year-old cemetery. The city administration then uses the gravestones as quarry stone.

Before the planned deportation of Jews from Salonika, the SS introduces the identification with a yellow star at the end of 1942.

In April 1941, the German Wehrmacht occupies Salonika, on the Aegean Sea in Greece, home to 50,000 Jews. Immediately after the invasion, the Einsatzstab Rosenberg, a detachment specializing in the theft of works of art, plunders the 500-year-old Sephardic treasures of literature and art from public and private libraries and synagogues. Greece is divided up between the German Reich and its Italian and Bulgarian allies. This situation delays the persecution of the Jews, because the Reich Security Main Office in Berlin wants the three occupiers to act in concert. But here, as in their own country, Italy refuses to follow the SS demands for deportation. Referring to the behaviour of the Italians, the Reich authorities agree to delay the action, including the one planned for German-occupied Greece. The first organized blow against the Jews takes place on 11 July, 1942: 9,000 Jewish men must assemble at the Plateia Eleftheria (Freedom Square), where German soldiers humiliate and abuse them. About 3,500 are drafted for forced labour by the military administration; by October, 250 of them have died. At the end of 1942, Berlin loses patience, registers all those Jews remaining in Salonika and sends members of the SS there. With support from the local military administration, the SS-Sonderkommando of the SS Security Service takes immediate measures for deportation, beginning in late February, 1943. The Jews of Salonika and the surrounding area are concentrated into ghettos and their property is confiscated. At first, the poorer ones are sent to the fenced-in ghetto near the train station in the Baron Hirsch quarter. After the start of the transports on 15 March, 1943, Jews repeatedly are brought here before their deportation. Up to mid-August, 1943, the Reich Security Main Office in Berlin organizes 19 transports carrying a total of approximately 46,000 Jews from Salonika to Auschwitz-Birkenau and Treblinka. Most of them are murdered immediately by asphyxiation with poison gas. In Auschwitz-Birkenau, the SS selects 4,200 women and 7,000 men deemed fit for forced labour; they are later murdered. On 28 April, 1943, 128 Jewish women are selected as "prisoners for experimental purposes", that is, for medical experiments. The Jewish Council and the Jewish ghetto police of Salonika are sent in August 1943 to Bergen-Belsen concentration camp; half a year later, with the help of the American Joint Distribution Committee, they are evacuated to Palestine.

To deceive the Jews of Salonika into believing they are being taken to a work deployment in Cracow, they are forced to buy third-class train tickets to Auschwitz-Birkenau.

At the same time, deportations continue from the Netherlands. On 5 March, 1943, after a three-day journey, the first train from Westerbork arrives in the Sobibor extermination camp. In the course of July 1943, 18 more trains arrive, carrying a total of 33,208 Jews, including one transport on 8 June with 3,017 people, almost exclusively children with their mothers.

In the Kovno Ghetto, large "operations" cease in 1942 and in early 1943. But sporadic deportations and shootings increase the sense of helplessness and threat, as does the daily terror of forced labour and malnutrition, not to mention the news from other ghettos. The Jewish Council, set up by the German administration, tries to create a sense of normality within its narrow confines, above all because the ghetto inhabitants work for the German armaments industry. On 1 November, 1943, the SS takes control of the Kovno Ghetto – as in Shiauliai and Warsaw. The Jewish administration is dismissed, the ghetto turned into a concentration camp and placed under the appropriate administration in Berlin. Forced labour is also stepped up. The results are "selections" of ghetto inhabitants. The SS take the elderly, children and the sick to camps in Estonia, such as Klooga, or shoot them in Fort IX near Kovno – as in the "Kinder-Aktion"

Deportation from Kovno to Estonia on 26 October, 1943.

The destroyed ghetto district of Kovno in the summer of 1944.

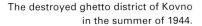
The deserted Lodz Ghetto, early 1945.

("Children's Operation") of 27 and 28 March, 1944, when German SS personnel and Ukrainian auxiliaries round up 1,300 Jewish children and elderly people. The 73rd transport from France, made up of 878 Jewish men, arrives here in mid-May 1944; some of the Jews are shot in Fort IX, while the rest are taken to Tallinn in Estonia and murdered there. Up until the German withdrawal in early July 1944, the commandant of the Kovno camp deports some 8,000 prisoners westwards from the former ghetto to the concentration camps at Stutthof and Dachau; the emptied camp in Kaunas is burned down.

In May 1944, the SS clear the Lodz Ghetto. This ghetto, too, is now a de facto forced labour camp, with at least 77,000 residents. Apart from children and the elderly, 90 percent of its inhabitants are working in factories.

On 23 June, 1944, deportations to the Chelmno extermination camp resume – under the pretext that Jews were to be transferred for work in the German Reich. But Chelmno is overloaded, so from 7 to 30 August, 74,000 Jews are sent directly to the gas chambers of Auschwitz-Birkenau. Those Jews remaining behind, the "cleanup squad", must gather Jewish property and prepare it for transport. In the autumn of 1944, 40 to 60 lorries leave Lodz daily for the German Reich.

In the summer of 1944, the extermination at Auschwitz-Birkenau reaches its peak. Up to 20,000 people per day are murdered using the poison gas Zyklon B. Aside from the transports from Lodz, the victims are Jews from France, Belgium and the island of Rhodes, from Polish Galicia and the Radom district. Within a few weeks, more than 437,000 Slovakian, Romanian and Hungarian Jews also arrive.

Hungary, which was previously allied with Germany, is occupied by the German Wehrmacht in March 1944. Though anti-Jewish measures have been in effect here since 1938, the Budapest government – like Italy's – has refused to hand over their country's Jews to the Germans. Now the last great Jewish community in German-occupied Europe – the Jews of Hungary and annexed areas – is to be struck. Adolf Eichmann comes here himself to organize the deportations to Auschwitz-Birkenau, no doubt because the Red Army is coming steadily closer. After Allied air raids in early April 1944, the deputy Hungarian Interior Minister orders that the Jewish community of Budapest make 500 apartments available within 24 hours to non-Jews. On the same day, Eichmann raises this quota to 1,500. In June 1944, only a few houses on dark, narrow and remote streets remain for the use of Jews. 17,500 Jews are deported from Budapest to Auschwitz, where most of them are then murdered. On 20 October, 1944, Hungarian nationalists, the Arrow Cross, drag all Jewish men between the ages of 16 and 60 – 22,000 in all – from their homes and send them on a death march to Austria. At the end of November, a ghetto is set up in Budapest. From December 1944 through January 1945, members of the Arrow Cross shoot between 10,000 and 20,000 Jews on the banks of the Danube. At this point, the Red Army has already completely surrounded Budapest. When the Soviet soldiers enter in mid-January 1945, some 70,000 Jews remain in the Budapest Ghetto.

In August 1944, members of the Polish resistance in Auschwitz-Birkenau took clandestine photographs. The images show Jewish prisoners burning bodies north of the gas chambers of Crematorium V (above) and naked women in the forest in front of Crematorium V (below).

Meanwhile, the SS have long been busy dissolving the remaining camps in the East and sending the prisoners on death marches into the still intact interior of the German Reich. Stutthof and its satellite camps are emptied after the Red Army offensive against East Prussia in mid-January 1945: some 13,000 inmates are concentrated in Königsberg. On 26 January, one day before the Russians reach Auschwitz, the SS in charge in Königsberg lead about 7,000 Jewish women – most of them from Lithuania and Hungary – through the city on a 15-kilometre route to Palmnicken, on the Baltic coast. Of these women, 2,000 to 2,500 die or are murdered during the march. On the night of 1 February, 1945, German SS and their foreign auxiliaries drive the remaining 4,500 to 5,000 Jewish women onto the frozen Baltic Sea at Palmnicken and murder them with machine-gun fire; this is the last great massacre in this war of extermination. Yet, until the capitulation of the German Army and the cessation of military action on 8 May, 1945, tens of thousands of camp inmates are herded through the remainders of the Reich. Untold numbers die on these marches, or soon afterwards of exhaustion.

Deportation of Budapest Jews in late October or early November 1944. The Jews are walking in a line along Joseph Ring Street. Here too, Jews are forced to wear an identifying star.

Lodz, Amsterdam, Kovno, Kamenets-Podolsk, Babi Yar, Minsk, Odessa, Salonika, Budapest, Chelmno, Belzec, Sobibor, Treblinka, Auschwitz-Birkenau, Stutthof or Palmnicken – the genocide committed by National Socialists and their helpers took place in thousands of locations. From Gurs in the French Pyrenees to Budyonnovsk near the Caspian Sea, from Oslo in Norway to the Greek island of Corfu, but especially in Polish and former Soviet lands – both on the edges and in the centre of the German sphere of influence – the responsible elements of the SS, the Gestapo, the military and civil administration with their German and foreign auxiliaries carried out a comprehensive programme of extermination. With the goal of complete extermination, Jews were deported, shot and murdered with poison gas. The policy of persecution and extermination was also applied to Sinti and Roma, who were classified as Gypsies; to Soviet prisoners of war; to civilians from almost all European countries, particularly Poles, Russians and Serbs; to political and ideological opponents and resistance fighters. In the occupied areas of eastern Europe – as in Leningrad – the German authorities intentionally let millions of people starve to death. In addition, those who did not fit the National Socialist image of human perfection, such as people with disabilities or homosexuals, became victims of the terror. In the end, between 5.4 and more than six million European Jews were murdered. There was almost no place in occupied Europe unaffected by National Socialist violence – but, where public awareness is concerned, the vast majority of these places remain unknown.

Europe with the border lines of 1937,
with the number of Jewish victims.

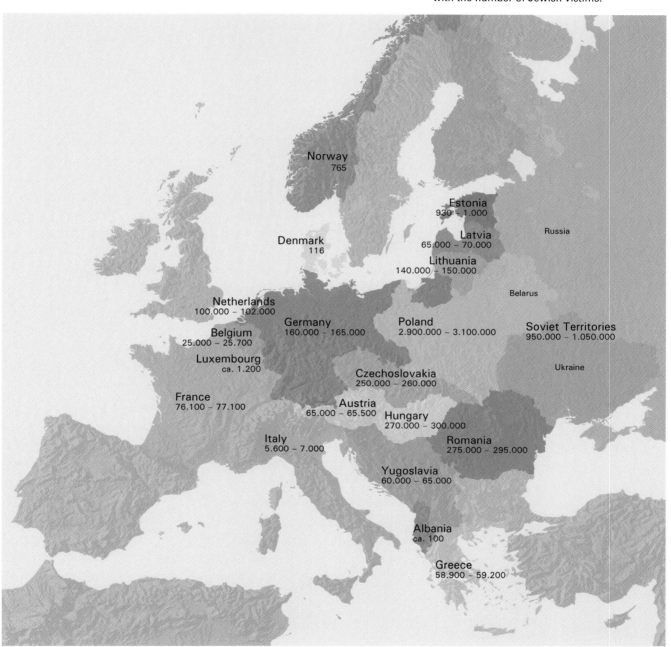

Norway
765

Estonia
930 – 1.000

Denmark
116

Latvia
65.000 – 70.000

Russia

Lithuania
140.000 – 150.000

Belarus

Netherlands
100.000 – 102.000

Germany
160.000 – 165.000

Poland
2.900.000 – 3.100.000

Soviet Territories
950.000 – 1.050.000

Belgium
25.000 – 25.700

Luxembourg
ca. 1.200

Czechoslovakia
250.000 – 260.000

Ukraine

France
76.100 – 77.100

Austria
65.000 – 65.500

Hungary
270.000 – 300.000

Italy
5.600 – 7.000

Romania
275.000 – 295.000

Yugoslavia
60.000 – 65.000

Albania
ca. 100

Greece
58.900 – 59.200

Bibliography

Wolfgang Benz (ed.), *Dimension des Völkermords. Die Zahl der jüdischen Opfer des Nationalsozialismus* (Munich, 1996).

Martin Gilbert, *The Routledge Atlas of the Holocaust* (London, New York, 2002).

Ulrich Herbert, *Nationalsozialistische Vernichtungspolitik 1939-1945* (Frankfurt/Main, 1998).

Raul Hilberg, *Die Vernichtung der europäischen Juden,* 3 vols. (Frankfurt/Main 1990).

Dieter Pohl, *Holocaust. Die Ursachen – das Geschehen – die Folgen* (Freiburg i. Breisgau, Basel, Vienna, 2000).

Tomasz Szarota, *U Progu Zaglady. Zajscia Antyzydowskie i Progromy w Okupowanej Europie* (Warsaw, 2000).

NATIONAL SOCIALISM, WAR AND GENOCIDE OF THE JEWS

Today's pluralist, liberal and democratic societies are inconsistent when it comes to dealing with the past. On one hand, historical events have less impact than ever when it comes to scientific and technological developments in the worlds of production, communication and consumption. On the other hand, the longing for history – or for an historical anchoring of human thought and actions in the "age of globalization" – has increased dramatically. This relates not only to the "great" historical events or personalities, but also to aspects of everyday life, of study and work, of family and neighbourhood, of coping with old age, illness and death. Our understanding of what is considered historically worth preserving has broadened remarkably in recent decades. There now are many other "lieux de mémoire" or "sites of remembrance" – alongside classical memorials and national holidays – that can occupy a place in the cultural memory of a nation or region.

Admittedly, when one speaks of a "culture of remembrance" in Germany, as well as in many other European states today, one usually does not mean "sites of remembrance" in this blanket sense. Rather, one is referring to the memory of the enormous crimes of the 20th century and their victims. In Europe that means, above all, National Socialism, the Second World War and the murder of the European Jews – and, since 1989/90, of the crimes of the communist dictatorship. Occasionally one also hears complaints about a generalized "culture of remembrance" that fails to distinguish between the communist and the National Socialist past. True, in both cases one is dealing with totalitarian systems and their victims. But it becomes problematic, if the differences between the political systems and the crimes they committed are blurred.

With respect to the memory of National Socialism, conditions for the politics of remembrance after the Second World War were very different in the various countries affected. In western Europe and especially in the USA, the public image of National Socialism and its crimes was determined above all by the horrific photographs taken at the liberation of the concentration camps in Bergen-Belsen, Buchenwald and Dachau, as well as by the findings of the International Military Tribunal in Nuremberg. In addition, there were the immediate experiences of the bombing and the terror of occupation, of deportations and massacres, of resistance and military and political successes. Doubtless the worst such experiences of war and terror occurred in eastern Europe and parts of south-eastern Europe. Particularly in Poland and the Soviet Union, the "Third Reich" had pursued an imperialist and racist war of annihilation, the likes of which had not been seen before. Tens of thousands of cities and towns were destroyed; entire regions were laid waste. The number of dead in Poland was six million, including about three million Jews; in the Soviet Union, according to new estimates, it was 27 to 28 million (including almost 20 million civilians). Here, one needed neither photos and films of the camps nor an international court to understand the nature of the National Socialist reign of terror. One had first-hand experience of the crimes in one's own country. One had direct exposure to the brutality of the war and the occupation. The suffering of the population that survived was almost omnipresent.

In the Soviet Union, however, the main focus was on the victory in the "Great Patriotic War". Most important were the achievements of the Red Army, as well as of the civil population, in the struggle against an enemy that initially had been a clearly superior military power. Politically, the victory over National Socialist Germany was used as irrefutable evidence that the future belonged to Soviet-style socialism. At the same time, the war formed a point of departure and a political justification for building a Soviet sphere of hegemony in the countries of eastern and south-eastern Europe, countries that the Red Army had freed from National Socialist rule. Thus, the Soviet politics of remembrance was not first and foremost about the victims of the war, unless these were the dead and wounded soldiers of the Red Army. Rather, it was about the victors. Even memorials honouring dead soldiers were designed to highlight heroic struggle and victory. Memorials, almost always monumental, also symbolized Soviet power and claims of hegemony.

This tendency to glorify the "Great Patriotic War", a tendency which began immediately after the war, would define the politics of history in the Soviet Union and most of its dependent "Peoples Democracies" until the break-up of the communist bloc. In the Russian Federation of today, the remembrance of the war as a politically integrating element has actually gained ground, because it is no longer possible to find societal consensus regarding the October Revolution of 1917. Public opinion polls have shown that, towards the end of "Perestroika" under Gorbachov, most Russians considered the "Great Patriotic War" – and not the "Great Socialist October Revolution" – as the most important historical event of the 20th century. Thus, on the fiftieth anniversary of the end of the war, an enormous "victory park" and a new "Museum of the Great Patriotic War" were built and opened to the public in Moscow.

Under these conditions, the murder of the Jews played as small a role in the landscape of Soviet memorials as it did in the official politics of remembrance. The fate of the Jewish people was considered one element in an overall history of terror and suffering, a view that did not justify emphasizing any one group of victims. Small, artistically modest

Kiev, summer of 2004:
The central memorial in the park dedicated
to the memory of the massacre of Babi Yar.
Additional, smaller memorials in the park
focus on the murdered Jewish children and on
the sixtieth anniversary of the mass shooting.

memorials that surviving Jews erected soon after the war in their home-
towns or in locations of mass shootings, were often removed in the
years that followed. There were no major memorial projects, and even
at Babi Yar, the huge ravine near Kiev where, in September 1941, more
than 33,000 Jews were shot within two days, the authorities stubbornly
resisted efforts to create a memorial. True, Yevgeni Yevtushenko's 1961
poem, »Babi Yar«, caused quite a stir, even inspiring Shostakovich to ded-
icate his 13th symphony to it. However, the basic tenor of Soviet policy
remained unchanged. Khrushchev raged against Yevtushenko in 1963 for
creating an impression that "only Jews were victims of fascist horrors,
when, in fact, Hitler's butchers murdered many Russians, Ukrainians and
Soviet people of other nationalities". When a memorial eventually was
erected in Babi Yar, its inscription referred to the "citizens of Kiev" who
were murdered there. There was no concrete reference to the Jews.
It was rare to find explicit references to the fate of the Jews on memorials dedicated to the victims of National Socialist rule, such as those in
Minsk. Since the end of the Soviet Union, interest in the fate of the Jews
under National Socialist occupation has grown noticeably in Russia and
some of the other successor states. But the effects of decades of sup-
pressing the unique tragedy of the Jews, the only people threatened with
total extermination, linger on.

Kiev, summer of 2004: A memorial in the form of a menorah, also in the Babi Yar park, makes it explicitly clear that the victims were Jewish.

Poland's politics of remembrance with regard to the persecution and extermination of the Jews are of particular interest. The first memorials to the victims of the National Socialist terror were built in the concentration and extermination camps of Majdanek and Auschwitz. Soon after its liberation in July 1944, at Majdanek, its buildings largely still standing, the first large memorial with a museum was built. A good half-year later, Auschwitz and the Stutthof concentration camp were added to the list of memorial sites. But there was no special recognition of the Jewish victims. In Poland, even Auschwitz was considered for decades to be a "Memorial for the Martyrdom of the Polish Nation and Other Peoples", as the Polish Parliament put it in 1947. This is probably why the decision was taken in late 1946 that the museum would not be in Auschwitz-Birkenau (the location of the extermination camp), but in the main camp (Auschwitz I). For all practical purposes, Auschwitz did not exist as a location of the extermination of European Jewry, either in official Polish remembrance politics or in public perception among the post-war generations. The memorial, dedicated in 1969 in Auschwitz-Birkenau, referred in many languages to the "victims of Hitler's murderers", but the genocide of European Jews went unmentioned. In 1967, the Jewish pavilion, one of two dozen exhibitions organized by nation, was shut down. After the Six-Day War, the anti-Jewish "purges" in Poland reached their peak. When the pavilion was reopened in 1978, the Polish Culture Minister explicitly reemphasized that Poles and Jews were persecuted equally ("among those slated for extinction, Poles and Jews were first on the list..."). Basic changes in this position were not implemented until the middle of the 1990s, after rather bitter political conflicts over whether to classify Auschwitz as a place of Polish, Catholic or Jewish suffering.

But the picture of Poland's engagement with the fate of Jews during the period of National Socialist rule is indeed more contradictory than suggested by a look at Auschwitz and Majdanek. As early as 1946, memorials were erected in the ruined city of Warsaw, both in memory of the 1943 uprising by Jewish resistance fighters in the Warsaw "Ghetto" and on the "Umschlagplatz", the square from which the Jews of Warsaw were deported to the extermination camps. Both memorials were created by respected artists and had a clear message: the victims were referred to not generally as "Polish citizens" but as "Jews of Poland", and the inscription was in Polish, Yiddish and Hebrew. This was followed in 1948 by the first memorial dedicated to the Jews, recalling struggle and heroism as well as tragedy: artist Nathan Rapoport's large monument marking the fifth anniversary of the "Ghetto Uprising" was commissioned by the Central Committee of Jews in Poland, with state support. The inscription

Warsaw, May 2004:
Monument dedicated to the memory of
the Warsaw Ghetto Uprising in 1943.
It was erected as early as 1948, amidst
the rubble of the destroyed city.

reads: "To the Jewish people – its fighters and martyrs". The memorial was not uncontroversial, but over time it won a certain respect both in Poland and among world opinion – from when Willy Brandt dropped to his knees there, to when Pope John Paul II visited the site. Even among members of Solidarity, the Polish opposition movement, this place took on symbolic significance.

In more than a few Polish communities, surviving Jews who returned to their home towns in the first post-war years created simple but often moving memorials using stones from destroyed Jewish cemeteries: small mounds and walls made of fragments of gravestones. One of the most impressive memorials is on the grounds of the former Treblinka extermination camp, where almost one million Jews were murdered. There, between 1959 and 1964, sculptor Frantiszek Duszenko and architect Adam Haupt created a national memorial. Their arrangement of 17,000 granite stones with an eight-meter-high, split granite block at its centre represents, according to its creators, "an effort to depict the largest cemetery of the genocide". Unlike those at Auschwitz and Majdanek, this memorial stated unmistakably at its entrance that the "people murdered in this camp were almost without exception Jews". Experts from Poland and abroad consider the Treblinka memorial, its monumental simplicity having lost none of its exceptionally powerful effect on visitors, to be "probably the greatest of all Holocaust memorials" (James E. Young).

The changed quality of the commemoration of the Jewish victims of genocide became clear in the 1980s, when Poland invited Jewish organizations from throughout the world to Warsaw to mark the fortieth anniversary of the "Ghetto Uprising". A citizens' committee formed for the preservation of Jewish memorials, and took the initiative for a "Memorial Path of Jewish Martyrdom and Struggle" and for a new memorial on the "Umschlagplatz" in Warsaw. The path, marked with 19 stone blocks dedicated to individuals connected with the uprising (the inscription reads: "On this path of suffering and death [...] more than 300,000 Jews from the Warsaw Ghetto were forced into the gas chambers of the extermination camps.") was opened in 1988, as was the memorial, which presented a silent, dignified space for reflection. Since then, interest in recovering the history of the destruction of the Jews has increased steadily in Poland, to the extent that – according to some writers – there are more Jewish memorials in Poland than in any other European country. Of course, the large memorial sites and museums in Auschwitz and Majdanek have been remodelled extensively in recent years.

In western Europe and the USA as well, the remembrance of the murder of European Jewry stood for a long time in the shadows of the general war experience. One celebrated the victory over National Socialist Germany, honoured one's fallen soldiers, abhorred the war crimes that the Germans committed. The persecution and murder of the Jews was considered part of these crimes and appeared not to receive any particularly prominent consideration outside Jewish communities. Generally, it took until the 1970s or 1980s before remembrance of the genocide of the Jews separated itself from general remembrance of the Second World War and the crimes associated with it. Only at this relatively late date did the opinion begin to prevail that the events now referred to internationally as the "Holocaust" were "unique" and signified an unprecedented "break with civilisation". From that point on, to a rapidly expanding international public, Auschwitz stood for "absolute evil". It became the "symbol of the 20th century".

Of course, the development of the politics of remembrance displays numerous national characteristics within Europe's democratic societies. Nevertheless, some general tendencies may be read from the examples of France and Italy, where one focused both on the soldiers who fell in battle against Germany and on victims of German war crimes. Monuments and memorials were erected at the sites of major massacres and other acts of terror. In addition, both right after the war and in the following decades, there was a very pronounced interest in basing the new political order on a tradition of anti-fascist resistance and national struggle for liberation. Thus was born the myth of a nation united in resistance, although in Italy the fight against the German occupation was also a civil war between anti-fascists and fascists, and in France the Allied military victory was used by the "Résistance" as an excuse for bloody revenge against collaborators. Since the 1950s, both countries have focused on remembrance of resistance fighters, but even more so on those deported and the survivors of the German concentration camps, with no distinction between those deported on political or "racial" grounds. The dominant theme is the comprehensive "remembrance of the camps", the "univers concentrationnaire". In Italy the history of the deportation was acknowledged in 1959 through the first large exhibition initiated by the "Associazione Nationale Ex Deportati Politici Nei Campi Nazisti (ANED)" (National Association of Former Political Prisoners in Nazi Camps). In France, a national "Mémorial des martyrs de la déportation" was created in 1962 on the Île de la Cité in Paris. In both cases, it was not deemed important to differentiate between the deportation of Jews and non-Jews.

For several decades in both countries, there was a broad consensus that Jewish victims of National Socialism did not merit a special place in the national memory – an understanding clearly shared by the majority of surviving Jews. With the exception of a few important authors, the murder of European Jews was itself a subject of discussion neither by the public nor on the political level. Only in the 1980s and 1990s was there a fundamental change. Remembrance of the genocide of the Jews quickly took on growing importance. Criticism of the behaviour of one's own citizens and authorities was also given new weight. In 1993, France declared 16 July – the day in 1942 when Jews were deported from Paris – a national day of remembrance. And when in 1995, President Chirac used this memorial day to speak of "France's responsibility" for the deportations, 16 July became "the first official 'negative' memorial in the history of France" (Henry Rousso). Similarly, with the establishment of 27 January as a "Day of Remembrance" for the Jews in Italy, public attention was drawn to the Italian racial laws and their consequences. One spoke both of "la memoria ritrovata", the "rediscovered remembrance" of the Jews, and also of one's own guilt or complicity.

Museum of Resistance and Deportation, Forges-Les-Eaux (Normandy), 2004: numerous regional museums built in France since the end of the 1990s combine these two thematic focuses.

Since then a national Holocaust memorial has been created in France. The only comparable exhibition within Europe is the Holocaust exhibition of the Imperial War Museum in London, which opened in summer 2000. The "Mémorial de la Shoah" in Paris opened to the public in January 2005 and contains the "Mur des Noms" – a wall of commemoration with the 76,000 names of the Jews deported from France –, a museum and a research centre.

If one looks for institutions which set the international standard for the remembrance of the murdered Jews, one looks to "Yad Vashem", the great Israeli national memorial in Jerusalem, followed by the "United States Holocaust Memorial Museum" in Washington in the 1990s. The idea for a memorial in Jerusalem was first proposed in 1942. A resolution of the Jewish National Assembly in June 1945 could not be enacted, because of the struggle for the establishment of the Jewish state. But a law was passed in 1953 establishing Yad Vashem as the "Memorial to the Heroes and Martyrs" and simultaneously as a national "memorial authority" to be the "custodian and creator of national remembrance". While there was no lack of successful initiatives for very effective memorials, monuments, stones and plaques in Jewish towns and villages as well as in kibbutzim, Yad Vashem now became the official representative for the national politics of remembrance. As early as 1951, the decision was taken to hold a "Day of Remembrance of the Holocaust and Heroism" on the 27th day of the Hebrew month of Nissan, marking the Warsaw "Ghetto Uprising" of 19 April to 16 May, 1943. A supplementary law, passed in 1959, established a two-minute nationwide silence on this day. With the sounding of a siren, every movement on the streets and squares is halted. For a moment there is a kind of living monument of collective memory. Already in 1954, the international organization B'nai B'rith (Hebrew for "Sons of the Covenant") began to create another kind of living memorial in the Jerusalem area, a "Forest of Martyrs", in which a tree would be planted for each of the six million dead. The central monument, created in 1971 by Nathan Rapoport, bears the inscription, "In memory of the martyred six million and in acknowledgment and celebration of the rebirth of Israel".

This touches the core of Israeli memorial politics: the connection of mourning for the victims of genocide with pride in the rebirth of the nation. This link explains the heavy emphasis on Jewish resistance, on struggle and "valour", whose participants are interpreted as a kind of herald for an independent Jewish State. From the 1960s onwards, the focus on the murder of the European Jews intensified further, partly because of the Eichmann trial in Israel, which aroused national and international attention, and partly because of the immediate threats to Israel's existence during the Six-Day War and the Yom Kippur War. This was reflected in the notable expansion of Yad Vashem, which had been enlarged steadily since its first large building opened in 1957, and which at the same time took on new tasks. The result was a large, diverse, structured memorial landscape in which, by applying the tools of landscape architecture,

Paris, summer of 1998:
The "Mémorial des Martyrs de la Déportation"; built in 1962 in the city centre, on the eastern tip of the Île de la Cité. It is dedicated to the French citizens deported to German concentration camps.

science, fine arts, modern technology and education, the dead would be remembered, "for the future" as well. All of this was developed on the basis of steadily growing archival documentation and collections, of the long-term preservation of all accessible knowledge and materials. It should be stressed that this national memorial – despite all the renewal and expansion – in principle is considered incomplete. That is a major reason why Yad Vashem continues to gain in importance in the international development of memorial sites.

In the last 25 years, the international politics of remembrance regarding the murdered Jews has been influenced most powerfully by the United States of America. This began with the four-part television series "Holocaust", first broadcast in April 1978 in the USA and later in many European countries. It not only achieved ratings of 50 per cent and more in the USA, but also had a ripple effect. It influenced the founding of numerous Holocaust chairs, Holocaust research and study programmes at American universities, the inclusion of Holocaust education in high schools and colleges of many states, as well as a rapidly increasing number of Holocaust museums. This development reached its internationally recognized zenith in 1993, with the opening of the national "United States Holocaust Memorial Museum" in Washington.

It was not always so in the USA. Holocaust remembrance there did not develop gradually, but rather occurred in great leaps. In the first two decades after the Second World War, not only was the term "Holocaust" not used as it has been since the second half of the 1960s, but there was also virtually no public discussion about the genocide of the Jews and its meaning for the present. Even leading representatives of American Jewry encouraged silence as the language of Holocaust survivors living in the USA. In Jewish communities, "survivor" was not yet a badge of honour, and for a long time there was little interest in the experiences of these people. Thus, in public opinion in America, the Jews were regarded as one victim group among many. Heated public discussion was prompted first by the Eichmann trial in Jerusalem, which was televised in the USA, and by the Broadway production of Rolf Hochhuth's play "The Deputy", in which the Vatican's silence regarding the genocide of European Jewry was presented critically. Particularly deep was the impact of the wars for Israel's survival in 1967 and 1973. The Yom Kippur War, in particular, generated a new awareness of Jewish vulnerability because, while she had won, Israel no longer appeared invincible. In light of the continued threat against Israel, the Holocaust appeared to many American Jews as no longer a purely historical event, but as a possible, frightening future.

Major Jewish organisations now drew the conclusion that remembrance of the Holocaust must never fade, that "Holocaust programmes" of all kinds were needed urgently. In addition, in the face of the great religious and cultural divisions within the Jewish population in the USA, the historical experience of the Holocaust was now deemed the most important thing they had in common, a basis or at least a starting point for an overarching Jewish identity.

The first memorial event for victims of the genocide of the Jews and the Warsaw "Ghetto Uprising" was held in New York City during the Second World War. In the first few years after the war, however, efforts to have a memorial to the Jewish victims erected in a public park in Manhattan failed. The era of Holocaust memorials and memorial sites, which today almost every large city in the US possesses, began only in the 1980s. To name but two important examples: in San Francisco, the controversial Holocaust memorial by George Segal was dedicated in 1984; and in 1985, Nathan

San Francisco: The 1984 Holocaust memorial by George Segal remains controversial because of its portrayal of human figures – both alienating and naturalistic.

Rapoport's "Liberation" memorial, depicting a US soldier carrying a concentration camp victim, was installed in Liberty State Park in New Jersey, within sight of the Statue of Liberty. At around the same time, the story of Holocaust museums begins in the USA. At the end of the 1970s, the "Martyr's Memorial" of the Jewish Federation in Los Angeles was the first and only Holocaust museum in the USA. Fifteen to 20 years later, there was a wealth of such museums in larger American cities, the most important ones being the "United States Holocaust Memorial Museum" in Washington, the "Beit Hashoa – Museum of Tolerance" of the Simon Wiesenthal Centre in Los Angeles and the "Museum of Jewish Heritage" in New York. The Washington Museum is the most outstanding, not only nationally, but also internationally, thanks to its concept and architecture, its exhibitions and collections, and also to its extraordinary public success since its opening in 1993. The establishment, programme and sponsorship of this utterly unusual museum project, whose preparation began in 1978 under President Carter, makes it abundantly clear that remembrance of the Holocaust is at this point a concern no longer for American Jews alone, but for American society as a whole. Later, with the founding in 1998 in Stockholm of the "Task Force for International Cooperation on Holocaust Education, Remembrance and Research", the effort was undertaken to extend the level of "Holocaust education" reached in the USA to as many lands as possible.

In Germany, the challenges of remembering the history of National Socialism and the Second World War were always different from those faced elsewhere. Germany had not only lost, but had also started the war, and was responsible for the enormous crimes committed during the war. Here, the National Socialist regime was no foreign occupying power, but rather, was freely supported by the great majority of the German people. It was a terror system that – within the borders of the Reich, at least for a time, – was supported by nearly all those who were not themselves persecuted or felt threatened. True, support dwindled as military failures mounted, as the number of dead and wounded German soldiers rose dramatically, and as the allied bombing created growing fear and panic among the civilian population. Nevertheless, the German people remained to the end astonishingly loyal to the "Third Reich" and their "Führer". Thus, the unconditional surrender in May 1945 was seen by most, not as a liberation, but as a "collapse" and "catastrophe".

In the first post-war years, it was almost exclusively surviving opponents and victims of the National Socialist system who tended to the remembrance of those tormented and murdered by the regime. They put up the first, often provisional, memorials in former camps and other places of suffering. They also organized the first memorial events. However, the mass of the population remained preoccupied with their own suffering during air raids, in flight as refugees or as prisoners of war, and with the food shortages that began with the end of the war. In these circumstances, there was practically no interest just after 1945 in preserving important sites of National Socialist history or in establishing prominently visible memorials. In the western occupation zones and the early Federal Republic of Germany, including West Berlin, one was content with a few symbolic sites: the former concentration camps in Bergen-Belsen and Dachau, the execution site in the Berlin-Plötzensee prison, and a memorial dedicated to those killed after the 20 July, 1944 attempt on Hitler's life, in the "Bendler-Block", the former office of the Supreme Command of the Wehrmacht in Berlin. For decades, efforts to confront National Socialism critically remained the affair of a small minority. Prominent sites of the terror regime, such as the headquarters of the Gestapo and the Reich Security Main Office, the site of the People's Court, the villa in which the Wannsee Conference took place, or the headquarters of the "euthanasia" murder programme, were still unnoted when the first major trials of National Socialists took place, in West Germany (the "Einsatzgruppen [Mobile Killing Squads] trial" in Ulm, 1959, and the "Auschwitz trial" in Frankfurt, 1963-1965), and when, at the end of the 1960s, the student movement and the Brandt government engaged in the first public debates about the legacy of National Socialism. The memorial at the former concentration camp at Dachau opened in 1965 on the initiative of the International Dachau Committee, a survivors' group, and was, for a long time, the only permanent exhibition of national significance.

In contrast to developments in the early Federal Republic, in the Soviet zone of occupation and in the German Democratic Republic, the theme of "anti-fascism" played a prominent programmatic role from the very outset. Much more radically than in the west, institutional and personnel ties with the National Socialist regime were severed, although "de-nazi-fication" was also instrumentalized as a tool for imposing a socialist-communist society. The political elite in the GDR counted themselves, alongside the Soviet Union, among the victors, who thus bore no responsibility for the deeds of National Socialism. In the first instance, it was "fighters against fascism" who were regarded as "victims of fascism". Consequently, in the first months after the war, it was hard even for Jews to be recognized as "victims of fascism". In the mid-1950s the GDR leadership decided to build massive "national monument and memorial sites" on the sites of the former concentration camps at Buchenwald, Ravensbrück and Sachsenhausen, which were to be opened a few years later. These memorials, on which internationally renowned artists collaborated, emerged as the most important symbolic sites of the official "anti-fascism" of the GDR; the "red triangle", the badge of political prisoners in the National Socialist camps, was omnipresent in exhibitions, while all other prisoner groups were kept in the background. In addition, political resistance in the camps was given disproportional attention as compared with the massive suffering and death. The politics of remembrance expressed in the "national monument and memorial sites" was centrally guided by the GDR leadership and barely changed in the decades that followed. Only in the final years of the GDR were some new emphases and distinctions made.

In the Federal Republic, the 1980s brought a breakthrough in the public discussion of the National Socialist period. In no small way influenced by the American television series "Holocaust", broadcast in Germany in early 1979, the conviction spread that consideration not only of the murder of European Jewry, but also of the entire National Socialist past, had been suppressed for too long, and that it was high time to catch up on what had been neglected for so long. Attention was drawn primarily to the sites of persecution and murder of the Jews, as well as to the remaining evidence of Jewish history in Germany. Attention was now also focused on the "forgotten victims": on the ill and victims of forced sterilization, on homosexuals and Jehovah's Witnesses, on the "Gypsies" (Sinti and Roma) and victims of German military courts, and not least, on the Soviet prisoners of war and forced labourers rounded up from many countries. Importantly, public interest now focused not only on the victims, but also quickly turned to include the perpetrators and the places in which the Gestapo and SS, National Socialist authorities or special courts operated.

The new interest in history during the 1980s generally came "from below", was critical of the prevailing view of history, saw itself as a part of the democratization process – and it was concrete: it focused on historical sites where the events occurred. By the end of the 1980s, this interest in a critical investigation of the history of National Socialism had become broadly accepted, and even the political world now made its contribution. Almost all projects that could grow out of citizens' initiatives were financed with public funding. Within a few years in the old Federal Republic, a many-tiered landscape of remembrance had sprung up, oriented toward historic sites and thus, by its very nature, decentralized, dedicated to the memory of the victims and to education about the perpetrators. With this process came an intensification of historical research, which continually broadened and deepened the painful insights into the criminal dimensions of National Socialism.

There were widespread fears that the end of the GDR, German re-unification and the creation of a new national state, would lead to a rapid waning of interest in the National Socialist past and thus to the atrophy of the landscape of remembrance, which had so recently come into being. But the public confrontation with the National Socialist past did not merely continue from the beginning of the 1990s onward, it actually intensified. Thus, in 1999, the German Federal Government, together with the German Parliament, from which the initiative came, presented a "memorial site concept" signifying the beginning of a national politics of remembrance over and above that of the federal states. The Federal Government since then has participated in financing all the memorial sites, which had their origins in the GDR's "national monument and memorial sites" in Brandenburg and Thuringia, as well as the large Berlin institutions that served as national, rather than local or regional, reminders of the National Socialist period: the "Foundation Topography of Terror", the "Memorial Site to German Resistance" and the "Memorial Site House of the Wannsee Conference". In connection with the annual budget provided for "memorial site funding", the Federal Government has also contributed considerably to the building and renovation of the concentration camp memorial sites in Bergen-Belsen, Dachau, Flossenbürg and Neuengamme as well as many smaller memorials sites – from places where the ill were murdered, to camps for prisoners of war and forced labourers, to regional Gestapo prisons. The political and societal need for an ongoing confrontation with the National Socialist past – for remembrance and warning, for research and education – is no longer contentious in Germany, at least in principal.

In the old Federal Republic, remembrance of the persecuted and murdered Jews has held a unique position from the very beginning. In 1952, the "Luxembourg Agreement" regulated the "restitution" contributions of the Federal Republic. Knowledge of the murder of six million Jews even forced the bourgeois right wing, including many former National Socialists, to make a clear political break with National Socialism. For a long time, however, the suffering and death of European Jews remained a completely abstract topic for most people, and questions about the perpetrators were quickly – and all too comfortably – narrowed to Hitler and his closest associates, to the SS and the Gestapo. Publications like The Diary of Anne Frank, plays and not least court cases, prompted passing public debate, yet here, too, the breakthrough did not come until the end of the 1970s. Since the 1980s, the number of memorials and memorial sites dedicated to the Jews has increased steadily, and by the fiftieth anniversary of the anti-Jewish violence in November 1938, nearly all cities in the Federal Republic had sites dedicated to the memory of former Jewish communities and their members.

In the autumn of 1988, a grass-roots initiative in Berlin promoted a "Holocaust-Memorial" that would commemorate not only the persecution, expulsion and murder of German Jews, but the genocide of European Jews as a whole. After prolonged, sometimes heated confrontations, the citizens' initiative finally became a national project. In the summer of 1999, the German Parliament resolved to build a "Memorial to the Murdered Jews of Europe" in the centre of Berlin, according to the design of New York architect Peter Eisenman. It would be linked with an "Information Centre" that would offer basic information about the victims of the genocide and about the murders.

As a national memorial, it will state in unequivocal terms the commitment of German politics and society in the former and present German capital, never to evade remembrance of National Socialist crimes. However, it must not be forgotten that Berlin has many other locations where the Jewish victims are remembered and information is given about the perpetrators. Even before 1990, there were several memorials in Berlin recalling the persecution, deportation and murder of Jews, particularly at sites of destroyed synagogues, as well as places where Jews were collected together and from where they were deported. The 1990s saw the arrival of a large number of additional memorials, almost all of a high aesthetic quality: in 1991, the memorial at the commuter railway station S-Bahnhof Grunewald, by Karol Broniatowski; in 1993, 80 signs on the streets and squares of the Bavarian Quarter in Schöneberg, by Renata Stih and Frieder Schnock; in 1995, three memorials: the sculpture commemorating the protest by women in the Rosenstrasse by Ingeborg Hunzinger, the empty underground "library" on the Bebelplatz, site of the book burning (among the "burned poets" were many Jewish writers) by Micha Ullman, and the "mirror wall" in Steglitz by Wolfgang Göschel and Joachim von Rosenberg; in 1996, "The Abandoned Room" at Koppenplatz by Karl Biedermann and Eva Butzmann, and on the Oranienstrasse in Kreuzberg, the first of Berlin's "stumbling blocks" by Gunter Demnig, reminders of people from the neighbourhood who were deported and murdered; in 1998, at the goods railway station Grunewald, "Track 17" by Nikolaus Hirsch, Wolfgang Lorch and Andrea Wandel; and lastly, in 2000, at the entrance to the underground station U-Bahnhof Hausvogteiplatz, "A Sign of Remembrance of the Fashion Centre Hausvogteiplatz" (there were many Jews among the proprietors and employees in the Berlin fashion trade) by Rainer Görß. In addition, there are memorial plaques on numerous buildings in the centre of the city, and also, of course the popular exhibitions at large Berlin memorial sites (Topography of Terror, The House of the Wannsee Conference, The Foundation New Synagogue Berlin – Centrum Judaicum) and museums (German Historical Museum, the Jewish Museum), but also in smaller institutions, including the "Otto Weidt Workshop for the Blind" in the Rosenthaler Strasse.

Memorials and monuments always have the dual task of honouring the dead and ensuring that history not be forgotten. However, they can fulfil these functions only if society, or at least a large portion of it, heeds their message. Thus, remembrance is dependent on universities and schools, political parties and large societal institutions doing their part to keep interest in history alive. Remembrance of National Socialism in Germany is not only about remembering the dead and honouring the victims of terror. With no less intensity, we must also confront the perpetrators and the political-social conditions that made such crimes possible. Remembrance bound with extreme national guilt for National Socialism in general and for the murder of European Jewry in particular, must not be seen as a handicap or as backward thinking. Rather, such remembrance is better able to convey the message that the protection of human rights and civil rights, and the safeguarding of a liberal and democratic political order, must enjoy the highest priority. By knowing the consequences of the National Socialism perversion of the political order and disregard for all rights, coming generations will understand their duty to work all the more insistently to safeguard and improve the democratic and legal order of our society. These politics of remembrance do not face backwards; rather, they serve the present and the future.

Literature

Burkhard Asmuss (ed.), *Holocaust. Der nationalsozialistische Völkermord und die Motive seines Gedenkens* (Berlin, 2002).

Christoph Cornelißen/Lutz Klinkhammer/Wolfgang Schwentker (eds.), *Erinnerungskulturen. Deutschland, Italien und Japan seit 1945* (Frankfurt/Main, 2003).

Monika Flacke (ed.), *Mythen der Nationen. 1945 – Arena der Erinnerungen,* 2 volumes (Berlin, 2004).

Johannes Heesch/Ulrike Braun, *Orte erinnern. Spuren des NS-Terrors in Berlin. Ein Wegweiser* (Berlin, 2003).

Volkhard Knigge/Norbert Frei (eds.), *Verbrechen erinnern. Die Auseinandersetzung mit Holocaust und Völkermord* (Munich, 2002).

Claudia Lenz/Jens Schmidt/Oliver von Wrochem (eds.), *Erinnerungskulturen im Dialog. Europäische Perspektiven auf die NS-Vergangenheit* (Hamburg and Münster 2002).

Peter Novick, *The Holocaust in American Life* (Boston,1999).

Peter Reichel, *Politik mit der Erinnerung. Gedächtnisorte im Streit um die nationalsozialistische Vergangenheit* (Munich, 1995).

Peter Reichel, *Vergangenheitsbewältigung in Deutschland. Die Auseinandersetzung mit der NS-Diktatur von 1945 bis heute* (Munich, 2001).

Henry Rousso, *Frankreich: Vom nationalen Vergessen zur kollektiven Wiedergutmachung*, in: Monika Flacke (ed.), *Mythen der Nationen. 1945 – Arena der Erinnerungen*, vol. 1 (Berlin, 2004), pp. 227-56.

James E. Young, *The Texture of Memory: Holocaust Memorials and Meaning* (New Haven, 1993).

James E. Young (ed.), *The Art of Memory: Holocaust Memorials in History* (New York, 1994).

Shimon Mendel
from Romania was deported
to Auschwitz in 1944 at the
age of 59 and murdered there.

ACKNOWLEDGEMENTS

In anthologies such as this one – "Material on the Memorial to the Murdered Jews of Europe" – the merits or shortcomings of the whole reflect the sum of its parts, and in turn reflect on the merit of the entire compounded volume.

The word "material" is chosen deliberately. It is difficult to convey systematically and fully in 180 pages the million-fold murder of the Jews in all its facets, from the point of view of the victim to the analysis of the perpetrator. However, it was not our intention to provide a mere compilation of tangible information. This would have meant the loss of the desired effect: to convey as clearly as possible at least the contours of the scenario of horror. The thematic structure of the exhibition in the Information Centre suggested the structure of this volume. It is thus no accident that the leaders of the expert commission and the board – Prof. Richarz, Dr. Benz, Dr. Jäckel and Dr. Rürup – who developed the memorial exhibition's thematic structure, together with their mentor, Prof. Quack, through years of sometimes controversial work, have contributed to this volume. I thank them and Prof. Quack, who represent the other members of the commission and the board, for managing to convey the dimensions of the National Socialist genocide – in all its monstrosity – within the limited space of 800 square meters.

From the very beginning, the Foundation's academic staff was limited to a small number of highly qualified scholars: Eva Brücker, Dr. Ulrich Baumann, Dr. Jürgen Lillteicher and Uwe Neumärker. Through the spring of 2005, with great personal dedication, they converted the instructions of the expert commission and the board into an exhibition of photographic and text material, the like of which has rarely been seen before.

They represent the requisite highest quality of the younger generation of historians, as do their colleagues outside the Foundation, Prof. François Guesnet (University of Potsdam) and Dr. Dieter Pohl (Institute for Contemporary History, Munich). The latter, in his contribution, illuminates the current state of research on the statistics of the genocide and thus provides a rejoinder to the denial of history that is often repeated under various guises. Together, Ulrich Baumann and François Guesnet reconstruct entire Jewish cultures that were destroyed by racism, showing how these cultures developed in Europe for centuries before the war.

To be seen both as a great honour and evidence of the close cooperation between Yad Vashem and the Foundation for the Memorial to the Murdered Jews of Europe, is the contribution of Avner Shalev and Alexander Avraham on the meaning of names in Jewish tradition, and their preservation through the remembrance of individuals, even in the tragic case of mass murder: the "Pages of Testimony".

An entire room in the exhibition is dedicated to the work of Yad Vashem. Jürgen Lillteicher's meticulous research for the Room of Names, with some 3,000 individual biographies, would not have been possible without the support of Yad Vashem.

We also thank the following for their support:

Norbert Aas, Joel Alpert, Vadim Altskan, Andrej Angrick, Paul Antmann, Dietmar Arnold, Ulrike Bär, Julian Baranowski, Ella Barkan, Margit Bartfeld-Feller, Giles Bennett, Gunnar Berg, Martin Bergau, Roza Bielauskiené, Alexander Brakel, Bjarte Bruland, Valerij Brun-Zechowoj, Judy Cohen, Jack Cossid, Christoph Dieckmann, Adamo Chicci, Joachim Dort, Gérard Dreyfus, Maraglit Efrati, René Del Fabbro, Bodo Farnsteiner, György Fehéri, Stephen Feinstein, Ingo Gedde, Michael Haley Goldman, Gábor Hirsch, Nikolaus Hofinger, Marc Hofman, Yves Hofman, Avram Gafni, Hans Werner Goldberg, Hanna Greenbaum, Nerijus Grigas-Pluhar, Elly Gross, Isidor Grüngras, Nomi Halpern, Martin Hartwig, Frank Hertweck, Klaus Hesse, Brigitte Holzhauser, Thomas Irmer, Jan Jagielski, Sven Juengerkes, Larisa Ivanovna Junina, Ronny Kabus, Jack Kagan, Sally Kalwary, Florian Kemmelmeier, Matthias Kern, Frauke Kerstens, Elisabeth Klamper, Peter Klein, Verena Kleinschmidt, Anna Kleynman, Adi Kodym, Marcel Konstantyner, Andreas Kossert, Robert Kuwałek, Olivier Lalieu, Jean Laloum, Karsten Linne, Hanno Loewy, Leonore Martin, Jürgen Matthäus, Clément Millon, Hanna Meyer-Moses, Fruma Mohrer, Reinhard Müller, Bogdan Musiał, Eftihia Nachmias, Stephen Naron, Naftali Oberhand, Berit Pistora, Lutz Prieß, Ioanid Radu, Maren Read, Maurice-Philip Remy, Frank Reuter, Volker Ries, Nelly Romanenko, Joanne W. Rudof, Rafael Pijade, Florrie Pot, Rūta Puišytė, Evelyne Salis, Thomas Sandkühler, Christoph Schölzl, Manuela Schulz, Piotr Setkiewicz, Lior Smadja, Irena Steinfeld, Krzysztof Tarkowski, Thorsten Taubner, Larissa Traspova, Michail Tyagly, Daniel Uziel, Sabina Van der Linden, Tamara Veršitskaja, Margers Vestermanis, Jill Vexler, Martina Voigt, Sven Vollrath, Elana Weiser, Andreas Westphal, Roy Winckelman, Tomasz Wiśniewski, Alexander Wolters, Michalina Wysocka, Christine van der Zanden, Ton van Zeeland, Hansjakob Ziemer, Moshe Zilbar, Volker Zimmermann

Yielding to pressure, Prof. Eisenman, architect of the memorial, abandoned his principle of withholding more than minimal analysis of his own work. His essay on architectural theory in this volume is more an insight into the workshop of his mind than an "official version" of the planning process. To him we owe our thanks for a memorial that defies every attempt to label it, and whose completion stirred renewed reflection even among critics. The memorial surprises by achieving the impossible.

Dr. Günter Schlusche also deserves thanks. In addition to his work with the construction, he has become a de facto historian of the creation of the memorial, and the data bank search path he developed with Jeannine Fiedler provides information on the history of the creation of the memorial to all those interested.

Dagmar von Wilcken turned images, texts, film and narrative into a high-quality exhibition. Combining "thinking with the eyes", tactile intelligence, and the ability to patiently bring together disparate views, von Wilcken is responsible for the entire presentation. She and Sibylle Quack describe the links between content and audio-visual concept in this volume.

Dagmar von Wilcken's importance to the exhibition is matched by that of Ben Buschfeld as the designer of this volume. For his stubborn and insistent interventions as graphic designer, aiming to make the volume readable, and for achieving a lively balance of text and image, he deserves thanks. The ever-thankless task of editing was linked in this case with project management. With her many excellent suggestions – from the choice of graphic designer to publisher – Jeannine Fiedler never rested, and the results speak for themselves.

Of course we must also thank the publisher, the Nicolai Verlag. Right from the beginning, the Foundation was determined to offer this volume of material as well as a volume of photographs at a comparatively low price in the Information Centre. The Nicolai Verlag met this requirement, and the reasonably priced result is of high quality.

Both the exhibition in the Information Centre and this volume of material cannot depend on tertiary or secondary literature. Both must rely directly on source material. This avoids the confusion of repeating errors – however small – that may arise from failing to check attributions in earlier research. In Germany, we all remember what happened with the first edition of the "Wehrmacht" exhibition.

We therefore owe our thanks to a great number of freelancers, correspondents and colleagues, particularly from eastern European archives, whose thorough research into original sources led to surprising discoveries of images and texts, most of which are found in the "Room of Places". Thanks also go to more than 400 memorial sites in Europe, whose staff supplied original information about the sites and the historical context of their work. Most important in this regard is the cooperation of the Foundation "Topography of Terror", through which a public data bank was developed.

A growing problem for academic work is presented by the increased economization of the granting of rights. As the results of academic research are usually of limited economic value, rights management thus has become essential to the success of the exhibition. Here, Stefanie Fischer rendered a great service, taking on this task in addition to her main work in museum education.

Finally, the greatest thanks go to members of the families who survived and helped us, both through the chance to speak with them and through the loan of important material from the time before and during the genocide. This is found in the concrete family histories in the exhibition, as well as in this volume of material.

In the dedication of her book, "The Last Album" Ann Weiss says:

... [this book is] ...
a grave marker, and final resting place,
to the millions whose stories we will never know,
to the thousands whose names are recorded nowhere else,
to the hundreds whose photos appear in this book,
and to the blessed memory of my mother.

The exhibition has gained authenticity through the acquisition of some 1,200 recorded conversations and interviews with survivors that the Fortunoff Archive of Yale University (Prof. Geoffrey Hartman) — the most relevant oral history archive on the persecution of the Jews — began collecting in 1980.

The transfer, digitalization, and processing with a mind to problem solving, would not have been possible without the financial support of the Federal Cultural Foundation. For this, both Caroline Ehmke and Hortensia Völckers receive warmest thanks.

In many respects, the audio-visual transformation of the Foundation's work is also a result of cooperation with ZDF — from the choice of speakers, to the studio recording of the personal histories recounted in the Room of Names, to the technical concept for digitalizing the videos of the Fortunoff Archive, up to and including operability. But here one must highlight Susanne Gelhard's long-term documentation, which practically formed a visual memorial of the memorial. We have always encountered extremely helpful and knowledgeable colleagues at ZDF — and naturally also the goodwill of the directors. Representing these many contacts, we wish to name Berlin Production Director Heinz Gummelt, Technical Director Rainer Ahrens and Jan Dottschadis for the successful technical transfer of the Fortunoff interviews.

HANS-ERHARD HAVERKAMPF, DIRECTOR,
FOUNDATION FOR THE MEMORIAL TO THE MURDERED JEWS OF EUROPE

Alexander Avraham was born in 1958 in Romania; educator in language and literature; graduated from University of Bucharest and Hebrew University of Jerusalem; since 1984 worked on collection of "Pages of Testimony"; since 1991, director of Yad Vashem's programme on data bank documentation of names of victims; represented Yad Vashem as advisory expert in numerous international commissions on the assets of Holocaust victims, including: the Volcker Commission, ICHEIC, Foundation "Remembrance, Responsibility and Future", the Generali Fund in Israel; Director of the Hall of Names, Yad Vashem.

Ulrich Baumann was born in 1967 in Trier; doctorate in history on the coexistence of Jews and Christians in rural Baden; worked with Conference on Jewish Material Claims Against Germany, Shoah Foundation and Jewish Museum in Berlin; research on history of businesses in the Weimar Republic; since 2002, researcher at the Foundation Memorial to the Murdered Jews of Europe.

Wolfgang Benz was born in 1941; studied history, political science, art history; 1969-1990 worked for the Institute for Contemporary History in Munich; co-founder and -publisher of the journal "Dachauer Hefte"; publisher of several series of books; since 1990, Professor at the Technical University of Berlin and Director of the Centre for Research on Anti-Semitism; 1992 recipient of the Geschwister-Scholl Prize; President of the Society for Research on Exile; numerous publications on German history in the 20th Century.

Peter Eisenman was born in 1932 in Newark, New Jersey; architect, college lecturer and author; his prize-winning office, "Eisenman Architects", has built apartment houses, college and educational buildings, stadiums and museums; currently Louis-Kahn Professor for Architecture at Yale University and guest professor at Princeton University; 2004 received Golden Lion at International Architecture Biennial in Venice for his life's work.

François Guesnet was born in 1962; studied eastern European history, Romance languages and Slavonic studies; doctorate in history from Albert-Ludwig University, Freiburg; worked several years at Simon-Dubnow Institute for Jewish History and Culture; assignments abroad, including Poland, Israel and the USA; research emphasis: Jewish history in eastern Europe; guest professor of historical sociology of culture at the University of Potsdam.

Eberhard Jäckel was born in 1929; 1967-1997 Professor of Modern History at University of Stuttgart; member of the Board of Trustees of the Foundation for the Memorial to the Murdered Jews of Europe; numerous publications on 20th Century history, including "Hitler's Ideology" (1969, 1981), "Hitler's Reign" (1986), "Death is a Master from Germany" (with Lea Rosh, 1990), "The German Century" (1996), "Jews in the Secret Nazi Background Reports 1933-1945" (with Otto Dov Kulka, 2004).

Uwe Neumärker was born in 1970 in Berlin; 1997/98 worked in publishing, followed by lecturing and writing; 2000/01 cultural assistant at Institute for Foreign Relations in Memelland (Lithuania); research and publications on eastern Prussia; since 2002, researcher at the Foundation Memorial to the Murdered Jews of Europe.

Dieter Pohl was born in 1964; PhD in philosophy; researcher at Institute for Contemporary History in Munich; research and publications on history of the mass crimes of National Socialism; on Stalinism; and history of former East Germany.

Sibylle Quack was born in 1951; studied political science, German studies and philosophy; doctorate in 1981, focusing on Paul Levi and Rosa Luxemburg; 1979-1987 worked with German Federal Press Department; 1988-1992 worked with German Historical Institute in Washington, D.C.; post-doctoral degree in 1992; from 2001, unscheduled professor for political science at the University of Hanover; 2000-2004, Director of the Foundation for the Memorial to the Murdered Jews of Europe; from 2004, working with Federal Representative for Culture and Media.

Monika Richarz was born in 1937 in Berlin; 1970, doctorate in Jewish history, Free University of Berlin; 1972-1979 Research Fellow at the Leo Baeck Institute, New York; 1984-1993, Director of Germania Judaica, Cologne; 1993-2001, Director of Hamburg Institute for the History of German Jews; 1996 named professor at the University of Hamburg; research theme: Jewish social and cultural history, 18th to 20th Century.

Reinhard Rürup was born in 1934 in Rehme/Westphalia; 1962 doctorate in Göttingen; 1970 post-doctorate at Free University of Berlin; 1970-1975 Professor of Modern History, Friedrich-Meinecke Institute of the Free University of Berlin; 1975-1999 Chair in Modern History at the Technical University of Berlin; 1992-2004 Research Director of the "Foundation Topography of Terror" in Berlin; numerous guest professorships (including Berkeley; Harvard, Jerusalem, Stanford, Oxford); focus of research: formation of middle-class society; history of revolution; history of the Jews and anti-Semitism; National Socialist dictatorship; history in public spaces.

Günter Schlusche was born in 1950; studied architecture at Technical University of Berlin and city and regional planning at London School of Economics; 1981-1987 project coordinator of International Building Exhibition with Josef Paul Kleihues; 1995, doctorate at Technical University of Berlin; since 1996, coordinator for planning and construction of the Memorial to the Murdered Jews of Europe, from 2000 on behalf of the Foundation; member of German Work Federation Berlin; numerous publications on planning and construction.

Avner Shalev was born in 1939 in Jerusalem; studied modern history of the Middle East and geography; graduated from Israeli Defence Forces Command and Staff College and from National Security College, Israel; served in Israeli Defence Forces as Brigadier General; military positions include: 1973 Director of Office of Chief of Staff during the Yom Kippur war, and Director of the Educational Corps; appointed Director of Art and Culture Department of Israel's Ministry of Education and Culture, and Head of National Art and Culture Committee; since 1993, Director of Yad Vashem.

Dagmar von Wilcken was born in 1958; studied design and visual communication; in 1987, earned diploma from College of Art in Berlin; freelance exhibition designer; numerous exhibitions for Bauhaus-Archiv, Berlin; 1995-2004 design of permanent exhibition, "Tracking Injustice", for the Documentation and Information Centre (DIZ) Torgau; numerous projects for Foundation New Synagogue – Centrum Judaicum Berlin, including the exhibition "Jews in Berlin – 1938 to 1945"; 2001-2005 design concept for exhibition in the Information Centre of the Memorial to the Murdered Jews of Europe.

Field of Stelae

area:
19,073 m²

dimension of stelae:
0.95 m width, 2.38 m length,
heights from 0 to 4.7 m
tilts from 0.5° to 2°

number of stelae:
2,711 stelae made from high quality
concrete (self compacting concrete)

of which

83 stelae with heights greater than 4.5 m
220 stelae with heights from 4 to 4.5 m
249 stelae with heights from 3.5 to 4 m
320 stelae with heights from 3 to 3.5 m
232 stelae with heights from 2.5 to 3 m
259 stelae with heights from 2 to 2.5 m
400 stelae with heights from 1.5 to 2 m
469 stelae with heights from 1 to 1.5 m
334 stelae with heights from 0.5 to 1 m
33 stelae with heights less than 0.5 m

and

112 ground level stele slabs
(mostly placed in the public walkway)

position of the stelae
in 54 North-South axes and
in 87 East-West axes

weight of the highest stele
(4.7 m): ca.16 t
average weight of a stele: ca. 8 t

area covered by paving stones:
ca. 13,100 m²

paving material:
concrete paving stone (special production
series/ size 10 cm x 10 cm)

illumination of the field of stelae:
180 ground level illumination boxes
(2.38 m long, 0.10 m wide)

access for disabled
esp. wheelchair users: 13 passages
with a maximum slope of 8 %,
marked with specially cut paving stones
and with cast iron ground level markers
(wheelchair symbol) on the border with
the public walkway

trees planted in the field of stelae:
41 trees on the western side
towards Ebertstrasse

of which

11 Kentucky coffee trees
(Gymnocladus dioica)
8 Devils Walkingsticks (Aralia spinosa)
7 Black Pines (Pinus nigra)
7 Linden trees (Tilia vulgaris)
5 Silverbell trees (Halesia carolina)
3 Juneberry trees (Amelanchier laevis)

Information Centre

total area:
2,116 m² including inner and outer walls,
stairs and technical rooms

of which

778 m² exhibition rooms
106 m² lecture rooms
46 m² book shop
166 m² office rooms,
reception room and cloakroom

Building Costs

27.6 Mio Euro
from Federal funds

of which

13.9 Mio Euro for the construction
of the field of stelae

10.3 Mio Euro for the construction
of the information centre

1.1 Mio Euro general building costs

and

2.3 Mio Euro for the exhibition,
for furnishing and equipment

Dates

25 June, 1999 resolution by
the German Bundestag

1 April, 2003 beginning of construction

12 July, 2004 roofing ceremony
for the information centre

15 December, 2004 last stele
put in place

10 May, 2005 opening ceremony

Archiv der Hansestadt Rostock,
p. 51 c.

Archiv der Zeugen Jehovas,
Moers, p. 35 top

Dietmar Arnold, Uwe Friedrich
(Berliner Unterwelten e. V.), Berlin,
S. 18 bottom

B. Aust, i. A. des Senators für
Stadtentwicklung und Umweltschutz:
Die städtebauliche Entwicklung Berlins,
Berlin 1986, p. 17

Beth Hatefutsoth, The Nahum Goldman
Museum of the Jewish Diaspora,
Tel Aviv, p. 146 top, c.

Jack Cossid, Chicago, p. 100 top

Beit Lohamei Hagetaot, Holocaust
and Jewish Resistance Heritage
Museum, Israel, p. 55 bottom l.,
56 bottom r., 64 top, 85 bottom, 106,
107 top, 113, 114

Belorusskij Gosudarstvennyj Muzej
Istorii Velikoj Otečestvennoj Vojny,
Minsk, p. 133 c. r., 142 top

Bildarchiv Preußischer Kulturbesitz,
Berlin, p. 51 l.

Bund der "Euthanasie"-Geschädigten
und Zwangssterilisierten, Detmold,
p. 35 bottom

Bundesarchiv Berlin, p. 67
(Nürnberger Dokument NO-51-5193;
BA NS 19/1570, Bl. 9 bottom and Bl. 10),

Bundesarchiv Koblenz,
p. 18 top, 53 top, 60 l.,136

Centre de Documentation Juives
Contemporaine, Paris, p. 121 bottom

Comité international de la Croix-Rouge,
Genf, p. 144 bottom, 145 top

Deutsches Historisches Museum,
Berlin, p. 51 l.

Dokumentations- und
Kulturzentrum deutscher Sinti und
Roma, Heidelberg, p. 53 bottom

Dokumentationszentrum des
österreichischen Widerstands, Wien,
p. 57 top r., bottom

Gérard Dreyfus and Evelyne
Dreyfus-Salis, Frankreich,
p. 90 bottom, 91, 107 bottom, 108 top

Eisenman Architects, New York,
p. 10, 11, 12, 13, 25, 26

Fils et Filles des Déportés Juifs
de France, Paris, p. 7

Gedenkstätte und Museum
Sachsenhausen, p. 30, 65, 97 top

Generallandesarchiv Karlsruhe,
p. 102, 103

Geschichtswerkstatt Bayreuth,
Ekkehard Hübschmann, p. 38

Imperial War Museum, London,
p. 53 bottom l., 64 bottom l.

Institut für Zeitgeschichte, München,
p. 58 top r., bottom

Instytut Pamięci Narodowej, Główna
Komisja Ścigania Zbrodni
przeciwko Narodowi Polskiemu,
Warschau, p. 55 bottom r.

Joods Historisch Museum Amsterdam,
p. 49, 77 bottom, 98, 99 bottom,
112, 132 bottom

Jack Kagan, London, p. 97 bottom

Matthias Kern, Frankfurt/Main,
p. 152, 153

Robert Kruse, Berlin, p. 22

Landesbildstelle Berlin, p. 23 top

Dirk Laubner, Berlin, p. 14

Gunter Lepkowski, Berlin, p. 45-48

Lehnartz Bildarchiv, Berlin, p. 19 bottom

Lietuvos centrinis valstybės
archyvas, Vaizdo ir garso dokumentų
skyrius, Wilna, p. 133 top r.

Magyar Nemzeti Muzeum Torteneti
Fenykeptar, Budapest, p. 148

MMCD interactive in science,
Düsseldorf, p. 132 top, 135 bottom,
137 top, 149

Moyzeio Fotografiae Thessalonike,
p. 133 bottom r.

Musée de la Résistance et de la
Déportation, Forges-Les-Eaux, p. 156

Nederlands instituut voor
Oorlogsdocumentatie, Amsterdam,
p. 49, 135 top

Niedersächsisches Staatsarchiv
Aurich, p. 51 top

Państwowe Muzeum Auschwitz-Birkenau,
Oświęcim, p. 61 top, 86 top
(Bestand Sonderkommando, Bd. 78,
Bl. 94 and 95), bottom (Bestand
Sonderkommando, Bd. 135, Bl. 5),
145 bottom, 147, 175

Florrie-Pot Peereboom, Amsterdam,
p. 93, 94, 99 top, 108 bottom

Rafael Pijade, Holon, p. 92

Privatbesitz, p. 78 bottom, 85 top

Rossijskij Gosudarstvennyj Voennyj
Archiv, Moskau, p. 138-141

Günter Schlusche, Berlin, p. 23 bottom

Senator für Bau- und Wohnungswesen
Berlin – Landeskonservator (Hg.):
Die Kunstdenkmäler von Berlin,
Bezirk Kreuzberg: Karten und Pläne,
Berlin 1979, p. 16

Senatsverwaltung für Stadtentwicklung,
Abt. III, Berlin, p. 20, 21

Senatsverwaltung für Stadtentwicklung,
Architekturwerkstatt, Berlin, p. 27

Smalfilmmuseum Archives,
Hilversum, p. 111

Stadtarchiv Bielefeld, p. 56 top,
56 bottom r.

Stadtarchiv Heppenheim, p. 50

Malka Malach witnessed the 1939
German invasion in Dabrowa Gornicza,
Poland. She did not survive the war
and persecution. The exact circumstances
of her death are unknown.